This book may be k

WITHDRAWN

The Stars at Noon

The Stars at Noon

~~~~~~

by
JACQUELINE COCHRAN
With Floyd Odlum *as Wingman*

An *Atlantic Monthly Press* Book
Little, Brown and Company · Boston · Toronto

FIRST EDITION

ATLANTIC—LITTLE, BROWN BOOKS
ARE PUBLISHED BY
LITTLE, BROWN AND COMPANY
IN ASSOCIATION WITH
THE ATLANTIC MONTHLY PRESS

Published simultaneously in Canada
by Little, Brown & Company (Canada) Limited

PRINTED IN THE UNITED STATES OF AMERICA

※※

BACK in 1938, Jacqueline Cochran, affectionately known to everyone in aviation as "Jackie," was awarded the General "Billy" Mitchell Award as the American pilot who during the previous year had made the greatest individual contribution to aviation. Sixteen years later, that same remarkable woman by unanimous vote was awarded the Gold Medal of the Fédération Aéronautique Internationale for the outstanding accomplishment in aviation during 1953. I know how prized a possession that Gold Medal is because I am the proud possessor of one awarded to me in a previous year, for being the first to pass the sonic barrier and to fly faster than the speed of sound.

Much has happened progressively in aviation during the sixteen years between these two awards to Jackie and a measurable part of this progress has been due to efforts of the few pioneering pilots who willed and won. Among this group Jackie has a high place.

If speed flying is a man's prerogative, then Jackie Cochran is the exception because she has stood toe to toe with the men and fought it out without fear or favor. Few people realize that she holds practically all the recognized *men's* international speed records for propeller-driven planes. Not content with these laurels, she went out in the spring of 1953 to set a few records with jet-propelled planes.

It was my privilege to follow Jackie in a "chase" plane during her record speed runs in the Canadian built and powered Sabre-jet and in her preliminary test flights, and to act as her principal instructor in the handling of jet aircraft. A "chase" plane is taken into the air to accompany and observe experimental aircraft during test flights. As the chase pilot, I know the many problems, sometimes of a serious nature, that Jackie had to contend with. It is truly remarkable that, with less than six hours flying time and only thirteen take-offs and landings in the Canadian built Sabre-jet, Jackie set three world's records and dived three times past the sonic barrier to beat the speed of sound. And if the high speed in rough air on the last flight had not set up such a vibration as to cause a bad leak in one of the main fuel tanks — which luckily I saw from my chase plane and reported to Jackie by radio — she probably would have taken on one more record.

During all of the record flights that Jackie flew, she showed courage and skill that was outstanding. The low altitude and high speed together with very rough air required skillful flying that few pilots, male or female, can produce. Jackie came through with flying colors and still managed a sweet, ladylike smile for the ground crew, and not a single strand of her blond hair was ever out of place.

Jackie and I had one experience that can never be duplicated. I as the first man to pass the sonic barrier and Jackie as the first woman to do so each took a Sabre-jet, climbed to nearly fifty thousand feet of altitude and put the two planes, almost wing tip to wing tip, into a full-power vertical dive past the barrier, as a sort of supersonic duet.

I salute Jacqueline Cochran as a good pilot and a fine person who has often had to accomplish things the hard way. Her many contributions to the progress of aviation have helped make our world a better and safer place in which to live.

"CHUCK" YEAGER

Edwards Air Force Base
Edwards, California

PREFACE

THE little girl you see in the center of the frontispiece is surrounded by some of the women she made herself into during the succeeding years. Reality was the result of ceaseless energy, sparked by imagination and determination. That is how dreams come true.

That little girl, now grown up in some ways but not in all, is the author of this book. She is also my wife and the most interesting person I have ever met.

Even if Jacqueline Cochran had been born with a silver spoon in her mouth, her outstanding accomplishments in aviation would well merit their telling. Her background and beginning only serve to make these aerial feats more remarkable. For more than twenty years she has been pushing high and fast into the little known and sometimes unknown frontiers of the atmosphere, bringing back bits of information which have speeded along the onrush of the air age.

But she has also out-Marcoed Marco Polo with her travels to most of the foreign lands on the face of the earth, always on the search for and seeing the unusual. A glance at a new spot on a map is usually, for her, the start of a new adventure.

From no shoes to the Diamond Horseshoe at the Metropolitan Opera House is a long way for a girl to go, even here in blessed America where we are more familiar with the stories of rags to riches than are our fellow human beings abroad. That trip from a symbolic start in poverty to a symbolic cushion in luxury has followed many interesting and adventurous bypaths.

On the interesting side it has made Jacqueline Cochran the table companion of the last four Presidents of the United States and the honor guest of royalty on several occasions. If she were writing this preface she would put first of all her private audience with the Pope. And I, a Protestant, the son of a Methodist minister, say she would probably be right in such a priority, because the ascendancy of man over all other living earthly things has been marked by the development of man's conscience, his ability to distinguish right from wrong and his concern with the humanities — at the heart of all of which will be found religion whether Catholic or Protestant or Jewish.

On the adventurous side, that trip caused Jackie to be the first woman to make a totally blind landing in a plane, the first woman to pass the sonic barrier and exceed the speed of sound, and the woman to lead men in numerous speed flights over a period of two decades. Along the way she served as pilot with the British forces during the war, then as a member of the staff of our newly formed Eighth Air Force in England, and then on the General Staff of our own United States Air Forces, where she organized, trained and led the more than one thousand women pilots known as "WASPs."

Along another bypath she watched the surrender by Japanese General Yamashita in the Philippines, interviewed another Japanese general in China at his base before he had surrendered, and then returned to Germany for the war trials at Nuremberg.

For her business accomplishments she was chosen in 1954 as America's outstanding business woman; and before that had been chosen on several occasions as one of our country's outstanding women leaders irrespective of business or profession.

Such a person must have many sides to her character and personality, some of which seem to contradict the others. I have said many times that Jackie is fearless, and yet she runs wildly from a snake, and I have seen her become almost hysterical from listening to a good old-fashioned ghost story. However, I have never seen her back away from real danger and I have constantly observed that she moves automatically toward the center of trouble. Certain it is that she is fearless of death and equally certain it is that she considers a barrier only something to surmount.

Perhaps an excerpt from a letter Jackie sent to me in 1949 will give an insight into her character and thinking processes more than anything I can say. When she wrote that letter, part of which is quoted below, she was gravely ill in a hospital in Vienna in a sector behind the Iron Curtain. She doubted that she would ever be well and robust again. Under these circumstances she said:

I am so thankful to God that you are better. I have Prayed so many many times that I might be permitted to take your sickness and that you might again have the fun and complete happiness that you once had. So now if you get completely well and I am sick with arthritis I will assume my Prayers have been answered and will not complain.

The person who said these things to me is the person for whom I acted as "wingman" in this book. My job was only to help Jackie dress her thoughts in language that approached grammatical correctness and to suggest elements of continuity here and there. If the result is something that will entertain many with the reading and help a few, Jackie and I will be pleased and fully repaid for our writing efforts.

FLOYD ODLUM

The Stars at Noon

CHAPTER I

I AM a refugee from Sawdust Road, which is located in the South close by Tobacco Road of theater and movie fame.

Until I was eight years old, I had no shoes. My bed was usually a pallet on the floor and sometimes just the floor. Food at best consisted of the barest essentials — sometimes nothing except what I foraged for myself in the woods or in the waters of the nearby bayou or the running "branch." Mullet and beans were the staples, with a bit of sowbelly added when we were in clover, with some black-eyed peas thrown in if and when we were on the crest. No butter, no sugar. My dresses in the first seven years of my life were usually made from cast-off flour sacks.

That was my life in the sawmill towns of northern Florida when I should have had toys and been getting schooling. It was bleak and bitter and harsh. But it taught me independence and the necessity of fending for myself. Particularly did I grow independent when at the age of six I overheard, by chance, a conversation in which "Mama" was engaged with another woman which disclosed to me the secret that I was not one of the family, but by a promise made I was never to know this. "Mama" was slovenly and lazy and her meanness varied from a normal high, when things were going well, to a feverishly high pitch, when we were on half rations — which was most of the time. The knowledge that I did not belong to her gave me a sense of happiness and exhilaration.

I could tell you in detail about Bagdad, Sampson, Millville and Panama City because I have lived in them all and other like sawmill camps and I have something close to a photographic memory. But they were all pretty much alike. Each was a sawmill with appendages. Some mills were two-sided, which means they operated two band saws rather than one. That doubled the accident rate, because a saw was always breaking apart or a belt flying loose or a splinter shooting off like a jagged bullet. One of the appendages was a company doctor who patched up the living and took care of the mill families for a standard charge of fifty cents per month, which did not include delivery of babies. This cost a little extra — so the neighbors helped each other with this routine. I delivered babies before I even knew that the stork was a bird.

Another appendage was the company commissary. We never saw money. The men were paid with "chips," which were tokens, good for rental of a company-owned house or for food and clothes at the company commissary. Many's the time I have seen a wife after the noon meal go with her "man" to the mill. This was not done for exercise or companionship, but to get chips for that day's work of his in order to get food for that day's dinner. That's how close to starvation many of them were running. If the worker reported back on the job sound in body after lunch, he could get a slip of paper showing that he had worked that day. He would hand this to his "woman" before going to the saws or slabs, and she would turn it in to "Chip Charlie" for chips. Chip Charlie was so fast at counting out the chips — each of which was for five cents — that no one could catch him cheating, least of all a person who couldn't read or count which included many of the women. The use of chips instead of money, good no place else except at the commissary, was a strong way of keeping people tied to the job. It was effective slavery. In fact, it was worse than slavery in some ways because the actual slave had continuity of bed and board, known nowadays as security, whereas these Sawdust Road people had bed and food only while the logs were coming in and the saws were turning.

Besides the mill and the store, there were the houses, ranging from good old plain board four- and five-room jobs down to shacks and shanties. But even in these camps there was a right side and wrong side of the railroad. The rich folk lived on the right side, where there was also a small schoolhouse. The rich folk consisted of the foremen, the doctor, the bookkeeper, the paymaster, the butcher, the storekeeper and the like. I lived on the other side of the tracks, but always. Usually a shack on stilts, down near the swamp, served as home. There was always a swamp and behind the shack there was always either a bayou as in Millville or a branch as in Sampson. The swamp and the bayou or branch and the woods were my stamping ground — and I stamped a lot. No wonder my hands and feet are large and strong and out of proportion to my body.

Going back beyond my memory there was, as I gleaned from bits of conversation later in life, a little tract of land near Muscogee, Florida, where we had an ox and some home-grown food. That comparative comfort near the town where I was born I came to believe had something to do with my real parents. My foster family must have soon dissipated this windfall from my real parents, for sawdust and slab piles marked their horizon from then on.

My first clear recollection was of a bedroom in the usual shack. "Papa" was sick with typhoid fever on the bed in one corner of the room. My pallet was in another corner. There were no windowpanes and we tacked up paper to keep the cold out of the room. Our only means of support with "Papa" sick was the work of my two "brothers." One had a crippled foot from birth and couldn't earn full pay. He stacked slabs for sixty cents a day. The older "brother," while working, could earn a dollar a day. I had two "sisters." "Papa" eventually got well and went back to the saw.

Fifteen years later, while working as a nurse, I heard that the whole family, including the two "sisters," was down with the flu. I hurried back to Sawdust Road to help them. "Papa" died and because there was no undertaker I laid him out in his only suit in a cheap pine coffin. I performed the same last service for two neighbors before getting back to my hospital. It was a more trying job than acting as midwife. But, after much thought, that is the way I want to be taken care of when I die. No embalming, no ceremony. Just a cheap pine coffin. In this way, my body can soon again become a part of the grass and flowers. I have tried again and again to commit my husband, Floyd Odlum, to this procedure for me but he just gets silent when I mention this or utters some evasive, noncommittal generality, the meaning of which seems to be that the dear departed should not trouble themselves in life about these things because funeral arrangements are for the benefit not of the dead but of the ones left behind.

Now that I have introduced Floyd, I should paint a word picture of him, but Floyd, acting as my "wing man," won't let me do this. I have, however, inserted bits and pieces about him here and there at pertinent points with which you can build up a partial mosaic of his character and personality.

If fending for one's self carries its satisfactions, I had my satisfactions rich and plenty for many years. They say if you want one really to enjoy the pleasures of heaven, just pitch him into hell first for a spell. Perhaps that sort of treatment is why I enjoy life to the brimful now, every minute of it.

Only because of these contrasts of my life — from rags to riches — is this story being written. It is a story of flights and fancies, of privations and places and perfumes and laces and of aces and kings and generals — all scrambled together.

The psychiatrists would probably have a field day over me. In fact, Karl Menninger, the king of them all, during dinner one evening years ago, got intrigued by my "psyche" and wanted to do a special research. I replied that even though I was perhaps or even probably the full-swing adult mobilization of infantile complexes, I had no intention of becoming a case history in his or any other person's card index. The advocates of the force of inheritance as opposed to the results of environment would have a hard time with me because of my unknown parentage. This fact never bothered me until I was about to marry Floyd. I thought he should know so I went south and got sealed letters from the two people then living who might know the facts. I gave them to Floyd and he handed them back to me, still sealed, and they still rest that way in my lockbox. I do not know what is in them. Having gone through my early years without knowing why my own parents were not around looking after me, I decided when I reached maturity that I did not want to know. But I thought Floyd had the right to know.

It seemed to be the job of the mills to take a beautiful virgin forest and sear it back first to stumps and then to waste sands. At least that is what I have often thought in after years as I have seen what happened to some of that part of our country through denuding it of trees and letting the rains and winds take over. When the mills in one camp would cut back, we would stay on part-time work as long as food lasted. When the mills shut down, we would move to another camp. Sometimes, we had to move on our own resources, which was pretty dreadful without transportation and without money. Sometimes, the mill and men would be moved nearer to the logs by the company. One of these moves, which happened to be from Bagdad to Millville by way of Panama City, gave me my first train ride. We were in the caboose and had to get off en route to help the crew gather "lighter knots" for the engine furnace. Lighter knots are the knotty and unsawable parts of pine trees and are full of tar. When we stopped at a little town, Negroes came on board, selling fried chicken and bread. But we had no money so went hungry. My eyes bulged when a man came through the train selling glass pistols filled with small balls of candy. I wanted one more than anything before or since in life but then such things were not for me.

Bagdad, Florida, which was my home for about two years, was not like the ancient capital of Persia. But on second thought, maybe it was because I have been to modern Persia and had a look around and for the ordinary folk it leaves almost everything to be desired.

While Millville was our goal on that first train ride (which was about a hundred-mile stretch as the crow flies but which took all day and into the night), we had to walk the last three miles from Panama City. I trudged through sand up to my ankles and thought I would not make it — what with an empty stomach for so long and no sleep. But finally we arrived at the same old edge-of-town, broken-down shack without windowpanes. It was like sitting through the second showing of a horror film. I went reconnoitering for food. A farmer lived nearby. Out back of a shed he had tubs of sweet potatoes being boiled for the pigs. My hunger was so intense I "borrowed" some of these potatoes and ate them on the spot. The next day, I found some "pine mass" in the woods. These are small nuts that drop out of the cone in the fall. They are tasty and nourishing. I have often wondered why they are not marketed. I occasionally get something like them now — called piñons — from the Indians in New Mexico and Arizona.

Two days later, I went to the waterfront and met some children whose father seined at night for mullet to sell and also to help with the family table. I was so woebegone and wanted some of the fish so badly that he gave me a panful to take home. They were filled with fine roe. I decided we needed some grease so I went to the farmer's house — the one whose sweet potatoes had filled my stomach — and asked to borrow a small cup of lard. He accommodated me, which was a surprise. In those days, in the wood camps, it seldom dawned on people to ask for things from others because of hunger. Hunger was a permanent status, common to all. Full of glee I rushed back to our shack with the fat and we had our first hot meal in over a week.

Work by the three men enabled us to progress from the shack to a company house and with our chip money we could get the necessities. Occasionally, using bootleg chips, we could get outside the commissary some fresh vegetables from the farmers or a bit of fresh meat at a big discount. For the most part only dried beans and similar staples and meat such as bologna could be had in the commissary. Oranges, even in that state of oranges, cost a nickel up in our section and were above our means. But broken-down chairs and rickety tables finally began appearing in our new house, along with mattresses. The finest quality mattresses we knew were stuffed with excelsior and the stuffing was done by ourselves. We were moving up the ladder again even if it meant pledging wages not yet earned which is a sure way to invite trouble. Along the way we had only a mojo lamp which consisted of a hollow stalk of corn stuck into a bottle with oil in the bottom. Through the corn stalk there was inserted a piece of cloth, preferably wool, to act as a wick. Toward the top of the financial ladder we managed a kerosene lamp to keep our mojo lamp company.

Even at this age of six, I had a feeling of resentment — not so much over having but little as the way that that *little* was managed. It would have taken only a bit of effort on "Mama's" part but this bit was lacking. Others with the same pay seemed to get along better with more cleanliness and more orderliness.

I used to do a bit of fishing or crabbing to help out or, more often, I would stand around and have some mullet given to me by fishermen who had been lucky. One day, I rushed over to a pig-sticking in a little clearing on the other side of the camp with the notion that somehow I would come out of it with some food. I watched them prepare the inner spare parts as food. It was sickening to me. They called some of this food "chitlins." Chitlins are the small intestines of a pig. When a pig is slaughtered, the intestines are cleaned out in the running branch water, then cut up into small pieces and boiled for a few days in salt water. Then they can be fried. The odor, both while they are being cleaned and while they are being cooked, is pretty awful. It was the odor that revolted me. Tripe is the aristocratic relative of chitlins, having as its source the lining of the cow's stomach rather than the pig's "innards."

Because of this early experience, I have never been able to eat any of the inner organs of an animal, like liver, kidneys or brains. I have since learned that perhaps the health of the poor in the South was maintained through this sort of diet, so full of vita-mins. The Eskimos could not get along with their blubber diet without eating the insides of the fish, and I mean everything. At the end of World War II in Greece, I also saw fish cooked and eaten whole. So, I guess it's all in the state of mind.

In these camps the men worked about fourteen hours a day in the summer, but in the winter the hours were shorter because there were no electric lights. Work would start with the first crack of dawn and stop when it got too dark to see.

My foster parents had no religion and never went to any church. Yet my earliest recollection is of going to Mass whenever the priest came to town (usually once a month), and this I did at the start on the instructions of my foster parents. I now assume they were bound by some sort of promise in this respect. Of course, after the first time or two, I went by choice. The Catholic priest who came to our camp was a good man who represented something big and wonderful and wholesome to me and I learned about godliness from him.

My Heaven in those days was a very physical place with golden gates and streets paved with jewels. It still is; and when the time comes, I'll eventually enter those gates with anticipation of the clean fun and adventure that must be awaiting a restless soul that the Heavenly Father will not just let float around slowly like a crowned helicopter in a sort of vacuum. I hope He will have much speedier and more adventurous chores for me to do. The only song I ever learned as a child and the only one I occasionally sing now with all the gusto of my youth and a fine southern hillbilly accent (which has left my tongue except when singing this song) goes as follows:

I'm livin on a mounting thats bountiful supplied, and
I'm drinkin from a founting that never shall run dry, for
I'm dwellin in Bueler Land.

"Bueler" Land is quite a place.

It was in Bagdad that I started to school. The teacher's name was Anna Thompson. I'll never forget her. About my third day in school, she started to whip me with a ruler. But she didn't get the chance of a second slap, for with the first I struck back and then took off at top speed through the door — not to return for a year, until there was a new teacher. There was no one around to make me go to school — least of all my "parents."

So, I just ran wild — a real harum-scarum ragamuffin, hunting the woods and fishing. I caught crabs and cooked them and on special occasions would stoop to "conquer" a chicken that seemed for the moment unbranded. I developed an interesting technique to catch these chickens. It consisted of a piece of corn with a hole bored through it by which it was attached to a long string with myself at the other end. The chicken having swallowed the corn would then be gently drawn toward me and sure death. The chicken didn't belong to me but the corn didn't belong to the chicken either.

A child with plenty of imagination always has fun even though it is in fancy. Most, if not all, fun is a state of mind anyway. I had fun, for example, with "Grandpa Whiskers" who, besides driving a team of horses about the town on odd jobs, liked the children and told them many stories. We all called him grandpa because of his white beard. He was everybody's grandpa. From him I learned that I had a navel because when I was very little, an Indian shot me in the stomach with an arrow. He also explained that in my excitement over this bow and arrow affair I had sat down suddenly on an ax and as punishment for this carelessness had become a girl.

Then there was "Aunt" Jennie Smart, a very ancient Negro woman without teeth. She was my childhood counterpart of "Uncle Remus" with her tales and superstitions. "Aunt" Jennie used to fall asleep with the slightest provocation and with her mouth open. I remember once feeding her a dry cracker and she fell asleep in the process of rather dry mastication of it. Her heavy breathing sent cracker crumbs flying in every direction and gave me great fun.

There was a long freight train that used to pass the door very slowly every day with its string of boxcars. It came from far-off places, I was told, and the cars had signs on them which were words. I learned my A B C's by watching the boxcars and began to figure out words. This was my first adventure into the literary world and it intrigued me. Furthermore, I had to make Anna Thompson sorry she tried to whip me and so kept me out of her school. One day I saw the house in which she lived being moved on wheels, and I hated her so, I kept hoping the house would fall off the wheels and crash to the ground. I figured she had whipped me because I was poor and didn't have as good clothes as some of the other children. But whatever the reason, no one

even then could whip me and get away with it for long. "Mama"
used to take it out on us children when she was in a mood. I
thought she picked on me because I was the smallest. One of
my "brothers" came down with a bad case of mumps. It was hot
summer and he had a high fever. I was sent down to "Bunk"
Greenwood's store with a chip to get some ice. I packed the ice
in sawdust and then with a piece of newspaper, but most of it
melted before I could get home. For this bad conduct on the
part of the ice "Mama" decided to whip me. I took things into
my own hands in the shape of a good chunk of firewood and we
talked things out with my eyes flashing fire. She knew I meant
what I said and she retreated, never to touch me again. She was
a coward to let a six-year-old girl get the best of her. She even
let up some on the older girls after that.

At about this time — that is to say, when I was six — I wandered far into the woods with a neighboring boy and his somewhat older sister and we got lost. The girl became hysterical and
nearly cried herself to death. Finally, exhausted, we went to
sleep. No one looked for us — we were just missing. We found
our way back the next day.

I saw my first electric lights in Bagdad. They were on the
principal street and I remember they seemed to stretch off into
eternity, although by day the street was only two or three blocks
long. I heard that there were other places with many such lights.
Also those boxcars told me there was a more substantial world
beyond and the stars and my dreams and imagination told me
likewise. I was determined to get away on my own.

The circus came to town. As I look back, it was a small carnival
but it did have an elephant and a bearded lady. I made friends
with the bearded lady and carried water for the elephant. I told
the people in the circus that I wanted to join up with them and
I bedded down, close at hand, waiting for the break-up of the
show. But in the morning there I still was on my pile of straw

with a sack over me for warmth — and the circus had departed.

My adventures with the circus did not end there, however. Years later I checked off my list of childhood frustrations and determinations this desire to ride an elephant. Covered with bangles and perched in all my happiness and glory on the head of the lead elephant, I led the parade at the opening of Ringling Brothers in Madison Square Garden. Floyd had arranged it through General Kilpatrick, head of Madison Square Garden, who in turn arranged it with Mr. Ringling. I had been desperately ill in a hospital in New York and was just back on my feet. Floyd was satisfying my childhood whim with this elephant ride as a sort of get-well present for me. I substituted for the girl whose job it was to ride on the lead elephant's head in the Grand Parade.

When I arrived about an hour and a half before the performance, the girl whose place I was to take was absent. The wardrobe mistress must have been in on the secret. She brought me the other girl's costume, which was too large (I was down to 104 pounds), but she made it fit with pins and thread. I used a ladder to get on the elephant's head. I noticed some of the girls got up on the elephants' trunks and then were lifted by the elephant from there to its head. While we were waiting for the start of the parade, the elephants swaying back and forth, the girl on the elephant next to me asked what had happened to the girl whose place I was taking. She went on to say I looked familiar and she wanted to know how long I planned to stay with the circus. I said it all depended on how well they liked my performance that night. I had been given a special rein for holding on, but I did not use it, and I think I rode as well as any of them. When we got back behind the scenes, the elephants all at once started making noises and swaying excitedly. A leopard had escaped from its cage. Elephants don't like roaming leopards but the trainers soon had them in hand. They brought me a ladder to dismount, but I had noticed the other girls were sliding down the snoots of their elephants, so down the snoot of mine I went, and in good form. I wanted to stay with the circus for a while, but Floyd kindly though firmly talked me out of it. I had an emotional upset when some years later I read that several elephants, including my own lead elephant, had been killed in Atlanta, Georgia, by some crank who fed them poison.

When the circus failed me in my effort to get away from Sawdust Road, I turned to the gypsies. I had been warned that gypsies would steal children if given a chance. There were some gypsies camped down the road, and I decided to give them their chance. It was a perfect solution. I wandered into their camp several times. They were never mean to me but would not let me join them. Finally they chased me away. This was a big disappointment, coming on top of the circus debacle.

Millville differed from some of the other camps in that, besides the branch and marsh, it had a bay and I used to wade out to the oyster bars and gather oysters. There were two little girls I used to play with during the hot summer months, bathing on the long bars which actually run out into the ocean around Millville and Panama City. I was just learning to dog-paddle with them when one day they drowned. I stayed out there all night and the next day while search was made for the bodies, which were finally found, half eaten. I never tried to swim again for years and I have never dog-paddled. Dog-paddling and drowning are linked in my mind inseparably.

Once when I was quite a small child I noticed a crowd of men going off into the woods with a Negro prisoner and I tagged along out of curiosity. The Negro was tied to a tree, wood was put all around him and after being sprinkled with kerosene it was set on fire. I was too young then to have any great feeling about the injustice or the loss of life, but I took away from that scene the very bad memory of the odor of burning flesh.

Several years later I saw two men legally hanged for a crime they had committed. These hangings then impressed me as wrong and revolting.

I remember that October was the best month for collecting oysters. I would wade to the bars and collect oysters by the hour. My hands were so tough I could shuck them barehanded better than any of the boys and I ate them until they were practically running out my ears. On these never-to-be-forgotten occasions in the life of a hungry girl, we would bring our oysters to the shore, pile them up on live coals over which we would put a chicken, if I had successfully enticed one to join our party with my string-and-corn trick. Then we would pile on more oysters and anything else the nearby patches had to offer — like late corn or squash. Then another layer of oysters on top. What feasts I had! I think my constitution today is due in part to these frequent seaside roasts.

The hot months brought mad dogs and one of my little playmates was bitten. It was my job then to keep a neighbor's cow out of a little cabbage patch we had. I borrowed a shotgun and put salt in the shell, instead of lead, and was ready for an attack from either mad dogs or cows. The neighbor's cow came first and I let fly with a gun so heavy I could hardly hold it in the air. The aim was good — the cow never came back — but the recoil of the gun put me flat on my back for the count of ten.

People all my life have been mostly kind to me. They took to me in my youth like people take to an unusual and striking-looking wild animal that wanders into camp to be fed and cared for. Besides "Aunt" Jennie and "Grandpa Whiskers" there was the company doctor who used to sit out in front of his tiny office with his chair tipped back, swinging his feet and gossiping. He would tell me stories. I had shed my baby teeth and my other teeth were coming in, but crooked. I was heartbroken. I did not want buck teeth and asked him to do something about it. He told me that if I had courage enough, he would pull two of the teeth. If I then kept pressing on the others with my thumb I would have pretty and straight teeth. His offer was quickly accepted and he pulled a lower tooth. The pull nearly lifted me out of the chair, and it hurt and the wound bled. But my pride was more compelling than pain so I had him pull the other. I practiced the thumb technique immediately and constantly and, as a result, I do have perfect and straight teeth, just as he said. White teeth were a rarity in those mill towns where the women used snuff and the men chewed tobacco.

A year after I bolted out of the schoolhouse I decided to try school again. I went to look things over. I liked the new teacher, Miss Bostwick, and so I stayed. She was the most beautifully dressed woman I had ever seen. Now as I see that dress in retrospect, I know it was very plain and old-fashioned, but to me at that time it was beautiful. It matched her character. She spoke in a different way, with a northern accent unknown to me until then. She was from Cincinnati. She was severe with the children and made them work and slapped them over the knuckles with a ruler when they misbehaved. But she was fair. She must have been psychic, because she did not punish me. After I had been at school two days, she said she would pay me ten cents per week if I would bring firewood each day to her room on the upper floor of a two-story boardinghouse, owned by the mill company. I was thrilled. I chopped the wood into little pieces and carried it to her room, which seemed so cozy with a little stove. To me her room looked like a palace. It was the first time I had seen a bedroom screen. She also gave me my first sight and taste of prunes which were stewing on the stove.

Each day I carried wood until the room was nearly bursting. She told me there was wood enough on hand but I kept on — I wanted an excuse to get back to her in that cozy warm room and talk to her. Soon she gave me a little dress to wear which she had ordered by mail. Now I could hold my head up with the other children from the right side of the tracks. Soon I started going to her before school in the morning and fastening her dress. After school I would tag along to her room and sit there by the hour while she read me books which were completely over my head. She taught me to read and told me of other people in other places. Why she got to Bagdad and took me into her arms, I'll never know. I guess she was just lonesome.

The first book she gave me to read was *David Copperfield* and I struggled through it. When I came to a word I did not know, which was often, I would copy it on paper and she would then tell me how to pronounce it and its meaning. When spring came and she left, my life became a void. I was terrified that she would not come back. But in the fall she returned and the same thing went on one more winter, which ended my attendance at school.

The priest taught me godliness and Miss Bostwick taught me the next thing to godliness, which is cleanliness. She taught me how to keep my body and clothes clean and how to fix my hair and she gave me a hair comb and a ribbon. Miss Bostwick was the greatest influence in my early life. She lifted the horizons for me and gave me ambition. She taught me about good and evil. I learned the same lessons from the priest and several years later also from a so-called "fancy lady," whose hair I used to dye. In later years, I went to Cincinnati and tried to find my Miss Bostwick. I wanted to see that lovely face again and put my arms around her and give thanks. Every Bostwick in the telephone directory I called. But none was my Miss Bostwick or even knew her. She is very alive in my memory. Because of what her help did for me in later life, there is no wonder that I once took a little beggar girl off the streets of Havana and put her in a convent school or that I have been keeping and educating three little poor boys in Spain.

I never do things by halves and this idea of keeping clean caught on in a big way. Each day I would put the washtub on the floor of our house, carry buckets of water to it from the pump, and give myself a good cold scrubbing. The other womenfolk in the house laughed and sometimes even sneered at me for these airs, but I kept right on.

About the time in spring when Miss Bostwick left for the north, the mill cut back and we moved down the ladder from our company-owned house into an abandoned shack at the bottom of the bayou, not far from the Negro quarters. There was an empty attic in that shack which had bats in it and the bedbugs seemed to come down from that attic as an army once darkness had arrived. I often thought it would be better to sleep with the frogs outside than with the bats and bedbugs inside. In fact my pallet on the floor was much safer and more comfortable than the "St. George" bed, which is a sort of shelf of rough boards built out from the wall with legs under the outer edge and a mattress of sorts for softness. That shack was even too much for the oldsters and with the first dollar in hand we moved. But while there I found another way of self-entertainment. There were two two-story buildings in town — the one where Miss Bostwick had lived and the other in the Negro quarter. On the second floor of the Negro quarter building, the Negro "jook" was located and there the Negro gay blades used to have a chitlin party every Saturday night. There was a tree just outside. I would climb into that tree and watch them through the window. There was a one-eyed Negro who used to play the piano well. He played what sounds to me like today's boogie-woogie. They carried on with great enjoyment — and I enjoyed it too, from my wonderful perch in that tree. One night I fell asleep and off my perch, but luckily no bones were broken. While the school for the white children was no more than rudimentary, there was no school at all for the Negroes.

I had a piece of great fortune during this period. Women who were about to have babies would ask me to stay with them and do their work for the several days before and after the birth. I have been cooking since I was able to stand on a box and reach the stove. I was then about seven or eight. I got up and cooked the men's meals before daylight and took care of the house and the expectant mother. For this stretch of duty, plus taking care of the children, and there were usually several, I got a dollar, which figured about ten cents per day.

One eighteen-year-old girl who was about to have a baby asked me to come and stay with her because her husband was back in the woods, logging. The night her pains came on she asked me to get a neighbor. But it was raining hard and I would have lost my way through the woods so she decided she could get along until daylight. But she didn't. I boiled water, took directions from her and acted as midwife.

By Christmas season, in this way and otherwise, I had earned about four dollars. But I had not been paid. There was a little stove in the commissary and I wanted it, which is a bad fix to be in without money. There was also a doll. For every twenty-five cents' worth of toys bought in the commissary, a coupon on the doll was given. The doll would go to the holder of the lucky number. I stood with my face to the showcase, looking at that doll, until I almost wore my nose off. I thought one of the other children would win it and anyway my pay for midwifery had not come in. But I did not pass up the slightest chance. I made rounds, drawing well water for women to do their washing. I worked until my hands bled. I was so small that if I had let too much water get in the bucket, I would have been pulled over the edge and into the well while trying to lift the bucket. So I would peek over the edge while lowering the bucket into the water so as to get it only partly full. After two weeks I had earned fifty cents. I went to the commissary and said I would like two tickets on the doll. They gave me some toys too, but most of all I got the two coupons which I dropped in the box. On Christmas Eve, wonder of wonders, I won the doll. So, what happened? My older "sister" had married when she was about fifteen and had a two-year-old baby. "Mama" and "Papa" took that doll away from me and gave it to this baby, whose name was Willie Mae. It broke my heart. But, as I have said, I have a memory like an elephant and a wrong is something to be righted. Years later, when Willie Mae was grown up and had a child of her own, I brought them both to New York to give them a new and better start in life. But I made it a condition that they bring the doll along and surrender it. I have the doll now, slightly refurbished and with new clothes. That doll represents a great deal to me — and it has several other dolls for company.

It was along about this same time that I conquered fear. I had been down the road in the afternoon, playing at the home of some children. Night came on. I had to pass a small cemetery on the way home and they said a ghost that was there would go after me; that I would get scared and come back. The wooden walk past the cemetery was raised over a low spot of ground and as I started along this raised section, the "ghost" rose up from the walk in front of me. I retreated and studied the problem. Between giving in to fear and returning to hear the jeers of my friends or fighting the ghost, I chose the latter. Gathering my courage and crying at the top of my lungs, I charged forward. The ghost rose to grab me but I kept right on to grapple with it. The ghost proved to be a calf with its hind legs down through a broken board. It was exhausted and resting but fear of me when I came along the walk caused it to rise on its front legs and struggle for freedom. I had won. All ghosts in life now are just scared calves, caught by the hind legs.

Things were going so badly on Sawdust Road that winter that we had to move again. We heard that in the cotton mills in

Columbus, Georgia, a boom was on and everyone could work. Again, we set out on that three-mile walk through sand to Panama City. Again, there was the train and the gathering of pine knots. We changed trains, in Dothan, Alabama, and sat in the cold wintry station hour after hour. I had no shoes or stockings and only a thin cotton dress. We had one blanket which we cut apart and I had a piece around me. We arrived in Columbus just before dark and rode up Broad Street in an open streetcar. It was the first time I had seen a streetcar. Broadway, New York, has always looked dim to me compared with Broad Street that night. Finally, we came to a nearby dreary suburb where the cotton mills were located. We knew we could all work because in that area there were many cotton mills, going full blast, so we moved into a house that had a bathroom, the first I had ever seen. So we had a house and a bathroom — but no furniture. We finally got some mattresses and blankets which we put on the floor and, next day, we got a stove — all on credit. I went to work immediately in the cotton mill. And so, good-by to childhood. At eight years of age, I became self-supporting and was on my way to independence. I had no shoes, but I had dreams. The pay was good — about six cents an hour. The hours were light — only the twelve-hour night shift. And I was supremely happy.

CHAPTER II

MY job in the cotton mill was to push a four-wheeled cart up and down the aisles, delivering spools of bobbin to the weavers. The weavers worked by the piece and in this particular mill made duck. An expert could handle six looms.

Up and down the aisles — all night long — I delivered spools to the weavers. I was not quite as tall as the cart I pushed. I would have to make a path down the middle of the spools of bobbin stacked on my cart and then, standing on my toes, I could see where I was going.

At the end of the first week, I had earned four dollars and fifty cents. I was rich and sat for a long time, thinking what I would do with it. "Mama" settled that question by taking it away from me. The next week I took the initiative. I gave "Mama" three dollars and kept a dollar fifty for myself, which I thought was fair. I bought my first pair of shoes then from a peddler by paying him fifty cents down and the rest on installment. I was thrilled with them — they were high-heeled. The next week I bought a pair of sneakers which I know now as tennis shoes. I needed those shoes because it was very hard walking up and down the aisles of the mill in bare feet.

At the end of two months I was given the job of repairing the warp. The warp is the part of the cloth that is in a huge roll in the back of the loom. Because the weavers worked by the piece, it meant money out of their pockets unless repairs to a broken warp could be made quickly. Running from loom to loom and making repairs was hard work but it paid a dollar a week more than the old job and my eyesight was good and my hands nimble and strong. I'm surprised that I along with the other workers did not get tuberculosis. The cotton "dust" from the spinning was in the air like a mist. Our faces were gray with it in the morning. Certainly our lungs took in a lot of this lint.

After a few months of this work, I was promoted to the inspection room where the material from the looms was put over a board and examined for flaws. Little flaws could be picked and combed out. Spots of oil or dirt had to be removed with a certain type of soap and water. Major flaws had to be rejected and the cloth cut and spliced. Then the cloth was folded into bolts, ready for shipment.

Other girls, some my age but most of them a little older, worked in the inspection room. They used to ask me what I was going to do when I was big. I told them invariably that I was going to have fine clothes and an automobile and be rich, buy things and see all the world. On Sundays I used to walk up and down Broad Street looking through the windows at the clothes. I have never seen anything since at any of the fashion salons in Paris that compared with these Broad Street clothes. Mine I had bought on installment from the same peddler who sold me the shoes. I remember I had a georgette blouse with a colored corset cover and a black wool skirt to go with those high-heeled shoes. At the age of eight or nine, I must have looked like a midget clown in that outfit.

I had been in the inspection room less than two months when I received my first executive position. Then I was still under ten. I was put in charge of about fifteen other children, to teach them how to inspect cloth and to supervise their work. When they came across a place they could not repair, I had to try it as an expert.

No worker seemed to be given much consideration by the management. Child labor and long hours were not the whole trouble. The lighting was poor and the ventilation bad, and the sanitary conditions were terrible. Old-fashioned "Chic Sales" houses were built out over the river which flowed past the mill. There were no rest rooms, no place to sit down from six o'clock in the evening until six o'clock in the morning, no place to go during the half hour given for midnight eating. I used to crawl into my cart for a few minutes after my bite to eat. I dozed one night and was awakened by a pinch from the foreman in a way that no girl should be pinched. I let fly with my fist and it hit him squarely on the nose. He left me alone after that and surprisingly enough did not fire me.

There was always more and more haste to get another yard of cloth out. Human beings did not count — only yardage. I have seen a whole family of man, wife and nearly a dozen children working together at the looms with the father rushing frantically around, spurring the others on so they could stock up as many bolts as possible before six o'clock in the morning.

And that is how labor unions were born. They were needed. Management — at least in these southern mills at that time — had a lot to learn. A labor union was formed in our mill and I paid one dollar for my membership card. No longer in good standing as a card bearer, I certainly well understand the side of the worker. That does not mean that I consider all union activities right or all labor leaders intent on looking after only the interests of their laboring flock. A leader in any field must know that he carries a heavy moral responsibility. The crying need today is for more, and then again more, honest, intelligent leaders in every branch of our industrial, political and agricultural life. There is nothing wrong with pressure groups, either. We all belong to one or another. But all the members of all the pressure groups together make up our citizenry and the good of all is foremost. In time, this young democracy will settle down. But here I am moralizing when I am not yet out of my childhood.

A strike was called in our mill. Twenty-seven mills were shut down when the world was crying for cotton cloth. Depots were set up by the union where a family like ours could draw about three dollars' worth of food a week. But we couldn't keep paying the rent and the mill people tried to get us all evicted. I picketed and must confess I threw bricks and participated in some of the riots, although I did not know what it was all about. I just wanted my good old job back. "Mama" no longer had control over me. I roamed about, waiting for work to start.

"Skeeter Flats" was a favorite place of mine during these days. For five cents one could see there some of the old-fashioned, high-action serial movies. And for the gathering and turning in of twelve "coke" bottles I could rustle the necessary nickel. The nickelodeon on "Skeeter Flats" was strictly a poor folks' affair. The real ladies of the town did not go to shows of that kind. I was fourteen years old before I was told that a "skeeter" was a mosquito to a "damyankee." During all this period I never stopped reading. This habit stayed with me from the time I started in Miss Bostwick's room. I used to read several hours a day with a dictionary at my side. During the strike, I read *Dracula* — not a very good book for a ten-year-old child to read. But I did not think of myself as a child.

The strike went on for three months. The workers were getting pretty hungry and tired of the beans and fatback issued to them at union headquarters. I was disgusted and talked to the fore-woman in the department where I had been supervising the group of children inspectors. She was a nice woman and advised me to get out of the factory and take a new start because I had energy and aims not possessed by the others. She told me to go and see a Mrs. Richler who ran a beauty shop. She said she would recommend me to Mrs. Richler to run errands, do odd chores and clean up the shop.

Mrs. Richler was a small, dark woman. I told her about my cooking ability and my love of work and the dexterity I had with my hands. I told her I could do things I really didn't know about. But my attitude was right. (It was like declaring a low handicap in golf and then having to live up to it on the course.) I got the job and went to live with the family — man, wife and six children. The house was nice. They were orthodox Jews and they ate kosher food, which I learned to make and like. On Jewish Sabbaths, when an orthodox Jew will not strike a match or do any cooking, I cooked all the meals for the family but every day I was up at five o'clock and helped with breakfast and the cleaning. Then I went to work at one of their three shops, cleaning the booths, making up big batches of shampoo and henna for the day. In a back room, unlighted except for a gas jet, I was taught to make transformations. Soon I started shampooing customers' hair and helped give permanent waves. A permanent was something new then, and it was expensive and took nearly all day. I worked from twelve to fourteen hours a day and received my room and board and a dollar fifty a week. Mrs. Richler took a motherly interest in me. I became quite familiar with the Jewish religion and she taught me the beginnings of a code of living, built on the start Miss Bostwick had made.

But I got my real lessons in morality from a "fancy lady" who came to the shop for hair dyes and permanents. She owned a "house" of which there were many in Columbus, Georgia, because of the mills. I believe this madam had been a schoolteacher. Certainly she was a person of education. She spoke well — with a northern accent — and she corrected my grammar and directed my reading. She told me how easy it was for a pretty girl to live without mixing shampoo and waving hair but how much better it was to work and maintain self-respect. She warned me about men and their ways. She had traveled a lot and told me wonderful stories about beautiful cities and lovely clothes. I was fascinated and made the work drag on as long as possible, practically dyeing her hair strand by strand, because I wanted to hear more. She always ended with a lecture to get where I was going in life the hard way. It's strange that my foundations in ethics and honesty and morality came to me not from my foster mother but from Miss Bostwick, the priest and a prostitute. They all taught me the same lessons.

We had many "fancy girls" as customers. They came in the front door while the respectable women, who wanted a little beautification, sneaked in the back way. The women in Columbus were the last in America to adopt the short haircut. That was because when a woman was picked up in Columbus for bad behavior, she was sent to what was called "The Rockpile" and her hair was cut short before they released her. Nice women, therefore, did not want their hair cut.

The operators worked on commission, usually getting forty per cent of what they took in. I would help them and thus speed up their work and in consequence their earnings. They themselves would pay me for this help out of their commissions. By helping the operators this way at this stage of my apprenticeship, I usually ended up the week with from eight to ten dollars. Invariably I gave exactly half of it to "Mama." My family was back on Sawdust Road. The strike had been a failure. The working conditions were worse than ever. I had now reached the point of sympathizing with "Mama's" lot and took over as her protector through subsequent years until she died. But now I had found this wonderful niche with Mrs. Richler, and I stayed on.

When I had been an apprentice for two years, someone started checking Mrs. Richler's shops for child labor. I had put my hair up and tried to look more than my thirteen years. In fact, I was the only girl she employed under sixteen. I overheard Mrs. Richler tell the investigator I was sixteen and that she was my guardian. I then promptly announced to her that I would go on full pay as an operator, or I would leave. She upbraided me for ingratitude, said she was teaching me a trade. I quietly pointed out that I had reached the point where I was bringing in more than two hundred dollars a week in income, though I was still getting from her only a dollar fifty in salary — plus what the operators themselves gave me. I said to Mrs. Richler that I had many friends among the clients and could go to another shop and take them with me. I told her I would be willing to continue to live at her house but would do no work except in the shop and during regular hours, that I would take room and board and thirty-five dollars per week — and further, I would work no longer in the back room with transformations and switches because they made me sick. She told me I was under age and could not work elsewhere. I replied that she had said she was my guardian and had certified me to be sixteen. She capitulated. I continued another year with her on that basis and saved every dime. Before the year was out I had several hundred dollars. What wealth that was for a snip of a girl.

One day I heard a traveling salesman for a beauty shop equipment company telling Mrs. Richler about a store in Montgomery, Alabama, where he could sell a permanent wave machine if only they could get an expert operator. I thought this would be a good way to start my travels. I walked into the room and said I was that expert.

So, when I was still fourteen years old, or perhaps a little less, I left Columbus for Montgomery and went to work as a permanent-wave operator in the beauty shop of a department store.

I was fortunate in finding a lovely place to live in Montgomery. I just went walking about the nice part of the city and when I saw a house I wanted to live in (it was 12 South Anne Street — I will never forget it), I knocked on the door and asked the lady

if she would take me for room and board. She was horrified at
the thought of taking anyone into her home but I talked on and
on, telling her I had never lived in a really nice house and I
thought it would be so pleasant if she would take me to stay with
her. She finally succumbed to my pleas and there I stayed as long
as I lived in Montgomery, until I went into training as a nurse.

At the store I worked on a strictly commission basis. My first
customer was Mrs. Lerton, the first woman to hold public office
in the State of Alabama. It took all day to give that permanent by
the old Nestlè method. But Mrs. Richler had taught me well and
it was a beautiful job.

During the long day's work, we did a lot of chatting. I had
become a most avid reader, starting with the classics under Miss
Bostwick's guidance and staying with them under the direction
of the "fancy lady." At the moment, I was deep in one of the
classics and this intrigued Mrs. Lerton no end. She came back
again and again and after a while she took an interest in me as a
person. She asked my age. When I replied that I was seventeen,
she expressed great doubt. I told her she could doubt if she liked
but she had no proof to the contrary. It was a good thing I rubbed
her the right way for she was a judge in the Juvenile Court and
a power in the community.

Mrs. Lerton became very interested in my welfare and I visited
with her a great deal. Through her and through my landlady I
met young friends, and through them I quickly met others.
Getting acquainted is not difficult for a person who likes people
and is not shy or introspective. My room and board took only a
small part of my earnings and I was saving lots of money. I
learned to dance and I bought a Model T Ford and went to
college parties. My Ford was an asset. It was also my first experience with engines and I personally ground the valves of the
engine in that Model T.

By the end of the first year in the store shop, I was earning as much as the manager and he was disturbed. But, inasmuch as I was on commission, every time they threatened to reduce it, I threatened to quit and they didn't have anyone else who could do permanent waving. I had arrived at a state of independence. I now had a profession and not a trade.

Meantime Mrs. Lerton was following in the path of Miss Bostwick and the madam, for she was instructing me in cooking, sewing and reading. I made clothes and did crocheting and needlework. I was good at it because I was adept with my hands. She finally persuaded me to go into training as a nurse. I told her that without schooling, I could not pass the State Board examinations, but through her influence at the local hospital I was admitted.

I stayed at the hospital three years. During my training my marks were poor in all academic subjects but I excelled in nursing. I was one of a few nurses who had two tours of duty in the operating room, and this by request of the top doctor. My memory was perfect and once I had set things up for an operation, I knew exactly what was wanted and when.

I did not like the sight of blood then, and I don't like it now. I don't think anyone likes the sight of blood, including nurses and doctors. But I had taken on a job which I thought gave me a constructive place in life, and that job involved helping in the operating room.

The most interesting operation I attended was a Caesarean on a midget from the Miller Brothers Carnival which wintered in Montgomery. The most humorous incident was that of the intern who kept drinking the milk I had for patients. I substituted some mother's milk one night and then quietly asked him if he knew what had become of it. He did not get mad. He got sick.

On my day off I used to go down in the wards and cut hair and shave the patients. The barber taught me to use a broadside razor. This was my contribution, my way of doing something extra for those in need and along lines that were suited to my experience and skills. I have an overwhelming compassion for those who, without fault, are unable to help themselves.

At the end of my training I did not take the State Boards but accepted a job with a country doctor in Bonifay, Florida.

Jobs were hard to get at this time and this one in Bonifay seemed right down my alley because it was in a sawmill section and had to do with mill people. I was going back to Sawdust Road again, but this time as a modern Florence Nightingale to help the people I knew needed help so much.

That mill district doctor apparently had great ambitions when he left school, for he had a room full of instruments but they were dirty and rusty and unsterile. His office was filthy and, on top of that, he had more than he could do. I had been with him a week, drawing three dollars a day, when we were called into the woods about fifteen miles out, where a man had a badly crushed leg from a logging accident. The doctor and I traveled out by logging train and did the amputation. We had instruments along, including a saw. I put fire under an old tub and boiled water in which to sterilize the instruments. Things were not too clean but the leg was sawed off and the man lived. I had to stay with him in the logging camp for four days. I had a chair fixed up to sleep in and every four hours the woodsmen would wake me up so I could perform my duties. One of the loggers would sit with the patient while I slept.

One night shortly after this nursing job in the logging camp I was called to a shack to deliver a baby. The doctor was away. He always seemed to be away. The shack was just like the ones I lived in as a child. The woman was on a "St. George" bed. Three children were sleeping on pallets on the floor. The only light came from a mojo lamp. I delivered the baby but there were no clothes for it. I had delivered many babies but this time it struck me the wrong way. I had had quite enough of being a mill-town nurse. I had neither the strength nor the money to do the smallest fraction of what had to be done for these people and I determined that, if I was going to do anything for myself or others, I had to get away and make money. The doctor wanted me to stay, but I had decided to go and said so. That was that. He even said he understood my attitude. So I struck out for Pensacola.

I chose Pensacola because it was the city closest at hand where I knew there would be beauty shops. Nursing was not repugnant to me but it seemed to me that I was adding as much to the happiness of others by making many of them beautiful as by making a few of them well — and I would certainly be doing a lot more for myself.

In Pensacola I applied for a job at a beauty shop that was just opening. The owner, Mrs. Stickley, told me I could work on commission, keeping for myself part of what I took in. The shop was a sorry-looking affair, so I put part of my own money into better furnishings and equipment. That is how I became Mrs. Stickley's partner. But she was a morose person who did not like much of anything, and I did not like the confinement, and after a few months I decided this small business had little to offer me in the way of prospects and so I pulled stakes. I answered an ad and got a job selling dress patterns and materials through various sections of the South. I had my car for travel.

I always had itchy feet. This, according to the Sawdust Road counterpart of Uncle Remus, meant I would travel. The traveling part of selling dress patterns suited me fine. As I went along in my car I improved my spelling from the road signs and at night with a good book in hand I would consult my dictionary. There were plenty of hitchhikers. I never passed one up. On one trip later between Miami and New York I let a hitchhiker drive and he ran me over the bank and the car rolled over, but no one was injured. Another time I picked up a man whose appearance and manners I did not like. At the next town I got rid of him saying it was my destination. The next day's papers showed a picture of Dutch Schulz for whom a search was on. Dutch Schulz was my hitchhiker of the day before. In later years I carried a hitchhiker all the way from Wyoming to Los Angeles.

I loved people and would talk my head off with anyone about anything. So I gathered a great mass of heterogeneous information and it all stuck. This passion for facts, important and unimportant, has substituted for a formal education. But for my part I still regret my lack of schooling. I have never really learned to spell well and I have never lost the telltale scrawl in my writing. A semicolon, to me, is still a small intestine. But Floyd says my vocabulary is amazing. Finding a new word is, to me, like finding a diamond. It immediately starts showing up in my conversation as if I had been born with it on my tongue. I sometimes get confused on the most fundamental rules of grammar but never fail to get the four-bit words in their proper context.

Selling dress patterns was interesting and made me money and developed my knack for salesmanship, but it held no future. So with a little spare financial meat on my ribs, I took over the operation of the beauty salon in the Edgewater Beach Hotel at Biloxi, Mississippi. A hurricane destroyed business in that part of Mississippi, particularly the class business at the winter resort hotel. So back I went to Pensacola and teamed up again with Mrs. Stickley. The business grew and I had a good time attending dances at the Pensacola Naval Flying School where I came to know many who later made their names as captains and admirals. About this time I took dancing lessons from a woman who had won the dancing championship for the State of Texas.

I had a frightful experience in Pensacola at this time which left itself deeply burned into my memories. I was living in a rented room on the ground floor of a private home in a good residential district. It was midsummer and hot. By appointment I had stayed downtown and given a working girl a permanent wave after dinner. Then I had gone home by a ten-cent taxicab driven by a Negro. My room adjoined, and by door connected with, a combination back porch and dinette. The windows of my room opened onto a back yard which merged into a grove of trees. After reading for an hour with the windows wide open for comfort I fell asleep. Shortly thereafter, I was suddenly awakened, presumably by a human touch. A burly Negro was standing over me. I could see his features in the moonlight. His hand was raised over me and held what looked like a knife. As I opened my eyes, he warned me that he would kill me if I uttered a sound. My reaction was immediate. I screamed at the top of my voice. He hesitated a moment then dropped the knife and fled through the window. The knife proved to be an ice pick which he had taken from the old-fashioned icebox on the back porch. The cigarette stubs and footprints under my window showed that he had waited restlessly all the time while I was reading. I moved upstairs the next day.

All beauty operators take the so-called trade magazines, which are intent on selling every type of apparatus — every type of new gadget. The beauty schools, including one in Philadelphia, advertised in these magazines, encouraging operators to come and take a refresher course and learn all the latest styles in hair dressing. I figured if I went to Philadelphia and took this course — then returned to Pensacola — all the people in Pensacola would think I had the latest from the North.

So to Philadelphia I went. I knew I could earn my living anywhere. I could get a job on commission in any city or good-sized town within a matter of hours and be on my own as to income. I reported to the school about seven o'clock in the morning. No one showed up until ten. The full course was, I thought, too expensive. The marcel-waving course was sixty dollars, so I decided to take that.

The next morning when I reported as a student, the manager

asked to see me. It seemed that I knew more than the school did about many branches of beauty work. She hired me as instructor and the school gave me sixty dollars per week plus a half of the five dollars I was paid for each private lesson I gave, and I managed at least a dozen such lessons a week. But I was never given back my sixty-dollar deposit. However, I was able to watch and learn about some points as to which I wanted instruction.

The first week in Philadelphia was tragic for me. After I had paid my sixty dollars to the school and my room rent, my purse was stolen on a streetcar, I think. I was not panicky. I tried to send a collect wire to the bank in Pensacola but the telegraph office would not accept it. The pennies I dug up out of the pocket and lining of my coat were enough to keep me from starving for a week. I bought some cheese and crackers, walked to and from the beauty college (it was miles from my room), and went without lunch. It was hard on the feet but probably good for the health. Being hungry was an old experience for me.

After three days of this diet of cheese and crackers, I had my first and only blind date. I was so hungry that when one of the assistant managers of the school said she and her boy friend were going out to a German club for dinner and would like me to go along with them and one of their friends, the old stomach took over and I accepted with alacrity. I remember only that I had an enormous, heavy German meal, and about an hour afterwards the dinner and I parted company. My stomach was in no condition to receive it.

Nine months in Philadelphia was more than enough because I thought it was almost taking money under false pretenses. It was my first exposure to how stupid people can be. The school high-pressured and sold courses to people who had neither the personal appearance nor the ability nor the intelligence ever to be beauty operators. Even worse, people were charged for a beauty treatment and then students were charged to work on such customers. I had left my car, some personal effects and my half interest in the shop in Pensacola, so I knew I would have to go back there. After about three months in Pensacola I just couldn't take it any longer. Mrs. Stickley was in no position to buy my half of the shop, amounting to about three thousand dollars, so I told her that when things were better for her she could do so. I sold my car and set off for New York. I thought I was ready for the biggest city of all.

I found a room for three dollars a week in back of a kitchen with kitchen privileges — near Broadway and Seventy-ninth Street. I took it because of the private shower. I hated the thought of sharing a bath with others. By putting a thin piece of felt around the door, I could keep the kitchen odors out. It had two windows and looked out on the park — and a large enough clothes closet for my few clothes.

I then started out to look for a job. We had all heard of Charles of the Ritz and I went there first. First I filled out an application blank giving my telephone number and address. Then I asked to see Mr. Charles. In answer to his question, I said I could do everything well. He said I didn't look old enough to be an expert, to which I replied that not only could I do things well but I could probably do many things better than himself. I did not like his manner. I thought he was egotistical and irritating. I was pretty fresh and confident of my ability. He was highly amused when I demanded fifty per cent of the take as a commission. He said I couldn't work for him on any basis without cutting off my long, curly blond hair. I said I would not cut it off even if he would turn his whole business over to me and with that I walked out. The next morning, he called and said he had changed his mind — I could go to work and still keep my long hair. I told him I had no interest in working for anyone who would attempt to impose on personal rights the way he had. So Charles of the Ritz lost a mighty independent operator. Mr. Charles is no longer living, but the company built around his name and Jacqueline Cochran are competitors in the cosmetics field.

The loss to Mr. Charles, so far as my services were concerned, became Antoine's gain. At least that is the way I figured it then. At that time Antoine was the rage in New York and his Saks-Fifth Avenue Salon was packed with customers.

With Antoine I caught on and started making good money. Before long I was going each winter season to his beauty shop at Miami Beach. I used to drive nonstop both ways to have the extra day to get located before reporting for duty.

I met many nice people through my work, both in New York and in Miami. But particularly, I had fun in Miami where I won many dancing contests and also, to balance it off the other way, took a prize at the county fair with my needlework. Molly Hemphill stands out in my mind in connection with Miami. Her husband, "Cliff," was a partner with our recent Ambassador to Spain, Stanton Griffis, in the financial firm of Hemphill, Noyes and Company of New York. The Hemphills liked to entertain and I was usually invited to their numerous dinner parties, as the much needed extra woman. Several nights a week, I would join them at one of the combination night clubs and gambling casinos. Cliff liked to gamble and had plenty to gamble with so usually after dinner and a dance or two, we would all go into the gambling room. I have seen him "on the rack" — that is, in temporary debt to the casino — at one time during an evening of play for thousands of dollars. Even a few dollars looked like a lot of money to a girl from Sawdust Road. Always, I drove my own little Chevrolet to the restaurant and would leave at midnight and drive home, for I was hard at work fairly early in the morning. I would always be offered money to play with by Cliff but never accepted more than twenty dollars. If I lost that, I quit and would not accept more. If I won, I would return the advance. Practically never did I lose. I have noticed since, while around casinos, that the small-spending woman who is there with a heavy-spending man usually wins while the man loses. The wheel just seems to go that way somehow and it just happens to be a happy combination that turns out well for the house. During my last season in Miami, I accumulated several thousand dollars over the tables. That was bad because gambling rather got into my blood. In later years, before I got better sense about these matters, I gave it all back.

I met Floyd at a party in Miami given by Stanton Griffis. Floyd was down there for a rest and had a cabana next to Stanton's at the Surf Club. Stanton asked him to the dinner and mentioned the actresses and other female luminaries who would be there. Floyd said he was too tired, but when Stanton completed the list of guests by telling of a pretty and interesting girl who worked in a store for a living, Floyd said he would go if he could be seated next to her. He told me in later years that he was too tired to face a conversation about the latest books or stage plays with experts in their line and felt he could have a comfortable evening, without such great mental effort, by talking with someone down to earth.

That night, I felt sure I had met up with my destiny. Standing in the lobby with Cliff and Molly Hemphill, where we were collecting for cocktails and just idling for a moment, I saw this thin, clean-cut man, later known to me as Floyd, walk into the lobby and go with very quick steps to the checkroom. I looked at Cliff and asked him why he didn't invite men like this stranger to his parties. Much to my surprise, a little bit later, I found this same man sitting next to me at cocktails and he started talking to me. Later we were seated together at the dinner table. He invited me into the casino for a bit of gambling. He bought one hundred dollars in chips and gave me twenty off the top. Strangely enough, it was the first night that I quickly lost — but

Floyd wanted me to sit with him while he played a little longer so, as an exception, I took some more chips and lost nearly a hundred before quitting. This quiet, serious man also quit after losing about three hundred dollars. I thought probably he was a clerk in a bank and I was concerned over his losses. He didn't look and act at all like the tycoons I had seen around that club all winter.

I think I got the idea about flying that first night during the table conversation with Floyd. I told him about my work in the beauty salon and how hard and confining it was and that I thought I would go on the road for a cosmetic house because I liked to travel and be out in the air. He said that with the depression on and competition so very keen, I would almost need wings to cover the territory fast enough.

Two days later Floyd gave a dinner party of his own at the Indian Creek Golf Club and made me the guest of honor among the twenty or more people present. In later years, he told me how the first time he went to Europe, he took on the big gambling table at Deauville and dropped thousands of dollars — and as a matter of principle then stopped gambling altogether. He had gone overboard that night in Miami with three hundred. Ever since, I have seen him limit his losses to fifty dollars, which he says is the cover charge for an occasional evening with friends who like to see the roulette wheel turn.

I saw Floyd only those two evenings in Miami. He went north the day after the dinner at which he gave me the seat of honor. Two months later I saw him in New York. He had said he would call me at Antoine's. It was against the rules to receive telephone calls during business hours but I had explained to the office manager that this one exception had to be made in my case or I would quit. Floyd called and took me out to dinner. It was the day I had selected as my birthday. When he learned during dinner of the anniversary I was celebrating he gave me a twenty-dollar gold piece he had in his pocket, which I still have in my lockbox.

Meantime I had been thinking about what Floyd had said to me in Miami about flying. I was near the top of my profession and I was tired of the daily conversation with customers — later so vividly depicted in Clare Booth Luce's *The Women*. I wanted to go higher than Rockefeller Center which was being erected across the street from Saks-Fifth Avenue and was going to cut off my view of the sky. I decided that if I could fly, I could really take on representation of a good cosmetic company and start a new career. This would help my itchy feet and make me more money and get me out of a line of work that seemed to lead nowhere.

So, one fine day in the summer of 1932, I decided to take the three weeks' holiday I had coming to me and learn to fly. I showed up at Roosevelt Field, Long Island, at the flying school. At that moment, when I paid for my first lesson, a beauty operator ceased to exist and an aviator was born. The idea of cosmetics stuck, however, and I have joined the two activities together.

※※

CHAPTER III

THE Roosevelt Field Flying School gave me a half-hour lesson free, as a teaser. That was my first experience in the air. I went up with a man by the name of Husky Lewellyn and he *was* husky. He was so big he could hardly get inside the plane and I wondered if it would carry us both. Without explaining a thing, he opened the throttle and we took off. Then after a few instructions he let me attempt to land the plane on the first circuit of the airport. I had caught on pretty well for some unknown reason. I was told it would take me two or three months to put in the necessary hours for a license. I said I had just three weeks to give to it. Husky expressed doubt that it could be done in that time but they took my money for the course and I went up again immediately. The next morning I was at the airport at seven o'clock. No one else showed up until nine o'clock. But I had a glorious two hours not only watching the sky which had taken on a new aspect for me and which I now knew I intended to conquer, but also browsing around the hangar looking over the planes and studying a mural on the wall painted by a woman pilot, Aline Rhonie, which depicted all the then "greats" in aviation and their exploits.

The following day, around midafternoon, Husky climbed out of the plane and said it was all mine to fly alone from then on. On the third day I went off on my first solo flight, when I didn't know the difference between a biplane and a monoplane. The engine quit on that first solo flight but luckily I made it back to the field on a dead stick. That gave me confidence. The next morning, as I was about to take off, a plane spun in across the field and my flight was delayed while the fragments of man and plane were being collected. On the very next day, George Gardner, then a government inspector but now president of Northeast Airlines, had me fly him over to North Beach Airport (now LaGuardia) where they were dragging some bodies out of the marsh at the end of the field. That landing, which these people had made short of the runway, was for keeps and taught me a lesson.

Short of three weeks I had my license but I was without any realization of my ignorance. I was full of plans. Just after I got my license, Canada invited the sportsmen pilots in the United States to an air meet in Montreal. My itchy heels and my new love of flying took over and I decided to attend that meet if I could get hold of a plane. I gave up my job with Antoine. M. E. Grevenberg (whom I later came to know as "Grevy" and a gypsy of the air if there ever was one) rented to me his Fairchild on the condition that I put up as security the full cash value of two thousand dollars. He said it was stupid of me to do the flight with my limited experience and asked to go along, but I always have felt that God takes care of the stupid. Anyway I wanted to try my wings. I bought air maps and had them explained to me. One old-timer said that the best thing for me to do would be to follow the Hudson River until I arrived at Lake Champlain and then to follow the lake until I came to Burlington, Vermont, where I should land, clear customs and ask for directions to Montreal. That was exactly what I did. I buzzed up the Hudson River on a beautiful day with unlimited visibility but, all of a sudden, I discovered I was following not the Hudson but a big canal. I retraced my steps, feeling a little apprehensive. Eventually I found the river again and finally the lake, the city and the airport. After clearing customs, I asked the airport attendant the way to Montreal. He naturally thought I was pulling his leg but I convinced him of my ignorance. He told me the compass course and the distance. Then I had to confess I didn't know how to read the compass. With that, he got some men out and they pushed the airplane around to show me the various readings on the compass and what they meant. I was told the general direction and that, about halfway there if on course, I would see two big silos. Fortunately the silos showed up and I got so intrigued with the compass when I saw those silos that I flew around and around them in circles, studying the compass and seeing what the readings were on it. I was something of a heroine at that air meet because my first flight away from an airport had been a fairly long distance and across the international border.

Grevenberg was at the meet by the process of air hitchhiking. He asked if I would give him a ride back to New York. I finally consented if I could take the control stick out of his cockpit so he would be only a passenger. Off we went. Pretty soon we were flying into almost a wall of haze. I looked back at him and he was pointing frantically for me to land. It's a good thing I did because otherwise I would not be here today. We landed on an airstrip, I forget just where. The weather was terrible ahead and unflyable for two days.

Flying was now in my blood as a career of its own. I had seen Floyd several times during the summer and he encouraged me in my flying. But winter was no time to carry on with my flying on Long Island. The aviation magazines told me the wonders of a Ryan Flying School at San Diego where the skies were always blue. In my car I headed for San Diego. When I reached Salt Lake City, I felt the need of a little refresher flight, so went to the airport and exhibited my license. The owner of an old Curtiss-Wright pusher plane rented it to me and off I went to fly all over the nearby Wasatch Mountains to see the fall colorings. The first light snow had just fallen, but the leaves were still on the trees and presenting their seasonal gaudiness to the few humans who could get up that high. There are so many wonderful things one can see while flying that earth-bound souls miss. After skimming the mountains I flew across the Great Salt Lake to an island in the middle of the lake where there were many buffalo. I flew low and chased them as if I were a modern Indian turning loose a stampede.

Soon I got disgusted with the San Diego flying school because I had to spend so much time on the ground for so little in the air. There were too many students for the number of planes available, and the blue skies were often foggy.

I found some of my old Pensacola Navy friends in San Diego with the fleet. Every Sunday evening, I was a guest on the *West Virginia*. Our recent Ambassador to Russia, Admiral Kirk, was a senior officer on that ship. Ted Marshall was the air officer attached to that battleship and one of the best pilots in the Navy. He listened to my complaints about lack of training and air time and said that if I would buy my own plane, he would direct a course of training the Navy way, and would give me flight instructions whenever the fleet was in port. I bought an old Travelair plane with a Gypsy motor for twelve hundred dollars. When the *West Virginia* moved to Long Beach, I also moved my flying headquarters there. So I was, in fact, trained in flying by the Navy. Paul Adams, then at the Long Beach Airport, now a captain on Pan American Airways, helped with my training during the periods while Ted was at sea.

In those early days a forced landing was usual. Every minute while in flight, one had to have an eye out for the best spot on which to make a landing in case of engine failure. I have landed on a substantial part of all the beaches and open spots in Southern California. One forced landing was through the fence to a road and into a parked car owned by the traffic judge. He fined me twenty-five dollars for unlawful parking. Another time I had the head of the flying school at San Diego in the plane with me. That time I landed on a narrow section of the beach down near the Mexican border.

Repeatedly I have been asked why I took up flying and have spent so much time and energy on it and have taken so many risks in the air. One might as well ask artist John Doe why he paints canvases with no thought of sales or why Richard Roe risks his neck, climbing to some almost inaccessible mountain to look for a new type of butterfly or an ancient grave. Each will attempt a rationalization of his actions. Flying got into my soul instantly but the answer as to why must be found somewhere back in the mystic maze of my birth and childhood and the circumstances of my earlier life. My determinations, based on incessant energy — my ups and downs of emotions — my likes and dislikes are all instantaneous and clear-cut from something deeper than the conscious mind. Whatever I am is elemental and the beginnings of it all have their roots in Sawdust Road. I might have been born in a hovel but I determined to travel with the wind and the stars.

Ted Marshall was on shore leave in Long Beach and we were in the apartment of Naval Captain and Mrs. Gaid Mitchell having cocktails when the earthquake hit in 1933. The front of the building we were in was shaken down. The elevators were torn apart. The sofa on which I was sitting landed against the wall across the room. We got down by fire escape. Notwithstanding the seriousness of the situation I had a great laugh because of the antics of a very fat woman who had become wedged in one of the main-floor windows. Her husband was trying to push her through and she was wiggling like a woman trying to get out of a tight girdle. What her husband needed was a man-sized shoe horn. I rushed from the wreckage of this building to the hospital to give nursing aid. For several days, until things quieted down, I slept and cooked in the yard back of the apartment house where I lived. Captain Mitchell of that earthquake party was leader of one of the Navy squadrons that flew out in the beginning of World War II with only a one-way fuel supply to meet and defeat the Japanese in the Battle of Midway. He was rescued after floating several days at sea. We have been close friends for years and I am his child's godmother.

It was through Ted that I became a rancher in that desert fairyland of Southern California, known as the Coachella Valley. I went down to visit his brother George, who was a rancher there, and to see the riot of spring colors. Two weeks later, when Floyd was on the coast, I asked him if he would go down and see the same glories of nature. As a result of these trips, independently made, each of us secretly asked George Marshall to pick up some land for us. Later, when Floyd and I were married and discovered each was a landowner in this desert, we joined forces in the "Cochran-Odlum Ranches." It was like making a fifty-fifty stew out of horse meat and rabbit — one horse to one rabbit. I had the twenty-acre rabbit and Floyd the thousand-acre horse. It was raw desert land then but now, due to our own efforts as the first human beings to till the soil, it produces heavily and has been run from the beginning as a business.

The virgin soil of our desert lies below sea level, having been dyked off from the Gulf of Southern California through the centuries by silt from the Colorado River. In time the water behind the dyke evaporated. But not quite all and in the lowest spot in the desert floor is the Salton Sea with its surface about three hundred feet below sea level and its water salty. Desert literally means a deserted place. But this is the wrong description. Even before man brought in his irrigation canals and date groves and citrus trees, the desert teamed with life. It's easy when musing about the desert to think in terms of coyotes, bobcats, pack rats, lizards and rattlesnakes. They are there in plenty. But the sun which in its harsher moods can bring on a summer heat of 130°

in the shade also has its softer side. Under its glare deep colors shrink into pastel shades, the white of the limitless sands merges into the grays and greens and purples of the sage and desert holly, the yucca and ocotillo, the mesquite and smoke trees. Spring with its multicolored carpet of verbena, Spanish bayonets, trumpet vine and night-blooming primrose cannot be bettered any place any time. The perfume of these native blossoms mingled with the fragrance of the flowers of the man-planted tangerine and grapefruit can be detected in the air a mile high. During April I can shut my eyes while flying and tell when I am over our ranch. The clear star-studded nights even in summer are usually comfortably cool and are ushered in by some of the most glorious and colorful sunsets ever born.

Ted Marshall and I laid plans to enter the London-Australia Air Race in 1934. The prize money was large and it was a chance for me to see more of the world. But Ted was transferred to Hawaii and there, within a few weeks, met death in his Navy plane. He didn't want to go to Hawaii. He seemed to have a premonition that he would never come back. I have never seen a man more devoted to his duty than Ted.

At the time of Ted's death I was in the East, and I now had a commercial pilot's license. I had sold my little trainer plane at a slight profit and had bought my first new plane, a Waco, for $3200. I decided to fly west in my new Waco to attend Ted's funeral.

Willie Mae — she who surrendered the doll to me — had a four-year-old daughter staying with me at the time and I took the child along for company on what was really my first cross-country flight. The Montreal trip had been mostly river following. Between Rock Springs, Wyoming, and Salt Lake City, Utah, I got lost. My compass was badly off true, due to faulty shielding of the radio, and as a consequence I was flying down the mountain range east of Salt Lake, rather than across it. Worse luck —

I got into a down draft of air in a cup in the mountains and could not rise above the crest. After desperately trying to get out of this predicament, I saw a little green spot below and headed for it. It was a patch of alfalfa and if there had not been an irrigation ditch running through it, I would have made the landing safely. As it was, I nosed over without damage to the child or myself but the propeller was broken. I managed to hire an old Ford from the farmer and drove to Salt Lake City for a mechanic and parts. Two days later, I flew that plane off the same spot and on to Long Beach in time for the funeral.

With Ted gone, I nevertheless determined to fly in the Australian Race, which meant a lot of preparation. As a preliminary, in the fall of 1933 I entered a women's pylon race at an air meet at Roosevelt Field. The flying in that race was high, wide and handsome. It was the only all-women's race I ever participated in.

About this same time Floyd came down with a dreadful cold in New York and wanted to get to Florida for a week end of sun bathing. I agreed to fly him down in my Waco. We became caught in murky weather over the Carolinas. I had never had any blind-flying training and had picked up just enough knowledge on my own to stay right side up while flying straight and level. I didn't dare turn back this day in the bad weather because I didn't know how to turn safely by instruments, so for forty minutes I flew straight ahead. When Floyd saw me cross myself for divine help, he knew we were in for trouble but calmly stated that he was tired and was going to take a nap. He told me afterward he did this to give me assurance but that he kept his off eye wide open, staring at the overcast and wondering fearfully about the outcome.

Floyd's throat was dry from that experience so when we got into the clear I landed in a cow pasture near a house and got some water. Then we landed on the beach near Orlando so Floyd could take a sun bath. The plane had no more than rolled to a stop when we were pounced on by two revenue officers who thought we were smugglers from Cuba.

I made up my mind, after that experience, that I would never again take up a passenger until I had mastered instrument flying. But there were no teachers available. Wiley Post was good and agreed to teach me but the lessons did not mature because he was too busy preparing for his round-the-world flight. So I bought a book on the subject and tried to teach myself. I hired a flying student to sit in the cockpit outside the blind hood I had rigged up and it was his job to look out for other planes and also to tell me if my own plane was getting out of control. The next time I saw that student he had become a captain on Eastern Airlines.

During that period and subsequently, I also put in much time in the pilots' compartments of some of our transport airliners. In those days there were no hostesses on the passenger planes and the copilot had to serve the meals and look after the comfort of passengers. The copilots hated this work and I struck a deal with many of them and their first pilots whereby I would do all this cabin work until the passengers had gone to sleep if I would then be allowed to do the flying for a few hours. Thus I became, in effect, the first hostess and that's what the passengers at the time thought I really was. I probably put in three hundred hours at the airline controls by this strategy and it was the finest sort of training.

Taking care of the passengers was not always easy. Little was known about need for oxygen in those days and I watched passengers and pilots get into trouble when weather forced the plane above 15,000 feet. Once I took a copilot's seat when he passed out from lack of oxygen on a flight between Los Angeles and Albuquerque. The captain was groggy too and made a rough landing. Nowadays, the crew must by regulation use oxygen above 10,000 feet.

Another time, I took charge of a mental patient between Salt Lake City and Los Angeles. He went to the toilet before we reached Las Vegas and didn't show up again. Because he had to be in his seat before landing, I finally opened the toilet door to pull him out, but he was not there. After landing, we found him crouched in the tail of the plane — all mixed up with and hanging on to the control wires. He had crawled back there through the inspection hatchway that led from the toilet to the rear of that old Fokker plane. The pilot had quite a time with that landing. On another occasion one of the Marx brothers tipped me at the destination because I had been so helpful during the trip. I thanked him, kept the tip, and put it in the collection box the next Sunday.

About this time the government canceled its air mail contracts with the airlines and the Air Force took over. Commercial pilots who had been flying the mail were grounded and a group of them on reduced pay were waiting for developments. Among them was Wesley Smith, one of the best instrument pilots in the country. I made a deal with him to give me his whole time for four months. (He turned his pay in to the pilot group to help them weather together their financial difficulties.) Instrument flying then became my daily routine and before many weeks, with Smith as my lookout, I was flying from coast to coast, entirely on instruments with the hood over my cockpit removed only for landing.

The cancellation of the air mail contracts had also caused TWA to cancel orders for some fairly long-range Gamma mail planes that Northrop Corporation was building. Jack Northrop was a friend of mine who had come to my rescue in 1933 when the Gypsy motor in my Travelair quit and a crack-up in Los Angeles resulted. He and Al Menasco, head of the Menasco Engine Company, had come over and made my plane flyable. I told Northrop then that I would never be satisfied until I had bought one of his planes.

Now, for the Australian Race, I bought a Gamma plane, installed gas tanks in the mail space to give it a 3000-mile range, installed a liquid-cooled Curtiss-Wright Conqueror motor and a specially built supercharger designed to increase the plane's speed at 14,000 feet from 220 miles to 240 miles an hour. It looked to me like a sure winner and I counted my profits, one way or another, into the hundreds of thousands of dollars. But I counted too soon. Wesley Smith and Royal Leonard (subsequently private pilot for Chiang Kai-shek) were going to serve as copilots with me, each going half of the way. The plane was ready to take to the air in Los Angeles only three days before it had to be put on a boat in New York. So, Leonard and I took off from Los Angeles as soon as the plane was flyable in order to get it back east. The take-off was at midnight. The supercharger, the first one ever installed in a private plane, gave way over Arizona and, although we were about asphyxiated with fumes, we made it safely to an emergency field. I went on east by transport plane to arrange shipment of my plane by boat and the Curtiss people came out to the emergency field to make repairs. The next night, Leonard took off again with the Curtiss-Wright Company's mechanic in the back seat and again the supercharger broke down, this time over New Mexico. Flares were dropped and a crash landing made. It cost the insurance company to have that plane rebuilt just what the plane originally cost me. Howard Hughes rented the rebuilt plane from me and in it made a transcontinental record and several other outstanding flights. In this same plane I had trouble in the 1935 Bendix Race. I had a fire in it in 1936, crashed in it later in the same year, had it rebuilt and then sold it to Bernarr MacFadden. The even then aging MacFadden damaged it in one of his first flights. Once again it was repaired and resold. Once again it crashed on the Teterboro Airport in New Jersey. The last I heard about that plane it was still flying in North Africa. Such is the endurance of some planes. But I did not have it for the 1934 Australian Race.

I knew that the Granville Brothers of Springfield, Massachusetts, had a special modified "Gee Bee" racing plane completed for the Australian Race, but their backers had failed them. I said that if their plane could be flown to New York and properly entered in the race, I would buy it. They hoped to get a military contract and a part of my deal was that I would get a royalty on all other planes of the same design that were sold.

The plane got to New York all right and on board the boat. But it was in an unfinished state and had not been tuned up or tested. Two mechanics worked on it on the way across the ocean and for a week in England. Late afternoon, thirty-six hours before the start of the race, Mr. Smith and I stepped into the plane to fly it for the first time. He took the front cockpit and the controls and I sat on a cracker box in the back cockpit because the rear seat had not yet been installed. After a very unsatisfactory ride, we arrived at Mildenhall Field just at dusk and landed so hard we thought we had broken a wing. The newsmen were on hand to greet us and we walked away from the plane quickly to hide the damage. There was none. It was just the way that plane always landed. In addition, its two landing wheels were so close together that a straight roll on the runway was next to impossible.

Dawn of the second day and we were off for Australia. Our first stop for gas was at Bucharest, Rumania, and we beat the entire field on that first lap. What a ride that was, in an untested and really unfinished plane. We were above an overcast and came down through it on instruments to locate ourselves accurately near Budapest before starting over the Carpathians. Right over the highest ridge of the Carpathians the engine sputtered and quit while I was shifting the fuel flow from one tank to another. Smith pulled his canopy open preparing to jump. My canopy was stuck so Smith did not leave the plane. I fiddled hurriedly with all the fuel line switches and suddenly the engine took again. I wrote Smith a note — it was too noisy on the plane to hear one another — saying that when the valve says "On," it means "Off." I had turned *off* the gasoline when I only intended to turn *on* a new tank. When we came in for a landing at Bucharest, one flap was stuck while the other one moved a little. That threw the plane out of balance. We climbed, went around, and tried again, with similar results. By that time, we had loosened my canopy and had agreed that if we failed on the third attempt to land, there was nothing left but a jump. Finally, we got both flaps back in flying position and came in very fast. It was a good long field and luckily so — we used it all — and our race ended right there. The Rumanian Air Minister, Radu Irimescu (who is now an American citizen and a business associate of Floyd's), was there to greet us because it was a restricted military airport.

Smith stayed on to get the plane in flying condition and to bring it back to the boat. I got to a store to buy a coat to cover my flying clothes and within a matter of hours, was on the Orient-Express for Paris. At the border of Hungary, in the middle of the night, my door was opened by officials and request was made for my passport. The officials could not speak English and I could speak nothing else, but it was clear something was wrong. They made signs that I would have to get off the train. I backed into the far corner of my compartment with a water bottle in my hand and prepared to fight it out physically, if necessary. Suddenly I thought of the Bucharest evening paper in my handbag with a front page picture of myself and the Air Minister. I showed it to them and then pointed to my flying clothes. The officials backed away and left me in peace. The next morning, I learned from the International Conductor that I answered the description of a jewel smuggler they were looking for and they were more than suspicious when my passport bore no permit to enter Rumania. I had not planned to enter Rumania, except for an airport stop, nor to leave by train.

Soon after we got that plane back to New York the factory pilot took officials of the Chilean Air Force up for a demonstration flight. I arrived at the airport ten minutes late so was only in time for the crash landing because something had gone wrong. No one was hurt, but my royalties on future orders went up in thin air. A year later, the plane was sold to the Mexican Government and Captain Sarabia — the Lindbergh of that country — used it to make a record flight from Mexico City to Washington. On his take-off in Washington, a few days later, for a record flight back, something happened. The plane dived into the Potomac just beyond the end of the field and Captain Sarabia was killed. I think I was one of the few owners of a "Gee Bee" who didn't lose his life in it. They were squatty, fast, and most unstable.

That Australian Race was for me a tragedy of errors. The original plane would have been good enough, without change, to win the race but my expensive supercharger put the plane out of the race. The cost, excluding the cost of the plane, was about twenty thousand dollars. I put up a substantial part of the money myself. Mabel Willebrandt put up the balance. She was then fresh from her job of enforcing Prohibition and a good leader among women, besides being a good lawyer. She was to get her money back first plus a percentage of all prize money and profits. When the supercharger broke down, Curtiss-Wright reimbursed all these expenses, which included entry fee, trip to England, refueling equipment and similar items. Mabel Willebrandt became my friend at that time and she now has a ranch next to us in the desert.

There was one other woman in the 1934 Australian Race — Amy Mollison, an Englishwoman. I had had special quick refueling devices installed in Bagdad and northern Australia, and when I dropped out of the race in Bucharest I wired ahead to have

Amy Mollison given the benefit of my refueling devices. During those early days she was England's foremost woman pilot. She later served in the British Air Transport Auxiliary and was killed in that service.

My time during 1934 could not be given over entirely to preparation for the Australian Race. Between the hours when I was flying or studying celestial navigation or Morse code I was busy starting my cosmetics business. Also one of my numerous operations caught up with me during the summer of 1934. A bad attack, which nearly doubled me up in knots, came on during an overnight stop in Albuquerque, New Mexico, on my way to California. I climbed in my plane at midnight and brought it into the airport at Long Beach on instruments and two hours later was on the operating table in Los Angeles. Long Beach was where I did so much early training and I knew the runways and approaches in every detail, so I chose that field rather than a Los Angeles one to get down on in an emergency. In addition to the other difficulties that night one of the wing fuel tanks sprang a leak. Because I had agreed to loan that plane, along with a pilot, to Mabel Willebrandt to go to San Diego, I climbed out of bed eight days later — unbeknown to the doctor — and brought the plane into Los Angeles for repairs. The stitches had not been removed from the incision. It was only after I had taken the plane into the air that I realized I was pushing nature too hard. But I recuperated from that operation and trained for the Australian Race at the same time; and when I took off in the race, I was only one hundred and four pounds in weight — twenty pounds under normal.

As to the cosmetics business, I started with a beauty salon in Chicago and a chemist and a laboratory in New Jersey. It is often said that to get anywhere on a wide scale selecting the proper personnel is of prime importance. If so, I moved correctly at the start. My chemist later became the head of the Association of

Chemists in this perfumery and cosmetics field; Peter Rivoli, one of the leaders in Antoine's, who besides being very competent held my respect as an individual, took charge of the salon in Chicago and is still there; and Miss Genevieve Crowley, who was office manager of Antoine's, came as my assistant. She stayed with me until she retired at the end of 1953.

If you are planning to start a cosmetics business, don't. That is, don't unless you enjoy business headaches and worries. But I shall tell you more about that later on. Just now I am only pointing out that I was a mighty busy person during the year of 1934, which was the year I started air racing.

With the experience I had in the Australian Race and in the preparation for it, I thought myself qualified for the next year's Bendix Race. My career of racing and record breaking had started.

CHAPTER IV

DURING those early years, just as now, the jobs as test pilots and airline pilots went to men, not women. The chances were that if a woman had been selected for this training, before she had returned a profit on the heavy investment in such training she would have converted herself into a wife and mother.

A woman in the air, therefore, had the choice of flying around in a light plane for pleasure or of obtaining for herself new fast and experimental equipment and determining the maximum that could be obtained from its use. I followed the second course. The objective in each such flight was to go faster or farther through the atmosphere or higher into it than anyone else and to bring back some new information about plane, engine, fuel, instruments, air or pilot that would be helpful in the conquest of the atmosphere.

For more than twenty years I have been exploring the atmosphere, with racing and flying for international speed records as the motivation. I have flown seven races and have gone after new records more than seventy times. Except for the London-Melbourne Race I did all this racing and record flying solo without copilot or other crew member.

But before I give some of my outstanding memories connected with these flights, let us consider for a moment the atmosphere itself. It is very complex.

If the earth were to be looked upon as the inside of a baseball, the atmosphere would be the leather cover. It clings to the face of the earth like a diaphanous veil, heavier on the inside where it exerts a pressure of more than two thousand pounds per square foot and exceedingly light on the outside where the lightest of fluff fades off into space. Space is populated by the universe of stars, planets, satellites and cosmic rays and goes on to infinity, which is boundless. That veil of atmosphere is about one hundred and fifty miles thick. From the face of the earth we humans look through it to the sun and the other heavenly bodies. It seems transparent and of gossamer quality. We see the close-by moon as earth's tallow candle. The underside of the veil holds back and uses the water vapor, gases and other exudations from the earth's face and keeps that face warm by night. The middle part, among other things, holds back or strains out rays from the sun and other points in outer space which, if they reached us, would make life impossible as we know it.

That atmosphere grows more wonderful to me with each trip I make into it.

Earth-bound souls know only that underside of the atmosphere in which they live, which is known to the scientists as the troposphere. The dust particles in this layer of air near the earth catch and reflect the rays from the sun and make things bright by day and oftentimes gloriously beautiful by sunset. But go up higher — above the dust and water vapor — and the sky turns dark and up high enough one can see the stars at noon. I have.

Man, in piloted planes and with pilotless guided missiles, is reaching higher and higher. The atmospheric pressure decreases quickly with increasing altitude so that man would blow up like a toad frog and burst like a bubble before getting much above fifty thousand feet except for the fact that man has provided artificial pressure around him to simulate conditions on the earth's surface. Oxygen also plays out fast as one climbs and therefore it must be carried along for breathing purposes and also at altitude it must be concentrated by compression out of the air for use in the plane's power plant.

Up there, where day is dark, will be found strange things. For example, there is a layer of ozone, in the vicinity of sixty-five thousand feet of altitude, which is poisonous to man but which filters out the worst of the sun's ultraviolet rays. In order to penetrate this ozone layer man would have to be specially protected.

Unlike the cover of the baseball, the atmosphere has many movements within itself, affected as it is by the whirl of the earth on the inside and the heat of the sun. It becomes within itself a myriad of tumbling and tossing, rising and falling segments, each seeming to be fighting the other but being in fact a part of an orderly whole. Jet streams are a comparatively recent discovery among the movements within the atmosphere. They are great rivers of air rushing at high velocity and, like the milder and more spread-out trade winds, according to a predictable pattern. Without warning I hit one of these jet streams once while climbing for high altitude and my plane was knocked almost out of control.

Man has learned a great deal about the air above him during these last twenty years but he has a great deal more to learn before that trip to the moon is undertaken and before human beings populate the sky — as they will in time, just as forms of life have adjusted to and populated the oceans and the land.

If I ever write another book, it will be the history of aviation from the moment of publication of the book back to the time when man first stood up on his hind legs, looked upward and envied the birds. The century posts in between are fascinating, from the imaginative flights of gods and men as depicted on early coins, to the drawings of Leonardo da Vinci, to the balloon and the glider and then the powered flight by Orville Wright on December 17, 1903. He piloted that powered plane for about twelve seconds for the first altitude, distance and speed records.

The least of my records makes his look pretty insignificant if measured by watch or tape. Orville Wright's great record — that of powered flight itself — can never be duplicated. We can only move on from the start he made and there is no end to the sky road.

We are still very much in the exploratory stage. Each day some so-called air barrier is surmounted or some new air frontier is crossed. Yesterday's impossibles have become today's commonplace and the obsolete of tomorrow. The sonic barrier is now behind us. Just ahead lies the heat barrier which causes planes and missiles to melt from the heat of the friction caused by very great speeds. At ten times the speed of sound — which means only about 7000 miles an hour and is not wishful thinking because that speed has already been exceeded in the wind tunnels with experimental guided missiles — the air temperature rises to twelve thousand degrees and the air actually becomes incandescent and glows as it passes over solid objects.

I am one of the comparatively small handful of people who traversed the air during the period when Orville Wright was still alive and interestedly watching. Only a very few thousand people in the United States had pilots' licenses when I took up flying. We learned from the experiences of each other and there was much that had to be learned for ourselves the hard and oftentimes dangerous way.

Were I to make the simple statement that I climbed to an altitude of thirty-three thousand feet, that statement in and of itself would mean nothing because I have often gone higher than that. But when I add that I did this in 1937 in a fabric-covered biplane without heating, without pressurization and without an oxygen mask, the elements of an accomplishment are added. I nearly froze; the pipestem between my teeth through which I tried to get an oxygen supply from a tank and connecting tube was inadequate for the purpose, and I became so disoriented through lack of oxygen that it took over an hour to get my bearings and make a landing. The difference between the pressure my body was accustomed to on the ground and the atmospheric pressure at 33,000 feet was such that a blood vessel in my sinus ruptured. All this was a part of the cumulative evidence that led up to cabin pressurization and mandatory use of the oxygen mask above certain altitudes.

There has hardly been a race or a record flight by me in which I have not tried out something new or experimental. Sometimes it was a new design of plane or wing, sometimes a new engine or a new fuel and sometimes a new airscoop or instrument or pulsating seat to help maintain the body's circulation or a new type of helmet or mask or spark plug. As I look back over the two decades, these tests and the information I developed from them have been my greatest satisfactions.

One great high spot in my memory is connected with my take-off in the Bendix Air Race from Burbank Airport, in Los Angeles, at three o'clock in the morning of September 2, 1935.

My Northrop Gamma plane, which had crashed before the Australian Race, had been rebuilt and equipped with an air-cooled Pratt Whitney engine. At great effort I had the Bendix racing authorities open the race to women provided I could obtain waivers from the male pilots. The plane, after repair, turned out to have a bad vibration which the manufacturer had been unable to fix. The day before the race I was asked by the Northrop and Pratt Whitney people to withdraw because of faulty equipment. I refused because I believed it essential under all the circumstances to make a take-off at least. One other pilot — Cecil Allen — and I chose to take off around three o'clock in the morning. The others got off in good order and with clear sky soon after midnight. Then a fog rolled in. Cecil Allen took off in a "Gee Bee" — like the one I flew in the Australian Race — and was killed at the end of the runway. The heavy load of gasoline and the fog were too much to contend with. I drove down the runway and viewed the wreckage. This was a mistake because the sight tended to unnerve me a bit. As an antidote and to give the appearance of nonchalance I walked into the airport restaurant and ordered a bowl of chili con carne. An official of the Civil Aeronautics Administration came into the restaurant and asked me to stay on the ground with the warning that otherwise I would be killed like Cecil Allen. I retorted that it was a bad suggestion and that if I were to meet up with that fate, I would come back and haunt him. That gave those around me a laugh and bucked up my spirits a bit. But chili con carne was not the right dish for that particular occasion and very soon it and I parted company out behind the hangar.

I climbed into my plane to warm it up. The photographers began flashing pictures which temporarily blinded me and added to my emotional strain. The representative of the plane company again asked me to withdraw. I left the plane and called Floyd on the long distance telephone to ask what I should do. In later years he headed the company that built the B–36 Intercontinental Bomber and the Convair Liners, but in those days his thrills and adventures in the field of aviation were vicarious ones through my activities. I was his aerial automaton governed by remote control. Floyd, that night, said there was a fine line between a course of action determined by logic and one dictated by great emotional urge. No one, he said, could quite draw that line for another. In his opinion it simmered down to a philosophy of life. My decision was to satisfy my emotional urge and go ahead, so back into the plane I climbed.

Down the runway I started, with a fire truck and an ambulance following close behind. The engine of my plane was not putting out the power I counted on. Halfway down the runway I knew it was a very close question whether I could become air-borne at all. I could not see the end of the field for fog but trying to stop at that point would have meant rolling up in a fiery ball a thousand feet beyond. With a prayer in my heart I pulled wide open everything the engine had. I felt the wheels leave the ground, which was like getting manna from Heaven. At the end of the field I was so low that my trailing radio antenna was caught and pulled off by the fence, leaving me no communication. Although off the ground, the plane still did not have flying speed sufficient to make a turn and I was headed westward. So, out over the Pacific I flew. Finally I made a shallow turn on instruments to get back on course. But I was not yet out of the fog or high enough to clear the mountains. So again with a shallow turn on instruments I headed for Japan. Finally I glimpsed a star and then many. Never did stars look so bright and friendly. The tail of the plane, where my cockpit was located, was vibrating badly and the engine had overheated with the overloaded climb. I settled back in my seat and throttled back. Soon San Antonio peak was behind me and then the Colorado River. Around daylight the Grand Canyon with all its colorful and majestic but awful ruggedness was just ahead. I was approaching a violent electrical storm known as a line squall. There would be no airports or landing strips for several hundred miles ahead — just wild peaks and canyons. At this point discretion took the play away from valor. A violent electrical storm is nothing to contend with in a vibrating plane powered with an overheated engine. I had accomplished my main purpose with the instrument take-off in fog, so I headed back for the nearest airport. Fuel had to be dumped. Fortunately the plane had been equipped with dump valves but unfortunately they had not been tested. When the valves were opened the escaping gas was in part sucked back into the tail of the plane. I was saturated and had to throw open the canopy and get my face into the wind stream in order to breathe. The velocity of the wind nearly took my head off but at least I remained conscious and made a landing. Back to Los Angeles I went to attend the funeral services for Cecil Allen. When reporters asked me what happened to me in the race I told them I just got tired and quit. I saw no reason to give an alibi which would put blame on the plane or engine. The manufacturers involved had done their best to stop my flight.

The episode just described stands out so prominently in my memory because I had given myself a great test and had not failed. If I had stayed on the ground that night I probably never would have raced again. In consequence there might not have been any women pilots' program during the war. More than all else, I proved something to myself and it's the down deep inside that one must live with. True it is that I had slapped the cheek of fate the year before over the Carpathian Mountains in the Australian Race, but that was the result of emergency in which predetermination played no part.

I often wonder what is meant exactly by a considered risk. If in advance one thinks about various possibilities of trouble and how to meet them in case of need, that would be consideration of the risk all right. In my own case I like to think that I pondered over the contingencies in advance but not very long. If one ponders too much, usually the risk will not be taken. In my own case the risks that I would consider would not be death so much as burns and painful or disfiguring injuries or damages to a valuable plane or harm to the cause of aviation.

Furthermore, in my case I never could ponder over the risks too much because I had to take a fast plane whenever it became available to me and make the best of it. I won the 1938 Bendix Race in a Seversky pursuit plane which I had never flown until that night, when, with a heavy overload of gas, I took off in the race. The plane was delivered from the factory to me just two days before the race and under the rules it had to be immediately impounded. It was a prototype that had not yet been tested. I tested it en route during the race. Its feature was that it had wings that were in effect integrated tanks so that most of the wings could be filled with fuel, thus adding range. It developed in flight that the fuel from the right wing would not properly feed the engine. By force on the stick I had to hold that wing much higher than the other from time to time in order to drain the fuel from that right wing into the left wing and from that left wing into the engine. When I got the plane back to the factory after the race a large wad of wrapping paper was discovered near the outlet of the right-wing tank. No wonder the drainage was bad. How, for example, could that particular risk be properly considered in advance? The paper in the tank could have been sabotage. Some thought so at the time. More likely it was paper pasted on the inside of the wing during manufacture which had not been removed and which worked loose from the action of the gasoline and the vibration of the plane.

When I landed at Cleveland after winning that race, one of the judges came out to the end of the runway by car to pick me up and take me to the platform in front of the great crowd of people present. He had to wait while I sat in my plane and tidied up my appearance with comb and make-up. He looked quite disgusted when he saw what was going on. I always tried when getting out of my plane, no matter how hard the trip, to look as nearly as possible as if I had just stepped out of a band-box. Even some of the women pilots did not appreciate this flair of mine.

After receiving an ovation by the crowd, I flew on to New York to make a transcontinental record and then took an airline back to Cleveland for the evening's festivities. A police escort met me at the airliner to take me to the hotel at high speed. But I insisted on lazying along in my car. The motorcycle cops asked me why I was unwilling to hurry along past the traffic. My reply was that I had enjoyed enough speed for one day.

The following year I had another Seversky to fly in the Bendix.

When it came off the production line on Long Island there was no test pilot on hand qualified to test it. I took it off for its first flight when I headed west for the starting point of the race. But the landing gear would not work so I had to put down at Dayton, Ohio, for several days of repairs. A thinner and therefore faster wing was the new feature in this particular plane. The aerodynamic peculiarities of this wing caused me plenty of trouble during the first few hours.

It's interesting how the configuration of wings has developed over the years. The flying qualities come from vacuum or suction over the wings as well as pressure of air underneath. Some of the old stunt pilots found that their planes were faster while being flown upside down. As a result the shape of the wing was reversed in later models. Much has come from the engineer and aerodynamicist but much good has also come from the process of trial and error in the air. The swept-back and delta-shaped wings of today on our fast fighter planes bear little resemblance to the wings I first used in flight.

Another Bendix Race — the one in 1946 — provided an abundance of memorable experiences. That was the first race following the war and was to be a battle between various makes of fighter aircraft, particularly the Mustang, the Lightning and the Thunderbolt. I bought a surplus Mustang (F–51) off the government stockpile for three thousand dollars. The idea was to take the machine guns out of the wing emplacements and to convert the wings into fuel tanks by giving them a plastic coating on the inner sides to make them hold gasoline. The other leading competitors with Mustangs did this but I was late in getting my Mustang and there was no time for such work. So I decided to carry exterior drop tanks. They would slow me up by about forty miles an hour until dropped, but in case of no wind or a head wind I could make this up after the dropping because I would have more fuel in reserve than the others and in consequence could pull more power. To get an extra amount of fuel I decided to use, not the drop tanks that were made for the Mustang, but the larger, longer drop tanks that were made for use on the Lightning. The air suction was so great between these long tanks and the nearby landing wheels on my plane that if I waited after take-off until the spinning of the wheels had slowed down I could not get the gear up at all. I made, in consequence, a very dramatic take-off because the onlookers saw my landing gear go into retraction at the very second that I became air-borne.

Nothing happened until I reached the border between California and Arizona. At that point my radio went dead in the middle of a check I was making on weather ahead. I turned and twirled and twisted everything connected with that radio to try to get it back into operation. Finally in anger and despair I gave it a good hard kick with my foot. All I got out of this was a very sore toe.

There was an overcast all the way to Cleveland, which meant I could not see the ground and without radio would have to fly a compass course. There was bad weather in the Grand Canyon area. I was flying at 24,000 feet and thought I could top the storm in front by climbing to 30,000 feet. The operating manual for that particular model of plane (which had previously been taken out of service by the Air Force) had warned me that prior to the time the fuselage tank of fuel had been drained down to less than thirty gallons the plane would go into an uncontrollable spin in turbulent air. I had no yearning for an uncontrollable spin. But when I got to 27,000 feet the engine quit. Then it started. It surged on and off and on and off. This action of the power plant with the sudden bursts of power followed by no power and then power again started my plane swinging backward and forward in the sky as if it were the seat of a swing attached to ropes several miles long. The plane had not been tested prior to the race higher than 25,000 feet. It so happened that the particular engine while being operated above 27,000 feet was subject to what is technically known as "cavitation," which is evidenced by a surging of power due to faulty utilization of the fuel.

I had no choice but to turn the nose of the plane down and head into that storm on instruments. I hit that front going full speed and while still rocking. Going on instruments under normal flight conditions is fairly routine procedure but doing so suddenly with the plane swinging so much as to be almost out of control was somewhat like diving into a pool of cold water from a platform that is on a long pole swinging in the breeze. I did not dare throttle back because that would have changed the flying attitude of the plane and would have necessitated change in trim for which there was no time. The instruments finally indicated that the plane was stabilized and within a few minutes I was beyond the storm. But trouble was not over.

The exterior tanks were such a drag on speed that they had to be detached and dropped as soon as empty. It was necessary to drop them before getting over populated areas. Because I was above an overcast and not able to pinpoint my position accurately I had to be on the safe side so far as endangering life on the ground was concerned. So I pulled the tank release controls while still over the mountain country and when they still carried fuel. The plane made a violent jerk — almost like a collision in the air. The release mechanism, designed for shorter, stubbier tanks, had failed to work properly. The connection between the front part of wing and tank released before the rear connection let go. The front ends of the tanks dropped away from the plane's wings while the rear ends remained fastened. The airstream caught the front ends with violence and swung them down, as a result of which the rear ends swiveled up and hit the trailing edges of my wings. These trailing edges were badly crumpled and torn in this collision between tanks and wings. I could not fully appraise the damage because from the cockpit I could only see the upper side of the wings. But what I saw was bad enough. To keep wind resistance on the wings down to the minimum and thus to get the last mile of speed available I had cellophaned the leading edges of the wings and all the rivet lines. Now I had pieces of wing sticking up two or three inches in places and acting as air brakes. Moreover the plane was badly out of trim and even after adjusting the trim tabs to the extreme, I had by force to hold the stick far out of neutral in order to maintain flying attitude. The major question was whether the plane would not disintegrate before I could get to Cleveland.

I reached the finish line six minutes behind the winner to take second place. The head wind I had hoped for that day had turned out to be a tail wind and this alone had cost me in elapsed time more than that six minutes as against the other Mustangs. The damaged wings cost me at least another ten minutes. So, all in all, I considered it a very successful day from my standpoint. An examination of the plane after landing showed that the damage was even worse than I thought while in flight. Furthermore, I discovered after landing that I had a lump on my head the size of a small egg. Whether I got it during the cavitation of the engine or while plane and tanks were exchanging blows I do not know. My concentration on the emergency problems combined with the excitement of the flight kept me from realizing at the time that I had been tossed out of my seat so hard that I had hit the canopy, even though I was bound down with both shoulder and belt straps.

One other thing is worth noting about that race. My flight map was a well-prepared set of accordion-pleated sheets fixed up like a book. On it I had not only my landmarks and radio check points but also my changes in compass courses related to minutes of flight. This last precaution was a result of consideration of the risk of an overcast combined with failure of the radio. But I had also considered the risk of sufficient turbulence to throw the map off my lap and so far away from me as to make it unrecoverable considering that I was immobilized in the seat. A heavy string tied the map to my leg against this risk. It's well I took that precaution because while the plane was being knocked about the map flew off my lap in the fuselage behind my seat. I had to fish it back by the same process I used as a child in capturing the chicken. Without the map and its compass course indications I would have lost considerable time. Several changes in compass course had to be made en route.

With the Mustang back in Los Angeles after the race I had another set of long drop tanks put on and accompanied by a camera plane the tanks were released over the ocean. The trouble I had experienced in the race was repeated. It would have been difficult to fix the mechanism to prevent this trouble. Anyway, the drop tanks were not equal, in terms of speed, to the plasticized wings, so I did a plasticizing job in preparation for the 1947 race. Floyd had been ill and at Mayo's during the summer of 1947, so I had no time for adequate preparation and loaned my plane to Bruce Gimbel. A propeller governor broke during his flight and the revolutions of the propeller were reduced so much that he came into Cleveland long overdue. I was at the finish line with his father and mother, Mr. and Mrs. Bernard Gimbel, and realized for the first time what Floyd went through when I was overdue in a race with no word. During the 1938 Bendix Race, which I won, Floyd knew my flight plan in detail. I came in twenty minutes later than expected and according to the plan I would have been out of fuel at least the last twelve of these twenty minutes. I could not contact the Cleveland radio tower and Floyd had visions of me strewn over the countryside. Storms had forced me to altitudes I had not expected to reach. At these altitudes the plane was slower but the consumption of gas was less. I landed with three gallons of gas to spare.

In races and record runs one usually figures the gas supply down to the last gallon. On five different occasions I have landed after a speed flight with less than two minutes of fuel remaining and once — on a record flight from New York to Miami — my engine went dead just as my wheels touched the runway. This was because of a risk I had not considered. When I reached my destination, a squadron of Navy planes was in formation flight over the airport and I had to circle before landing. One more round of the airfield and I would have been done in. The Miami Air Races were on and my flight was a part of the show. As I sat on the runway without fuel waiting for the machine to come out and drag my plane into the hangar, the Greve Trophy Pylon Race started and while the contestants were rounding a nearby pylon I watched two of my racing friends spin into death. It became my job on reaching the hangar to try to comfort the widow and children of one of the pilots. It was a bad ending for me of a successful flight in which I had bettered the New York–Miami speed record previously set by Howard Hughes.

That particular flight was full of the unexpected and dangerous. Because the plane in the standard form had not enough fuel supply for a wide-open throttle flight to Miami, the factory had installed an extra fuel tank just behind my seat and another specially built forty-two-gallon tank to take the place of the seat. I sat on the tank. But the plane had not been tested after this change because of lack of time and the tank back of me was in fact off center of gravity. The result was that when I took off at Floyd Bennett Field on Long Island the nose of the plane could not be kept on level course. Any movement of the stick resulted in overcorrection and in consequence I was headed for either high noon or the earth most of the time. This porpoising of the plane continued until I had nearly reached Washington and had burned that particular tank empty. (I have the seat tank in my trophy room as a memento.)

Racing is a dangerous game full of disappointments for most contestants. The honors and the prize money are attractive. But that is not what eggs the pilots on. It is a gnawing within themselves and a desire to contribute in a leading way to the cause of aviation.

It's satisfying, as I did, to try out a new fuel in 1939 and then three years later to hear from the White House that my reports had contributed in large measure to the decision to use this fuel during the early days of the war. I had the first homing device ever put in a private plane. It never worked properly but partly as a result of my reports subsequent ones did. I had the first turbo supercharger ever installed in a private plane. It blew up and wrecked my plane. But better ones were built and became standard equipment. In my Mustang, I pulled power on the Merlin engine for more than twice its rated output and did this for nearly twenty hours of flying time. The manuals said that a slight overpower could be pulled for not to exceed fifteen minutes in case of great emergency — which meant in a dog fight with the enemy in which life was at stake — after which the engine should receive an overhaul. I proved that engine to be a better product than the military thought.

In competition everything is pushed to the limit or beyond. After the 1946 Bendix Race the chief pilot for one of the airlines asked me how high the engine temperature went. My reply was that I deliberately refrained from looking at the temperature gauge during the entire flight because I knew I had to fly with everything pretty much wide open and I did not want to get distracted by seeing needles on the dials pointing in the wrong direction.

To tell all the exciting experiences that have come my way in flying would be to fill much more than a book.

There was the time the nose of my plane caught fire while I was about ten thousand feet in the air near Indianapolis. Because my cockpit was far back in the tail I thought I would chance a landing. I pointed the nose downward so that the smoke missed my cockpit and I headed for the airport after giving notice by radio. The field was cleared and the fire engines were waiting for me. I came to a stop beyond the end of the runway in a field of dry cut grass, which immediately caught fire. I jumped some eight feet to the ground and fractured a toe. The fire was soon put out. In those days most runways were fairly short. A hay field occupying the rest of the airport helped support the operating expenses and keep the dust down.

A week later with the plane repaired I took off from Indianapolis for New York with a heavy load of gas. The radio was not working and there were storms ahead, so I decided to return to Indianapolis for radio repair. As I was coming in for a landing with the flaps down, the engine quit and the flap mechanism broke so I could not raise the flaps and stretch my glide. I hit hard on the runway — so hard that it broke the metal plane in two. The two parts bounced in the air several feet and collided. Although I was covered with oil and gasoline I was not injured, refused to go to the hospital for a checkup and within twenty minutes was on a commercial plane bound for New York and a dinner appointment with Floyd.

A belly landing happens, I guess, to every pilot. Mine happened at Phoenix during the war. I had two passengers and the engine quit just after take-off. There was no chance for a turn back to the airport so I made a belly landing by putting the plane down on a nearby field with the wheels purposely left up. The plane was a complete washout but no one was hurt. It was a no-good plane anyway. It should have been in the graveyard for planes long before. On each of five previous flights in it I had made forced landings due to one mechanical trouble or another.

On a 2000-kilometer record flight I was making at high altitude, my oxygen system went out of commission but in the short period

before loss of consciousness I was able to break open the emergency connection and start the intake of full rich oxygen. I was
afraid the supply of oxygen would not last out the flight at this
rate of flow and radioed the nearest station to telephone Dr. W.
Randolph Lovelace II at Albuquerque for instructions. He is a
great authority in the field of aviation medicine. Within minutes I
had his instructions as to how to govern my breathing to conserve
the oxygen. The record was established and still remains on the
books.

Another time, while doing a 2000-kilometer record along the
western route of Trans-World Airlines, I ran quite unexpectedly
into a blinding snowstorm. The judges on the ground radioed
they had not seen me. I thought they said they had not seen me
make the turn at the halfway point, but Floyd happened to be on
a TWA plane headed for Los Angeles and was listening in over
the pilot's radio. He knew that I was trying to make two records
in one and realized that the judges were talking about the starting
point for the 100-kilometer course rather than the turning point
for the longer record. I had already throttled back to safeguard
the engine and had climbed over the snowstorm when Floyd sent
word to me from his plane via the tower in Los Angeles that I
had been seen making the turn and to keep going full speed. I
was told in later years that the flight in question proved the
merits of the plane to accompany bombers over long distances on
their missions and had a lot to do with orders for it as the war-
time Thunderbolt. I was flying the prototype through that snowstorm.

Twice the judges failed to see me cross the finish line at altitude
after successful record flights and the efforts on my part went for
nothing. On another occasion — which was a dangerous series
of runs at treetop level — the timing instruments failed to work
although they had been tested just before the flight.

At the conclusion of a speed flight in Miami, I made a perfect landing only to have the plane tear itself apart after it was slowed down on the runway almost to a walk. Fortunately, moving pictures were being taken of that landing from a truck that was following me down the runway. The pictures showed what had been happening to so many planes of that type with destructive effect. The tail wheel had jumped out of its lock so that it swiveled and had consequently thrown the plane into a shimmy with sufficient force to tear the wings and landing gear off. That near disaster for me probably saved the lives of a number of pilots because a correction was made in the tail wheel. Two days before, in that same plane, the pump for the fuel system gave out while I was doing a 100-kilometer record. I used the emergency hand pump and headed for the airport. That hand pump was difficult to work and by the time I landed the flesh on my hand was badly cut.

On another occasion, while high over the mountains just east of Los Angeles, in the first part of a long record run which required an overload of gas, the propeller governor broke. I radioed March Field across the valley to the south to clear the runway because I was going to attempt a dead-stick landing. It was ticklish business with the overload and no dump valves and a stretched-out glide of several miles, but I made the landing without incident. When I first radioed about my trouble and plans, General Ralph Cousins, then in charge of the West Coast Training Command of the Air Force, went to the radio tower at March Field and advised me to bail out. He stayed in the tower until I landed. The junior officer whom he sent to meet me at the plane on the runway startled me by saying he had heard about me so long that he expected to see an old woman at the controls rather than a young lady who looked like she had just stepped out of a beauty parlor rather than out of serious air trouble.

Some accidents have their humorous side. During my early days of flying, a girl in upper New York State appealed to Floyd for financial help. He asked me to fly up to her town in my single-motored Waco and make an investigation. Before I took off from Roosevelt Field on that mission, I went over my monthly bill from the hangar and expressed pretty strong words of criticism in the "front office" because I had been charged a dollar for a dust cloth obtainable almost anywhere for a quarter. I told the owner that he was the type who would skin a flea for its hide and tallow and ended the discussion by saying he had received the last of my patronage. An hour or two later, I had reached the field which was to serve as my landing spot. It was clearly marked as a landing field on my air map, and I circled and saw the wind sock before dipping down over the trees for a landing. When I was so low that I could not rise again above the trees and wires at the end of the field, I saw that it had been newly plowed and dragged. There was nothing to do but make the best of it. The wheels dug into the soft ground and the plane made a cart wheel and landed on its back. The propeller was broken and I surveyed the scene while hanging upside down in my seat belt. The man I had just told off at Roosevelt Field was the sales representative for the maker of that propeller and there was no other sales agency in the East. But I made good my buyer's strike and left my plane in that plowed field for nearly two weeks while getting delivery of a propeller from the Middle West. To add to that day's disgust, I found that the girl who had appealed for help was a phony.

I am often asked about the little things that take place in the cockpit during one of these races or record flights.

There is practically no time for anything but the necessities of flying. The cockpit is small and what little space is left after the pilot climbs in is filled with instruments. The pilot is buckled in and buckled down. With a helmet on and connected to the radio system and with the face covered with an oxygen mask, also connected to the plane by a long tube, the pilot looks like a man from Mars. There is no chance to move from the one position. The feet are occupied with the pedals. One hand is on the stick, the other is free to handle the radio, change gas tank connections, handle the throttle, and study the course map. My map was always in a folding book and, as I have said, tied to my knee. An extra gas tank was usually just back of me. The map had many marks on it so that, if necessary, I could continue on dead reckoning without sight of earth and without radio. Even the masts and wires for the radio were usually fastened inside the canopy so that there would be no avoidable outside resistance point in the air to slow me down. There was never any thought of food. In a small box inside the cockpit I usually carried a half-filled Cola bottle of water with a glass straw in it. Filled bottles would overflow from expansion of the water at altitude and the straw allowed me to take a sip without detaching my oxygen mask. A few small-sized lollypops were sufficient to keep my mouth moist. On occasion I had to switch to a small special tank of a combination of oxygen and helium gas during descent to keep open the Eustachian tube of a troublesome ear. The cockpit was usually terribly hot near ground level but one had to be clothed for an outside temperature of many degrees below zero up high. A series of zippers all over my flying suit enabled me to adjust partially to changes in temperatures. Try sitting down, strapped to a chair in one position for several hours and you will get a faint notion of what I mean, but only a faint notion, for the sitting is the smallest part of it.

The fighter planes have so-called service tubes for the men but these don't work for the female of the species. I tried various expedients but the most workable of all was to dehydrate myself before the race and then fight nature. During the later WASP days the laboratories at Wright Field worked out apparatus to meet this situation. The only one they had left in 1948 I borrowed for that year's Bendix, but the next day following the race it was destroyed when my plane crashed carrying my associate, Sam Held, with it to his death.

All in all, these races were no picnics. I have retired from racing because suitable fast equipment is no longer available to a civilian. But given fast, up-to-the-minute equipment and a race to enter, I guess I would be up and at it again.

On the drab side of these efforts at high speed was the preliminary training. Just like a prize fighter in the ring one could lose several pounds during a grueling flight and just like an athlete I trained. Because most of the speed and record flights took place soon after daybreak I had to be up and on my way to the airport during the wee small hours of the morning. Indeed I had to be at the field before midnight for most of the early Bendix races. For several weeks beforehand I would start going to bed a little earlier each day until at the last I was retiring around noon hour. I know the kind of a life a night watchman leads. I would start stirring about just as others were going to bed. Besides keeping to a heavy meat diet I did regular exercises to strengthen my shoulder and arm muscles and many a day I have started a round of golf at daybreak after having put in two or three hours of practice at night flying. In addition I always worked an hour a day for at least a week on instrument approaches and landings. Such procedure is more difficult in a fast fighter plane than in a transport job. Usually for this I would hire a Harvard trainer plane with two seats in tandem and would fly blind from the back seat with a copilot in the front seat to keep an eye out for dangers and to spot errors. In a Mustang fighter plane, for example, the pilot does not look at the runway below him while landing. He can only see fairly distant points out ahead like the horizon or the end of the field. In a very true sense the pilot "feels" his way down during those last few feet before touching wheels. A Harvard trainer plane provides wonderful vision from the front cockpit but during approach and landing the restricted vision from its rear cockpit simulates the vision from the Mustang's single cockpit.

These races and record flights were full of adventure but they do not crowd out of my memory the many wonderful experiences I have had during thousands of hours of poky air jaunts. My flying has been my passport to many wonderful places.

Not the least of these memorable places has been way up high in the sky above the murky dust-laden air that hugs the earth. The sun at twilight from up there, looking at it through that earth-bound veil, seems twice as bright and warm while rolling over the horizon with a smiling goodnight. The stars seem to hold their distance from the plane by only a mile or two. Often at altitude on a clear night, on seeing a particularly bright star ahead, I have suddenly started to change course in the belief that another plane was in my line of flight displaying its white navigation light. I have chased many a rainbow through the heavens and I have also chased a moon bow. That was during a night flight from Minneapolis to New York. After having climbed through an overcast with some ice in it I met up with the moon in its full splendor. It was just as full as a moon can get and for some reason it looked about a third larger than I have ever seen it before or since. The top of the clouds forming the overcast was thinning out and getting ready to break up and disappear. Suddenly I saw in the sky a huge bow of bright silvery light — like a rainbow only it was night and the bow was all silver in color. Then a second one appeared. They were so new and intriguing that I started to play around with them. I forgot all about where I was and the direction of my flight. Not so long thereafter I was in the studio of artist John Phillips in that artists' retreat known as Taos, New Mexico. There I saw a painting of an Indian standing on a ceremonial rock at the entrance to a large cave looking out into the night sky at a moon bow. Mr. Phillips said that he had seen this moon bow by chance while out during early fall watching the aspen trees by full moonlight. When Floyd saw the sparks from my enthusiasm about the moon bow, he bought the picture for my next Christmas and it hangs in our ranch home.

The northern lights I have seen on more than one occasion. They make one think of far-off places where these lights have their source — maybe where Santa Claus lives with his reindeer or maybe even in the corona of the sun. But the St. Elmo lights are like immediate insistent devil children of the northern lights, sent down to plague and to scare. Sometimes these lights will circle the nose of the plane or the propeller tips and follow along with the plane in flight. Sometimes they will roll over the leading edges of the wings and off the tips like balls of fire. I had no warning when I first met up with these freaks of electricity and my thoughts weren't pleasant. But the St. Elmo lights are harmless to plane and occupants and when this is known become an enjoyable occasional flight phenomenon.

The world is full of interesting places and some of the ones that are inaccessible to the ordinary traveler I have seen. On a trip in my own plane to Europe I stayed a day in Greenland and made a flight for quite a distance north over the polar ice cap. It is no place to go for a holiday. At this time an iceberg was floating around in a very big circle in the Arctic Ocean and a small group of scientists were housed on it making observations. I talked with them by radio while flying over the ice cap.

Many years ago I flew down in the Grand Canyon below the rim in an old Tri-Motor Ford plane. As passengers, besides Floyd, I had the Indian chief, the tribal pottery maker and the tribal painter, whom I had picked up in the Painted Desert and was taking to the Indian celebrations on the rim of the Canyon. Incidentally there was no airport in that wonderfully colorful area known as the Painted Desert — just a flat spot in the sand — and on approaching the Grand Canyon Airport for a landing I saw the field dotted with hundreds of wild horses.

Fortunately a dog had been trained by the airport operator to chase the horses off the runways on hearing the sound of an approaching plane.

Between Rome and Sicily I flew over and circled around the crater of the volcano Vesuvius and saw below, at the foot of the volcano, the excavated ruins of the ancient city of Pompeii. And I have flown in the far north of Europe during the long twilight when the sun just moves sideways for a time along the horizon as if too lazy to rise.

I have flown around and around the Taj Mahal, in India, by full moonlight. The gorgeous charm of the structure as a whole with the large square marble-domed central structure surmounted by the four smaller domes at each corner and with four minarets a little away from each corner rising like white fingers pointing to heaven will remain with me forever. I wonder why so many of the wonderful edifices in the world have been built as tombs for the dead, as was this one.

Yes, flying the slow gadabout way here and there about the world, seeing and marveling at its wonders, has its full measure of compensation. I expect I will be able to do that kind of flying for many years to come and for every such year there will be many new wonders to be seen.

CHAPTER V

SUPERSTITION seems a constitutional part of every Southerner, especially one close to the grass roots and the Negro revival meetings. I am chuck-full of superstitions. Some of them are in reverse. For example, I consider number thirteen lucky and it has been my official racing number for years. Number thirteen has constantly popped up in my life in a favorable way. When I turned the Sabre-jet back to Canadair, Ltd., in June 1953, and was having my time in it certified, I discovered that I had made thirteen flights. A fuel tank had cracked open, it is true, during that last flight (due to vibration from excessively turbulent air) but I had made another world record and had made a safe emergency landing. Check the number of chapters in this book or the number of pictures of me in the frontispiece. When I bought the "Beguine" special racing plane in 1949 and on Bill Odom's earnest insistence let him fly it in the Thompson Trophy Pylon Race in Cleveland, he agreed to take its old racing number off and put my number thirteen on; but I guess he was also superstitious about "thirteen" although the other way around. In any event, two days before the race he called me on long distance and explained that the paint job was so well done and so slick for racing that he hated to see it messed up just for the sake of change of number. I thought I understood his state of mind and told him for the sake of the paint he could leave the old number on the plane. He had very bad luck. His life was lost and the lives of two bystanders as well.

Every pilot has hunches and uses them on occasion. My hunches are pronounced and I learned in the process of time that they could be personally relied on to a very great extent. They had graduated to the class of real sixth sense or intuition and finally for a time — until I consciously and purposely submerged them — they apparently burst into full bloom as extrasensory ability. I'm not talking now about things related to spooks but about that real ability I believe to be inherent to some degree in most of us and quite highly developed in some few to receive and pass information without normal use of our senses, such as seeing, hearing, smelling, talking, and feeling. Duke University is well known for its studies in this field of extrasensory perception under the direction of Dr. J. B. Rhine. I'm one — or at least I was — of the people with this ability to a more than normal degree and I discovered it quite by accident.

But this is a ticklish and much misunderstood subject and I want, therefore, to preface my remarks with some generalization.

It's a simple matter today to pick up a little black object called a telephone, push the dial a certain way with your fingers, and talk to people hundreds of miles distant. But if you had been living a hundred years ago and had told someone that this kind of talking was possible and easy you would have been considered a fit subject for the asylum. For you to state that such talk made use of wires and electric current would not have helped you any.

But if you had pointed out that you could eliminate the wires altogether and, through the use of a little contraption called a vacuum tube, you could not only hear that person hundreds of miles away but you could see him as well, you would have been classified as one deluded or a witch. We have been using the vacuum tube for years and it is now fast giving way to the transistor which is so small that an entire radio set can be put inside a wrist watch. And in all probability the face of this wrist watch can serve as a screen for television.

What I have been discussing as today's realities were called in our grandfathers' day telepathy and clairvoyance and were seldom spoken about except in hushed tones.

The airplane in its own way is just as weird. Think how long it used to take a man to cross the American continent in the early days before even the pony express. That was Great-Grandpa's day. But now, during an average night's sleep for members of my family I can — using the speed that Major "Chuck" Yeager made in 1953 as a yardstick — fly from California to New York, have a good look around, and fly back to California again in time to awaken them.

In what I have just said I have been discussing commonplaces with us which did not exist in Great-Grandfather's day and only in part in Grandfather's day. From that time until now is but the smallest speck in a line representing the life of man. That line in turn would be but a dot in the life of the earth. Man has a mind that is constantly developing new powers and new things. If the mind of man can progress as far as it has during these few years in seeing and hearing at a distance, why can it not soon find the real key to the transmission and receipt of waves and impulses without the aid of any small physical object such as a transistor?

The point of all this preface is that what would have been weird and frightening psychic phenomena a few generations ago are completely accepted today as a part of our daily routine. It is sensory as yet because, whether it happens to be television or electric lights or telephone, we receive the impression through one of our five accepted senses. But maybe we have little transistors stored away in our brains or minds that work at times for some and will in time come into full bloom and work for all. To date it is called "sixth sense" on Main Street and extrasensory perception in the scientific laboratories — and there are many such laboratories, well-sponsored by universities, both here and abroad — where such parapsychological abilities and manifestations are being studied and made into rational and usable human traits. It is an old-fashioned notion that man is limited to five senses. There are many physical senses that in my opinion cannot be so classified and the physical senses are but a part of our total senses. Let's not put ourselves in capabilities behind the fish and birds and insects that can travel straight without sight and that can make and hear sounds that our ears cannot catch but which we can record on man-made instruments.

Floyd, as a hobby, had made quite a study of psychic phenomena over the years. He has a degree of intuitive ability himself, but, unlike me, has been careful never to play a hunch unless its truth is strongly indicated statistically and from every other known angle, and even then he says, in the words of Kipling, that one is likely to be wrong.

Years ago we had a friend with a reputation as a sort of nonprofessional medium. She came to our home many evenings and did what is known as table knocking, table lifting and similar things and on occasion would go into what is described as a trance. Floyd was intrigued by it, as a pure research study.

One night, this woman did what I considered a poor job of automatic writing and when she went home, I declared to Floyd that as pure showmanship I could provide a better exhibition myself. I like to act things out, so I got a tablet and paper and pencil and had my eyes bandaged with a handkerchief. I put the point of the pencil on the paper and for a moment held it still to properly impress Floyd before starting my act. Suddenly I started writing uncontrollably; my fingers broke the pencil in two and flung it into the air. I pulled the blindfold off, completely shocked. After composure returned, I tried again and once more the same thing happened. That was enough for one night, but the next evening we went at it again and successfully. I would write on and on but it was in a scrawling hand and we needed large rolls of wrapping paper to keep up with it. That automatic writing kept up at secret sessions between my husband and myself for several years but, after Amelia Earhart died, I stopped it and all allied activities for several reasons. Mind you, I am not saying or even indicating that the pencil was under control of any force beyond the grave or needed any force to move it except my own mind and body functioning together with some unusual end products.

One pertinent thing we noted about this writing. All mistakes in spelling I made while consciously writing were repeated in the automatic writing; and my tell-tale scrawl appeared on the wrapping paper. I was not conscious of what was being written, which indicates to me that my subconscious was expressing itself. I believe most people can do automatic writing. It seems to put memory on a broad, free-wheeling basis.

Even before this particular type of experience, Floyd and I had covered a wide breadth of associated experiences; I could often, for example, get him to call me on long distance by wishing it and concentrating on where I wanted to receive his call.

Also Floyd, almost at will, could carry on a conversation with me while I was asleep. These conversations became so animated at times that I would get up, open my eyes, move about and do odd jobs, often I would make hot milk toast. Once I took a speck of dust out of Floyd's eye. And on one occasion I wrote a short poem — my first and last attempt at verse — which Floyd said had merit. On request I would tell him accurately whether I had awakened or was still asleep. I never remembered these nocturnal episodes but Floyd gave me top rating for logic, consistency, memory and the ability to read his thoughts. He says he has in fact seen a dream walking.

In those days, I used to do a lot of night flying to quiet my emotions when upset. Who knows — maybe I have flown in my sleep, but I'm sure it wouldn't have mattered because I seemed to have all of my senses with me, except that of knowing in conscious memory afterwards what was going on at the time.

In the early period of this phase of my life, I made a trip from New York to California with Amelia Earhart in the Lockheed Electra which she used on her last flight. We were weathered in on the way and the trip took six days, which gave much time for conversation. I found that Amelia was following interestedly the work in the extrasensory field being done at Duke University and I told her a little bit about some of my own experiences. Shortly afterwards, she came down to the ranch for a few days' rest. The first night there, we heard that a passenger plane had disappeared en route from Los Angeles to Salt Lake City and Amelia asked me to try to locate it. We sat together for about two hours during which I gave names of various mountain peaks and the locations of roads and transmission lines and even of a pile of telephone poles up in the mountains near Salt Lake City. I also gave the location of the plane. Neither of us knew that area so Amelia called Paul Mantz in Los Angeles and asked him to verify names and locations on an air map and call us back. He called back with complete verification. Amelia, thoroughly excited by that time, dashed back to Los Angeles by car through the night and took off for Salt Lake in her plane at daybreak. She searched the area for three days and verified all my descriptions but found no wreckage of the transport and gave up. Next spring, when the snow on the mountain had melted, the wreckage of that plane was found within two miles of where, on the night it went down, I said it was.

A few weeks later, Amelia called me from Los Angeles with the news that a transport airliner en route to Los Angeles had gone down somewhere on the last leg of the flight. Would I try to give her the location? Within an hour, I called her back, told her exactly where the plane was, which way it was pointing down the mountainside and the condition of the occupants as between the dead, the injured and the safe. The plane was located promptly just where I said it would be; all my information proved correct. Only a few of my closest friends have ever heard this story or indeed any part of what is found in this chapter.

By this time Amelia was convinced that if we practiced together, I could locate her should she be forced down on her proposed round-the-world flight. So on one of her trips across the continent, she agreed to keep a record every hour on the hour as to where she was and I agreed to do likewise with respect to her location so we could compare notes. But I became engaged in some cosmetic problem and forgot until Floyd jacked up my memory on the third day. I then told Floyd what Amelia had been doing that day and he sent the report on to her. It was that she (and her husband George Putnam, who was with her) had landed the night before at Blackwell, Oklahoma; that it was fifty miles off their course because they had become confused by weather and radio; that they took off at nine o'clock in the morning for Los Angeles but stopped in Winslow, Arizona, for fueling. George Putnam wrote back that I had certainly made a bad miss that time. He said that while they did stop at Blackwell overnight, it was not because they were lost; that they took off at seven o'clock and not nine o'clock but that I did hit it right in saying that they stopped at Winslow for gas. George Putnam really confirmed the case. I didn't know what part of the country they were in at the time and had never heard the name Blackwell; seven o'clock their time was nine o'clock my New York time; and whether one is lost or not is more or less a state of mind as to which pilots can differ. A favorite expression of the old-time barnstorming pilots used to be: "I ain't lost but I don't know where I'm at." I never was too fond of George Putnam and that critical letter did not help matters — but I loved Amelia with a deep, true and loyal affection. She was a great flyer and an even greater woman. We were close friends and she spent most of the last few months before her last flight at my ranch, resting, building up strength in the swimming pool and on horseback and making preparations for her flight. We helped her finance the flight which she planned westward and when she crashed on the take-off in Hawaii, we helped her again to get the plane in shape for her flight eastward which ended in disaster. One of my prized possessions is a small silk American flag she gave me just before she took off. It bears a message to me. She carried it on several of her previous overwater flights. Her book *My Last Flight,* written in part by herself before her flight and in part after her death from notes she had made en route, was dedicated to Floyd.

I had plenty of "hunches" about that flight and none of them was on the optimistic side. I questioned whether the navigator she had employed, although an exceedingly fine man, was up to high-speed celestial navigation in a plane. I asked her to take him out to sea for quite a distance from Los Angeles and then, after flying in circles for a time so that he could no longer be oriented, to ask him to give her the course back to Los Angeles. She told me they reached the shore line halfway between Los Angeles and San Francisco. She took two navigators on the first leg of her flight to Hawaii and also took along Paul Mantz on that leg as copilot. Mr. Noonan, an old hand at navigation from the air in the Pacific area, went along with her on the rest of the last flight. My worries persisted after this early navigation episode. Before Amelia left, I gave her a bright-colored kite I had used in the London-Australia Race in 1934 to mark my location in case I was forced down. I also got her a set of fishhooks and lines and one of those knives with a blade for almost every conceivable purpose. While she was in San Francisco on a preliminary flight, I was driving Floyd to Palm Springs from the ranch one Sunday afternoon and remarked suddenly that a fire had started in one of the engines of her plane but it was being put out without serious damage. The story of that fire was broadcast on the radio later that day and appeared in the following morning's paper.

With all this ability and preliminary work with Amelia, why didn't I locate her when she went down? The answer is that I did, or at least I think I did, but can never prove it one way or the other, and besides it was all to no purpose. George Putnam was in my apartment in Los Angeles almost as soon as he could get there after the news of her nonarrival at Howland Island. He was extremely excited and called on me for the kind of help Amelia thought I might be able to give. I told him where Amelia had gone down; that with the ditching of the plane Mr. Noonan, the navigator, had fractured his skull against the bulkhead in the navigator's compartment and was unconscious; but that Amelia was alive and the plane was floating in a certain area. I named a boat called the *Itasca* which I had never heard of at the time, as a boat that was nearby, and I also named another Japanese fishing vessel in that area, the name of which I now forget. I begged Putnam to keep my name out of it all but to get planes and ships out to the designated area. Navy planes and ships in abundance combed that area but found no trace. I followed the course of her drifting for two days. It was always in the area being well combed. On the third day, I went to the Cathedral and lit candles for Amelia's soul, which I then knew had taken off on its own long flight. I was frustrated and emotionally overcome. If my strange ability was worth anything it should have saved Amelia. Only the urging of Floyd ever prompted me to try my hand at this sort of thing again and he hasn't urged me for several years for he knows it upsets me.

Once Floyd came home from the office and I told him an associate of his by the name of Parker Toms had just died in San Francisco. Floyd got the news by phone several hours later.

On another occasion while in New York I told him about a girl living in Hemet, California, who was sick and in trouble and wanted to come and see me at the ranch. I gave many details but could only give the girl's nickname. The next day a letter arrived from that girl, who was hardly an acquaintance of mine. The letter gave word for word what I had said the day before. Peculiarly enough, and probably importantly from the standpoint of an understanding of the strange "coincidence," it had only her nickname as signature and I had to check with mutual friends to get her real name.

What manner of ability this is, I don't know. Certainly, some of it is pure thought transmission, as proved by one experience.

Floyd and I were on our cruiser houseboat one Sunday afternoon, cruising down Long Island Sound and into the East River for a docking. I was tired and had fallen asleep in his lap. It was one of those emotional sleeps and he was worried about getting me off the boat so began trying to talk me awake. He said I should wake up because we would soon be at the dock. My reply was that we were not yet through Hell Gate and we still had plenty of time. He asked me if I could tell him when we would come exactly under the Fifty-ninth Street Bridge and I replied that certainly I could — and I did. Mind you, my eyes were closed this time. He then put two fingers up behind my back and asked me how many he had up. I told him the correct answer. He tried two or three more combinations, always with the correct answer from me. He then put up four and changed to two. My answer was four and when he said I was wrong and he had only had two fingers up, my reply was that he should not change his mind. That, perhaps, is the key to a lot of what I have told above. I was reading his mind.

Mabel Willebrandt was in on a number of these little episodes with me. One night in 1936, at her farmhouse in Maryland, I tried, mostly for her entertainment, to get something by way of forecast. It was to the effect that I would have a fire in the air that summer and would also have a bad plane crash. But I was unable to say whether or not I would be killed. The fact that I couldn't answer that led me to believe that my number was coming up and that Providence was just being kind in keeping the information from me. But it did not change my flying plans. I did have the fire and I did have the crash, but I was not killed and am here to tell this tale, which Mabel Willebrandt can verify.

One night while I was sitting in my room in Los Angeles with my friend and business associate, Miss Genevieve Crowley, and Floyd was in New York, I told her I could tell every place he had been and everything he had been doing that evening. I told his activities to her and she wrote them down. Then I called Floyd for verification. He had gone to the Plaza Hotel to attend a large dinner party and had returned to the apartment at twelve minutes past eleven o'clock. He knew the time because he put on the light in the living room to look at the clock. He then went to the bedroom to call me but could not get through so he took a bath, read a short magazine story and was getting ready to call me again when my call got through to him. It all proved correct in every detail. On another occasion, Floyd had gone to Choate School on a Saturday to visit his son. He was due back for dinner. At dinnertime I asked my secretary to dine with me, stating as the reason that Floyd had stopped at the hotel in Stamford for dinner and, in fact, would open the apartment door at precisely ten-eighteen. All this happened as I foretold. I guess some part of that cannot be mind reading but certainly it isn't "spooks."

These sessions over the years covered a wide range of subjects, such as a description of life after bodily death, the start of the war with Japan and what its end would be, the treachery of Soviet Russia and many things dealing with personal lives. Many forecasts were later verified by the course of events.

Floyd believes everyone has an inherent ability along the general lines which I have discussed — an ability which has perhaps been pretty well lost over the centuries through nonuse because it seems to have been quite common in ancient times. Even today tribes have a way of communicating important information to each other mentally over a space of miles. He remarks that if it could be developed again, it would make minor by comparison all the modern scientific advances I have referred to above and which are perhaps somewhat akin in nature. He has discussed the subject with outstanding neurologists, psychiatrists and scientists. He has many learned books on the subject and, at one time, sat with a carefully selected group to check an outstanding medium who seemed to have an honest reputation. The results, under controlled test conditions, were truly remarkable, but Floyd concluded that in the study of such phenomena there was nothing but a circle within which one would go round and round, usually with crackpots as companions, so gave it up even as a hobby.

So far as I am concerned, I continue to a degree to follow my hunches as such and to let the rest of it go by the boards in favor of a good sleep and a good day's work, flying or golfing, the next day. As for Floyd, he won't follow these hunches of mine, much less his own, saying it would be like hiring an erudite theoretical economist to tell him what is going to happen in the business world. He says they seem so right, in their reasoning backed by statistics, that they warp one's own hardheaded experienced judgment. Usually, he says, they are so wrong in retrospect.

So for me — except for so-called hunches — the world of seeing, hearing and forecasting without the help of the five senses, as we know them, has been laid aside. I have reported a bit of ancient, personal history and nothing more. But when I get to Heaven, if there is any way to come back, I am going to tickle Floyd's foot so hard and in such a way that he will know it is I and that I am still having fun.

While my intuition seldom fails me, there may be a wide difference between this intuition of mine and what is usually referred to as a sixth sense and even a wider difference between so-called sixth sense and the common or garden variety of hunches. Every inveterate gambler plays hunches and usually goes broke, so let the reader beware. Much is still to be learned about our powers in the extrasensory field but it seems to me best for most people to let those studies remain for the time being with the expert scientists who have already seen the glimmer of a great light which perhaps can brighten the pathway of man's future. Somewhere in this field may be found the scientific key to proof of man's survival.

Survival is a certainty, I believe. Therefore death is not something to be feared. I do not fear it. Dying is easy. It is living that becomes difficult at times. I do not feel sorry for a person who has passed on but if that person has been close to me I am sad about my own loneliness. I miss the departed friend but am not missed. Dying is as natural a step in a process of progression as being born or eating or falling asleep. I may have had a delightful day on the golf course or an unfinished piece of work at the end of the day, causing me at bedtime to wish that the day had been longer, but I don't yearn to sit up all night for this reason. In the same way I might wish to carry on a trifle longer with my present body and mind as a team to finish something immediate which can be helpful to others or interesting. But it would only be for a moment. I would be more likely to wish for a longer breathing period for an Eisenhower or an Einstein. But nature works effectively in another way than by extension of bodily life of a particular person.

There are those who, having read some of the things I have said up until now, might think that I have a harsh calloused attitude toward people and their troubles and pains. Quite the contrary. I almost blow apart with sympathy for those in pain or in trouble not of their own deliberate making — particularly the young. When news came to me of General Vandenberg's death, I wept uncontrollably. This was notwithstanding that I had prayed for months for his quick release from cancer.

I have mentioned in almost a passing way the crash death of Captain Bill Odom in my plane during the Thompson Trophy Race. You should have seen me at the time. I was in the judges' stand handling telephone reports from the back of the stands' pylons when the flash came through that Bill had crashed. I jumped into a helicopter that was just in front of me on the field and went out to the spot of the accident hoping that something could be done. I found a house on fire, with Bill and the plane, as well as some of the occupants, buried in the wreckage. Some news photographer arrived and snapped a picture of me standing there close by. I am in that picture the personification of abject desolation. For three days I stayed in Cleveland doing all the little things I could to honor Bill Odom's memory.

Three of my associate pilots — Max Constant, Sam Held, and Wallace Hurley — have all passed the last barrier in plane crashes. Their widows can well testify that I felt ever so deeply their loss and continue to keep my fine memories of them fresh in my own ways. But I repeat that they miss nothing, according to my way of thinking. They are not sad or regretful that they are no longer physically flying with me. I am the one who misses them and am sad and regretful.

CHAPTER VI

FOLLOWING the outbreak of World War II, I devoted my time assiduously to my cosmetics business and the ranch. But I was restless. England was in battle and the air war was on in a big way. I fretted as to how I could get into it but for some time could do nothing better than knit afghans for the Royal Air Force. I understood at the time that the airmen used these afghans for comfort and warmth in their forward base quarters while waiting in readiness for missions. After getting to England and looking around, I discovered they were not so used. They served as handy articles to be raffled off in the home-town church or town house.

Our country was being counted on to get flying equipment over to England in quantity and soon. This was being done by the British Ferry Command, working between Montreal and England with a stop for final fueling in Newfoundland. American pilots were being recruited as civilians to help in this flying work but the danger seemed great and we were still neutral. The Battle of Britain was fast coming to a head.

I was on the Collier Trophy Committee that year and in December its members met in President Roosevelt's office to watch him make the award to our choice. My candidates, namely Doctors Walter Boothby and W. Randolph Lovelace II of the Mayo Clinic and Major Harry Armstrong of the United States Air Force, had won the award for their work in aviation medicine; particularly in connection with pressure chambers, oxygen masks and high-altitude flying. I had watched their work carefully for several years, had acted as a guinea pig for them with all their models of masks, had submitted myself to tests in their high altitude chamber, and was generally convinced that the advance of aviation required much more attention to what goes on in the pilot's mind and body.

After the presentation of the trophy, several of us went to lunch with General H. H. "Hap" Arnold, including Clayton Knight, who was acting head of an American recruiting committee for the British Ferry Command. The conversation during lunch was devoted largely to the English need for planes and the great need for pilots. I was asked if I could not help in the recruiting effort and General Arnold, in an impetuous moment, turned to me and asked why I didn't do some of that flying myself — not only for the sake of the extra planes so to be delivered but to dramatize and publicize the need.

That was the opening I had been looking for and immediately I started plans to fly a plane across. I was convinced that our women pilots would be needed in the war effort. Women were already being used in local ferry work in England and I wanted to find out just what was being done by them and how well. On top of all this, I wanted to get to England and to the fighting front.

First I contacted the British authorities in Washington and through them an appointment was made for me with the Ferry Command officials in Montreal. They looked over my pilot's log book and flying record and said they could offer no objections as to qualifications but were frankly skeptical because of my sex. I used all the arguments I knew, including the possible helpful effect on the British public through a delivery of a bomber by a woman. The best I could get was a promise that I would hear from them later. Time passed and no word came. A new head of British Procurement in Washington came into power and Lord Beaverbrook was made head of Procurement in England.

Floyd and I had spent numerous evenings in Lord Beaverbrook's home in London before the war. Those dinners at Beaverbrook's were something to remember. Often, Winston Churchill
was there and practically always red-haired Brendan Bracken,
and also always Lord Castlerosse, who usually had his three-hun-
dred-pound body encased in an evening suit of colored velvet
with velvet shoes to match. Others, like ourselves, were the
transients for the evening. Churchill was then out of power and
gave over usually to reminiscing. Beaverbrook always led the
conversations. When he was not expounding he was starting an
argument.

Now Beaverbrook seemed to be my best bet to fly a bomber to
England. Floyd had in his files a letter from Beaverbrook, written
a little before the start of the war, giving numerous reasons
why there would be no war. I countered by cable, setting forth
that there was a war and England was in trouble and also giving
reasons why it would be good for all concerned to let me make
the flight. Beaverbrook agreed and wired his Washington people
to put the machinery in motion. The topside was thus in hand but
no one knows better than I that to get along it is not sufficient to
have the top echelon with you. The fellow down the ranks can
make or break the outsider trying to get in. That meant in this
case the chief pilot and the administrators in Montreal.

They agreed to give me a flight test and I had one of my pre-
monitions that trouble lay ahead. I didn't propose to be eliminated
on the reports of a flight test that I couldn't disprove. So, I first
went to the officials of Northeast Airlines and arranged to take
their captain's course and test. That line was already flying to
Iceland, by way of Newfoundland and Greenland, and did a
magnificent job all during the war. I went out with the chief
pilot while he gave the periodic check flights to several of the
captains on the line. It was an eye opener. I had been on many
test flights but never had I seen anyone get the rough treatment

those captains received. They had to be good. Getting them purposely lost and requiring them to locate themselves on instruments at night and to come back on the beam towards home base was simple. Putting the plane into a difficult position while flying on instruments, then stopping one engine while the pilot was working his way out of this trouble was tough experience. I was glad I went through it, however, because I got somewhat similar treatment on check flights at Montreal. For three days, I went through various flight tests. By the third day my right arm was sore from much use of the hand brakes while taxiing the plane. After the tests were over and the last landing had been made I told the chief pilot my arm was sore and asked him to work the brakes for me as an accommodation while we were taxiing the plane from the runway to the hangar. The report went in that I was quite qualified to fly the plane but it was accompanied by a recommendation against permitting me to fly because of possible physical inability to handle the brakes in an emergency. My arm had sored up after about *sixty* such emergencies.

The top brass thought this pretty trivial and gave the word that I was authorized for the ferry flight. Then hell broke loose. The pilots called a mass meeting and threatened to strike. They were a diverse set of people ranging from well-trained flyers, serving for patriotic purposes, to ham and homespun pilots who were in the big money for the first time. They included a pilot whom I had helped a couple of years before when he got "busted" off an airline. Another had been much publicized for his exploits although in the ferrying operation he had never accomplished much. Another old-timer who was there for a test went into the air ahead of me one day and when he landed he took the safety belt out of the plane so I could not complete my tests that day. I was not at the mass meeting but I got a detailed report. Captain Grafton Carlisle, with several transatlantic ferry flights already to his credit, had been selected as my navigator and he was satisfied with the arrangement. Carlisle and I had dinner together the night before the mass meeting and he told me what was brewing. The radio operator had also been selected and was quite happy to have me as pilot. (I took him across safely but on his next trip he was killed when a male pilot let the plane get out of control and crash on take-off. If that had happened on my flight it would have been charged to woman-pilot trouble.) At the mass meeting, some pilots claimed the Germans would be sure to shoot me down — others claimed that their own jobs would be belittled by letting a woman do the same thing. The truth is they were after more pay and thought the entry of a nonpaid amateur would interfere. They were getting handsome pay, tax free, as it was The publicity-minded pilot let it leak to a Boston paper that I was going to ferry a bomber, thinking that the publicity would stop me. Captain Carlisle tipped me off that another group was contacting the State Department to prevent the issuance of the special visa to me which I needed to get into the war zone.

The upshot of the meeting was that the authorities appointed me First Officer for the flight but required that the navigator, Captain Carlisle, who was also a fine pilot, take the plane off the ground and land it. That I thought ended the battle of the sexes, although in a rather unsatisfactory way, and we were scheduled to leave the next morning. My job, as First Officer, required me to check the plane, which I did very early so I could get to the American Consulate for my permit. By the time I got back to the airport, some equipment was disarranged. Lunch time came along. I wanted then to find out how to spring the life raft in case of emergency, only to discover that no plane as yet had been fitted with a life raft. At the last, the wrench for the oxygen system was missing for the second time. I saw one in a mechanic's pocket and paid him ten dollars for it. We were finally away late in the afternoon for Gander, Newfoundland. Carlisle took the plane off and then went to his quarters. The next morning my plane check showed the oxygen wrench missing again and one window broken in the pilot's cabin. The window was repaired but no wrench seemed available. Again I saw one protruding from a mechanic's pocket and this time, through force of orders, he turned it over to me.

The first trip down the runway for the transatlantic flight was a failure. Because of the heavy load of gasoline we passed the danger mark before becoming air-borne and had to stop. The second try was successful and we were off into the dusk and then into the night with a landing in Prestwick, Scotland, scheduled for the following morning. The moment the plane became air-borne Carlisle, having complied with instructions as to take-off, turned the single set of controls over to me.

Those trips were scheduled for a speed of 135 miles per hour. Sometimes a pilot would get a bit nervous and make greater speed. But a faster flight would consume more gasoline per hour and was consequently more dangerous. We plodded along, keeping to every regulation in the manual which I had studied religiously. Carlisle stayed at his station. The radio operator was in his compartment behind the pilot's cabin.

I'll never forget that night. Soon after dark, the main fuse for the lighting blew out. We got that replaced. Then the northern lights appeared. It was the first time I had ever witnessed the aurora borealis and from a plane it is weird and entrancing. The distant lights shot up out of nowhere in the north to give the appearance of the first crack of a strange dawn.

Flying the ocean at night didn't mean much. We were above an overcast and hardly saw the water. But just before daylight, we were heard or were spotted by radar and suddenly through the darkness tracer bullets came up in front and around us. There was sudden consternation on board. Carlisle rushed up to me and the radio operator came running out of his compartment with his Very pistol. He opened a hatch and by firing a certain colored bullet gave the signal of the day but this really served no purpose because the light could not have been seen from the surface of the water anyway and the firing at us was probably coming from either a German submarine or one of our own friendly ships. I thought maybe the pilots in the mass meeting in Montreal were right after all and the Germans were going to make a test case of me. Anyway, the tracer bullets stopped almost as soon as they started and no noticeable damage was done to the plane. After daylight, a hole opened up in the overcast and we saw a ship burning at sea, but could do nothing about it except to make a report by radio because we had no fuel to spare to enable us to go down and cruise around. Then we caught sight of the coast of Ireland in the distance and it kept creeping upon us and growing larger and larger and more friendly. From off the coast of Ireland to Prestwick, Scotland, was a tortuous air route. The route went one way and then another — without any real pattern — and the route was changed daily to make it difficult for enemy planes or submarines to intercept. At the end of twelve hours, we came to a stop on the runway. Carlisle, under the regulation, made the landing.

The clearance of the plane was fairly quickly done. The bottle of orange juice, the sandwiches and most of the lemons I had along were passed out to the help on the field and I only realized later what munificence was being distributed. The few oranges and lemons I took to London with me were like pure gold. My first meal at the pilot's hotel let me know what England was going through as far as rationing was concerned. Tripe was the main dish with some bread, potatoes, and tea for supporting cast. That tripe was chitlins to me and memories of that pig-sticking I had attended as a child overwhelmed me. I settled for a boiled potato and a cup of tea.

In London, I called first on Lord Beaverbrook and then on the head of the Ministry of Production. Lord Beaverbrook had me sit in his room with him for a couple of hours, presumably as one of his secretaries, while he conferred personally and by telephone with numerous very high officials including the Russian Ambassador. In the Minister's room there was the original of a cartoon that had appeared in the London papers of Beaverbrook as the Pied Piper of Hamelin, gathering pots and pans with which to make airplanes. I offered the Minister an orange for the picture. After some serious trading, he settled for two oranges and sent an armored car down to my hotel after them and to make delivery of the picture.

I checked in with Miss Pauline Gower, who was heading the group of English women pilots already at work, and with her covered their procedures, their places of work and all other details. It gave me a better understanding of how things might be done at home should a need for women pilots arise.

One of my unforgettable experiences on this trip was a visit to a fighter base to have lunch with the squadron before they started on a mission. Whitney Straight was the squadron's leader. All came back safely from that mission and Straight, who is now a top official in the British Overseas Airways, gave me his flight cap as a memento. In 1951 a member of that squadron called on me at the ranch. He told me that he and Whitney Straight were the only survivors of the group I saw off that day. However both of them had been shot down. I will never forget the look of determination on one of the pilots in that group. He was a Pole and had seen his mother and sister subjected to horrible experiences at the hands of the Nazis. I was later told that he forced a Nazi fighter plane down and meted out personal vengeance on that enemy pilot. I also brought home from England a piece of parachute that dropped a bomb near the Savoy Hotel where I was staying and damaged it. It was a British parachute, captured by the Germans at Dunkirk. Enemy raids were frequent while I was there. The custom of the old-timers like Quen-

tin Reynolds and others living at the hotel was to go to the base-
ment on first alarm. But I wanted to see these raids, and usually
headed for the roof.

The flight home was something to remember. Fourteen pilots
and a radio man sat on the bomb-bay floor of a B–24 Bomber,
flown by a British crew. Some loose boards served the purpose
of a floor. We each had a pallet to sit or sleep on. There were
no windows except two small ones off the tiny platform near the
rear of the plane which would accommodate about four people
sitting close together. The rest sat in semidarkness. Heavy head
winds were blowing so we flew low and just skipped the waves.
One of the passenger pilots got sick, probably more from the
thought of the waves than from rough air. Smoking on these
ferry hops depended on the whims of the pilot in charge of
the plane. On this trip, word came back that we could smoke. But
only a few had cigarettes. I had two packages and divided the
cigarettes equally among the group, which left me about three
which I placed on my pallet. Soon I took a snooze and when I
woke up, my cigarettes had been taken by someone. The trip
across was supposed to take about twelve hours with landing
at Newfoundland. At the end of fourteen hours, we became
somewhat nervous. No one can get more nervous than a pilot
when things go wrong and he is not at the controls. Word
came back that we were headed for Montreal. Later, this was
again corrected to Gander. The truth, I am sure, is that the
pilot was off course and didn't know just where we could get
in, if at all. Fuel was running low. Very little food had been
taken on board. It was in the form of a few cheese sandwiches, stowed in the toilet. I passed them around. Cigarettes
were gone but I had an ace up my sleeve. In my cigarette case
which I had along, there were ten. This time, I made a deal. I
would divide these once again but only if I could sit on the
platform and straighten my back a bit. Eventually, we landed at

Gander hours overdue and the next day I came on to New York.

I was a tired woman after a long hard flight and, on retiring, made the facetious statement that I would not get up before noon, even for the President.

At nine o'clock in the morning, I was called with the message that President Roosevelt wished me to be at Hyde Park for lunch that day. For a moment I thought it a joke but I kept the appointment with the help of a police escort. Besides the President and Mrs. Roosevelt, the guests at the lunch were the President's mother, Princess Martha of Norway and myself. After lunch the rest of us preceded the President into a sort of foyer where we stood and waited, except the President's mother who sat down. She rose, however, when her son appeared in his wheel chair. It was evident that she believed it to be her privilege, even if not duty, to arise and do honor to the chief executive of the nation. A few moments later President Roosevelt asked me to go to his office with him and we discussed England and the war for nearly two hours. I told him at the start that I was unfamiliar with protocol and he should tell me when to leave. Once or twice, I thought time had run out but he kept on. Besides explaining what was going on in England, as seen through a pilot's eyes, I explained to him why England could not tear up all her pastures and turn them into wheat and potatoes. I was on sure ground there because Floyd's brother, George Odlum, who is one of the great agriculturalists in England, had a cattle-breeding farm and had just made these things plain to me in terms of over-all economy.

A few days later, I was asked to the White House by Mrs. Roosevelt and discussed with her the question of use at home of women pilots. At the conclusion of this conference President Roosevelt sent me over, with a note from him, to see the then Assistant Secretary of War for Air, Mr. Robert A. Lovett, later Undersecretary of State. Mr. Lovett sent me to General Arnold and "Hap" sent me over to General Robert Olds, who was then just forming the Ferry Command, which later became the Air Transport Command.

General Olds wanted to get pilots wherever he could on an individual hiring basis and was agreeable to taking a few well-trained women pilots. I insisted that if women were to be used, and I was sure they would be, it should be on an organized basis. Otherwise, I was afraid the female effort would be a flash in the pan. I combed the lists and got from the Civil Aeronautics Administration the record of every woman pilot. A plan was formulated and submitted by me to use them, but it included training, organization, controls and regulations. Olds and I broke apart on that point and when he would not send through such a recommendation as part of his plan, I retired from the job.

I put my side of the case before General Arnold at a luncheon in his office. He agreed with me completely but also stated that the time had not yet arrived to use women pilots at all, so I should continue to plan in my own way against the later need but should do nothing actively about it for the present.

A week later, he called me back to Washington and said the British wanted me to recruit qualified women pilots and take them to England. He recommended that I do so to get experience for similar work later at home and to help the British. He said he would keep in touch with me and send word when the time had arrived to return and organize the women pilot program here.

This job of recruiting women pilots for England set me off on war work with a vim that never ended until the war was over and I had seen the ruins of Toyko, the surrender of General Yamashita in the Philippines, the trial of the German high prisoners at Nuremberg, and the cellar where Hitler is supposed to have said good-by to himself, his vanities and his ambitions.

During this whole period of more than three years, I spent less than ten nights in my own home, but quite a number of nights in hospital beds, for my work was interrupted by two major surgical operations.

My cosmetics business, then in its growing-pains stage, was allowed to rock along pretty much on its own, much to my cost in after years, for in those war days all one needed was the goods to establish the all-desirable retail accounts. Goods sold themselves.

The British wanted me to take to England up to two hundred women pilots, but I had gone over the record of every licensed woman pilot while working for General Olds and knew that this would involve a training program and other delays when speed was desired. Out of the approximately seven hundred women pilots, there were about seventy-five who were adequately experienced for prompt air work, but some of them, I was sure, could not or would not go to England. So I had the British agree to an original group of twenty-five to be augmented later if the use of women pilots did not mature at home.

I wanted those twenty-five, besides being good pilots, to be representatives of their country from the geographical standpoint and of such character as to be clearly a credit to the United States. I started a trek around the country in my plane and personally interviewed every likely candidate. After accepting them from my standpoint, they had to be medically checked and then checked by the British equivalent of the FBI. Then they had to go to Montreal for flight checks. I sent them to Montreal in groups of five or six and arranged for about forty in all for the tests.

My own secretary, Mary Nicholson, an old-time flyer, helped me with the routine of all this work and I then sent her to Canada with the last group. Passage was arranged for all by boat and when the last had departed I went to Montreal for my own flight check, after which I was to fly another bomber across to meet the groups on their arrival in England.

The first typhoid shot I had taken made me very ill. The next one caused a deep abscess on my leg. The day before I was to take my second ocean flight, I went to a Montreal hospital for a lancing of the abscess. A week later I crawled out of bed and returned to New York to take passage across in a British Overseas plane from Baltimore via Bermuda and Lisbon. I wasn't going to let a draining wound keep me from being on the job when the American women pilots arrived. A doctor friend gave me a quantity of sulfa powder and sterile dressings. For several weeks I pulled dressings in and out of that wound every day.

With the arrival of the twenty-five girls in England my troubles started in earnest. It seems that the higher English authorities had not consulted the people in charge of the actual routine of the ferry operations before asking me to sign the girls up on term contracts. Not having generated the idea, these operations officials were not very sympathetic and there were plenty of hurdles to surmount before getting the girls at work in the air.

First of all, the authorities decided there must be new medical checks. I asked to be the first for this examination, having gained in advance an idea of what was in store. When I presented myself in the doctor's office he told me to strip off my clothes. I told him that was not necessary, had never been done in the States and that I did not intend to comply or to permit the other American girls to do so. He asked me if I knew there was a war on, and I somewhat sarcastically replied that I had a faint glimmer of an idea about a war and that's why we were there, but the war didn't require stripping for a pilot's physical checkup. The doctor was adamant that things would be his way but I was also determined. I departed to seek the aid of higher authorities, intending to go step by step up to the top if necessary, for if I had backed down on this initial problem, I would have lost control of the many others to come up one by one. Miss Gower sympathized with me when I consulted her but she admitted she could do nothing about it. The commanding officer of the Air Transport Auxiliary, whom I next went to see, let me cool my heels in his outer office for several hours. I left word for him after this wait that I was off for the next higher echelon. He called me back next day and capitulated.

Then the question of written examinations came up. The girls were there to fly, not to write. Some of them had masters' degrees and knew their higher mathematics, but I had chosen them from a different angle and they had passed their flight tests. I argued all this and even used myself as the horrible example. I sat down with the man who was supposed to lay out these examinations and had him quiz me orally as to conditions relating to navigation in England, air lanes, captive balloons and the like. The authorities finally gave in on this point and only new flying tests had to be gone through, coupled with a period of indoctrination. Finally my group was put to ferry work.

That group did a wonderful job. Flying the corridors set off and hemmed in by captive balloons was not easy, particularly in sticky weather. The same could be said for flying planes in need of repair. Mary Nicholson, my secretary at home, was the only one to lose her life. The propeller flew off her plane and she crashed in rough terrain. Only one girl proved unsatisfactory to the British. She was really one of the best pilots of the lot, but through sickness at home or because of other emotional problems of her own, she failed to do her best and eventually cracked up a couple of planes. One time on a take-off she hit a hangar roof and in the collision lost a wing tip and then, while steadying her plane from this, she hit a telephone post beyond the hangar and damaged the other wing. Notwithstanding all this she still was able to circle the field and make a safe landing. Later on when I was in charge of women pilots' training with our own air forces at Fort Worth, Texas, and this girl had been released from English service, I had her given a refresher course at our training base at

Sweetwater, Texas, then put her at work with the WASPs. She served until the WASPs were deactivated, but later was found dead in bed.

Every type of plane was flown by this group of American women pilots. They would move planes from one base to another or from factory to field or vice versa. Their accomplishments were largely unsung even when compared to the little-known work of the WASPs at home, but they were noteworthy. I spent more time on the ground fighting administrative battles than I did in piloting planes in the air. That did not endear me to the authorities in the lower or field administrative echelons.

During this service in England as Flight Captain with the Air Transport Auxiliary (which I performed without pay on the condition that I would be released from my contract whenever asked to come home by General Arnold), my base was White Waltham. Air Marshal Arthur Harris, Commander in Chief of the Bomber Command of the Royal Air Force, had his home not too far away. He and his charming wife, now Sir Arthur and Lady Harris, set aside a room for my use. In addition, I maintained a flat in London where I could let the girls in my group go on their days off for a meal and a little diversion.

Food was a problem, but between the service posts and the ration cards and a few unrationed items we made out. Once I found a quantity of "hominy grits" in a store. No one was buying grits because the English didn't know what this cereal was. I laid in a goodly supply and on occasion got canned hams over from home. As a protection against bombs, I kept the hams and similar items in a bank vault and would draw them out as needed, like a capitalist goes to the vault and clips his coupons.

During my tour of duty in England, the U.S. Eighth Air Force was established in London. I knew my way around England pretty well by that time with respect to military channels and problems and how to get some things done, so was asked by the

Eighth Air Force to come over and help get them organized. I obtained leave of absence from the British for this purpose, and spent several weeks with the Eighth during its formative period. It was a most interesting experience and took me into every kind of problem, including the laying out of airfields and the working out of tables of attrition for fighter planes.

During this period I was invited one evening by an American officer to go into the plans room where some big drive was being planned. I refused, saying I didn't belong there and didn't want to know anything of a secret nature that was not a part of my work. A year later, while at Fort Worth on the staff of our own Air Force Training Command, I found an envelope on my desk one morning which contained my security record from two branches of our government. Both records mentioned my refusal in England to go into that planning room. I often wondered how our people knew. Our secret service was apparently better than most people thought. An American officer, at about the same time, made a remark at a cocktail party in London that was construed by some as a possible leak of important information and he ended up in no time at all back home in a very much demoted status.

While I was in England, General Arnold came over for conference with Air Marshal Harris and Admiral John H. Towers. A dinner was given for him at the Savoy Hotel where I had an apartment at the time. After the dinner General Arnold, Admiral Towers and Air Marshal Harris wanted to get off by themselves for a discussion and they asked to use my apartment. They invited me to stay on. The conference went on for hours. The whole air effort in the war was argued out. Things for the Allies in general and for England in particular were at a low ebb. The Royal Air Force had left in good operational condition only about forty fighter planes. The question of daylight versus night bombing was particularly at issue that evening.

The American Air Force was for bombing around the clock. The British thought daylight bombing would be too costly in loss of personnel and equipment. But the German air force and war potential had to be destroyed, and time was of the essence. The compromise was reached that the American force would take up daylight bombing and, for the time being, the British would stick to night bombing. That start was made and daylight bombing soon proved its worth in net results. I had been in on one of the important decisions of the war.

It was during that trip that General Arnold told me the time was approaching for use of women pilots at home and he would send for me before long to take on this organization.

Bombing of London was heavy in those days. The Battle of Britain was on. The sky at night was full of flashing planes, searchlights, and antiaircraft fire accompanied by the incessant sound of the sirens and the explosions of bombs. One night just before I left England the biggest raid of all was on. My house seemed to be in a sort of grandstand position and I got out of bed, wrapped a blanket around me and sat on the front steps. It was a long fight. The panes in my windows were broken from nearby bomb explosions. A house went to pieces a block up the street and then another hit came just a block below me. Even so, having traversed that particular area again since the war, and having compared it with the areas around St. Paul's Cathedral and in the financial section, I concluded that the damage around my quarters was not heavy. I often wondered whether Providence let St. Paul's Cathedral stand up while most everything around it was flattened. It seemed to me also that some mysterious force was at work to save Parliament buildings, the palace, the bridges and the power plants. London was pretty much a shambles at that time. People slept to capacity in the subways and cellars were at a premium. While not a fatalist, I held to the superstition that having done all that was expected of me my time would come only when my

number was up and so I went on my way without change of
routine, except as required by conditions about me.

It was in those days that King Peter of Yugoslavia, who had a
commission in the Air Transport Auxiliary, remarked to a friend
that he wished he knew how to go about getting an egg to eat.
The friend managed to supply him with a few bantam eggs.
King Peter and Queen Alexandra dined with us in our New York
apartment some years later and we recounted some English experiences. I told him that one of the wildest episodes I heard
about was the flight of two young pilots which ended on the deck
of a carrier with the small plane falling down the elevator. Then
I learned for the first time that King Peter was one of the two
culprits.

Another experience on the lighter side I must relate. My old
naval friend, Captain Paul Hammond, had an apartment in London. In a conversation with him and an admiral the talk went
back to the days at Pensacola, Florida, and then to southern cooking in general and southern fried chicken in particular. I said
that if Captain Hammond could arrange a suitable place and
someone would supply the white flour and chicken, I would cook
them up a dinner worthy of the memory of General Lee himself.
The apartment of our air attaché was obtained for the occasion.
The white flour showed up from an American cruiser, some
chicken came down by plane from Northern Ireland and I found
some odds and ends in the icebox. There were a dozen of us who
sat down to that dinner including a couple of British admirals. It
was a never-to-be-forgotten meal because of the circumstances
of its setting and arrangements.

Once I carried an English private practically all the way across
England in my car. He was hitchhiking and I was on official business. He carried in his hand a small paper sack during the whole
trip as if it contained gold. At the end he reached down into the
bag and handed me one egg. I tried to refuse it, but he insisted

he had two more. He had just taken his leave at the farmhouse of a friend.

The food problem was bad in England then, but I have been back twice since and I consider it not overly better now so far as the small householder is concerned. It's more distressing now, in any event, because there is at least so-called peace and the people in most other parts of western Europe have an abundance of food. In my mind I used to connect up an Englishman with roast beef, but not any more. I would now call him well starched, whether he hails from Oxford or not.

CHAPTER VII

THE pressure on our man power during World War II and the increasing use of war power made it certain that eventually there would be a need for women pilots. All my war work up until the time General Arnold called me home from England had been in preparation for this time of need.

The story of the WASP, and their war contribution, has never been told. It is a saga of real accomplishment. WASP is a synthetic word meaning Women's Airforce Service Pilots, as WAC means Women's Army Corps.

Women have played a role in aviation almost since the beginning. Madame Blanchard of France was a great balloonist at the start of the nineteenth century. Kätchen Paulus of Germany was beating all of her male contemporaries in competition and was looked upon as an air marvel during the latter part of that century. She made more than five hundred balloon ascents and about two hundred parachute drops. This took place before the renowned airplane flights by Orville and Wilbur Wright.

Harriet Quimby was the first American woman to hold an airplane pilot's license back in 1911, and she was soon followed by the two Moisants, sisters of the famous pilot John Moisant who crashed to his death in 1910. Then followed Ruth Law with a pilot's license in 1912. She made a women's altitude record of 11,200 feet in 1915 and in 1917 won a race by flying nonstop for

590 miles. Ruth Law tried unsuccessfully to join up with our own and the French Air Forces in World War I, and finally in an honorary uniform flew about the United States helping in recruiting and government loan drives.

Katherine Stinson was another early bird dating from about 1912. She flew in the interests of the Red Cross and similar efforts during World War I, now lives in Santa Fe, New Mexico, and was one of the timers at the Santa Fe turn when I did the 2000-kilometer record. Katherine and her sister, who learned to fly in 1914, opened a flying school and trained Canadian pilots while brother Eddie Stinson trained pilots at Kelly Field for our own air corps. The present Stinson private plane is named after him.

Phoebe Omlie came into the air picture in 1922.

Then Amelia Earhart came into the front view. Her first publicized flight was across the Atlantic in 1928, but she was in fact only a passenger on that trip and did not like the false credit. She cleared this up by her later flight across under her own power. Amelia had achieved an altitude record of 14,000 feet some years before this. It is not my purpose to write the exploits of Amelia, but only to mark her important place in the panorama of women flyers. During the Amelia Earhart era a substantial group of women pilots developed, including Betty Gillies, Louise Thaden, Blanche Noyes, Nancy Love, Helen McCloskey and Helen Richey, all of whom were good flyers.

When General Arnold sent word to me that the time had arrived to return home from England to take up organization of women pilots on the home front, I quickly closed out my work and arranged air passage. But after I had gone to the airport, word was sent to me that General S. H. Frank wanted to see me urgently and I should return to base. It was three days before I saw him, and the conference was merely a dinner with polite conversation about nothing in particular and thanks for my help to the Eighth Air Force. I wondered why I had been held over.

The night before my arrival home the Washington papers carried a release from Secretary of War Henry L. Stimson's office that a small group of women ferry pilots (WAF) would be formed in the Ferry Command under the direction of Nancy Love whose husband was administrative assistant to the Chief of Staff of the Ferry Command.

This idea of taking on a group of individual pilots without a special course of training and without some military organization was the reason why I originally broke with Colonel Olds before going to England. Furthermore, it was not in accordance with my discussions and understanding with General Arnold, so I was mystified.

When I walked into General Arnold's office to keep my appointment I had the press clipping in my hand and asked him what it was all about. He was mad all over and when mad, General Arnold could make the fur fly. He said that he had asked the Ferry Command to prepare plans for activation of a women's group, but expected to have such plans submitted to him and through him to me for study and approval. Instead, they had, as he said in no uncertain terms, gone around his desk to the Secretary of War with a project he hadn't approved except in principle and was not going to approve in detail. He called in the officers of the Ferry Command and told them to rework the project to my satisfaction. I, of course, realized by this time that the order from General Frank to wait over in England was but a method to stall my return to Washington until the WAF could be a *fait accompli*.

My conclusion was that the over-all women pilots' program would be set backward by canceling out the WAF and therefore that another way must be found to keep the work on course. A group would be needed in the Ferry Command sooner than any

THE STARS AT NOON

place else and the ones selected were generally the most experienced twenty-five women pilots available. Nancy Love was herself an exceedingly fine pilot, although I was reasonably sure that she did not go along with the idea of a large group of women pilots especially trained for various kinds of air work who would operate under military discipline. I proposed that the WAF be left as it was, but without enlargement for the time being, and that quite apart from the Ferry Command and under the Training Command a training school be set up to take women with some air time and turn them out as trained pilots for ferrying or numerous other flying jobs in the various Air Force Commands.

A suitable order was drawn up to put this into effect.

I was assigned as assistant to Colonel Luke Smith, who was at the time the General Staff Officer in Washington for pilot training. The Training Command itself had headquarters at Fort Worth and was under command of General Barton Yount.

Colonel Smith and I did not see eye to eye as to this woman-pilot problem, which increased the difficulties at the start and caused me many unhappy moments. The fact is that he had another candidate for my job who could be counted on by him for cooperation. His ambitions in this respect were scuttled by my appointment. He brought this young lady in ostensibly as my assistant but made her liaison officer between him and me, although he and I occupied adjoining offices. Finally he recommended that I be transferred to the Training Command at Fort Worth and I suspect he considered it a sort of banishment. I went gladly because the work had to be done in the field anyway and I considered any change would be for the better. General Yount and I later became the best of friends and this friendship lasted beyond the war and until his death. He told me that Colonel Smith in notifying him of my transfer said that the Training Command was receiving a bundle of trouble from a very determined and obstinate woman. There was trouble all right so far as Colonel Smith was concerned and it caused many a headache throughout the program in manifold ways.

I selected the Houston Airport as having the best all-round advantages for location to get started. Colonel Luke Smith tried to get me to select another location in Missouri, but the Training Command backed my choice.

Applications for pilot training were flowing in. I determined to interview each applicant personally. Soon this became too difficult and I had three assistants traveling around the country giving interviews, making selections and arranging for medical examinations.

We started with claptrap equipment consisting of every conceivable sort of primary and basic training planes. The girls housed themselves at nearby motels with free bus service to and from the airport. But the work was launched. The first class embraced women who had considerable air experience. The length of training for subsequent classes was to be variable depending on the capacity of the candidates. While the first course was to last only about twenty-three weeks we soon extended the training period to nine months.

Near the end of the training of the first class, I became very ill with abdominal adhesions and for several days it was touch and go for me in St. Vincent's Hospital in Los Angeles. An operation was avoided, but I was warned of probable recurrence. After a few days of recuperation at my ranch, I flew to Houston to present the diplomas to the first graduating class. I could not sit up to get from my ranch to the Phoenix airport — a distance of about two hundred miles — so I hired the local mortuary's "meat wagon" to transport me.

The Houston facility was at best a makeshift. The British had a fine training base at Sweetwater, Texas, which they were giving up, so we seized upon it for the women and the second class of trainees was transferred by air to the permanent home.

The WAC under Colonel Oveta Culp Hobby — later Cabinet Secretary Hobby — was having its growing pains at about this time. Many who had joined were using the technical right to resign afforded them by the shift of the Army organization headed by Colonel Hobby from the WAAC to the WAC and some dramatic move seemed to be indicated to offset this trend. Someone got the bright idea that women pilots should be made a subsidiary part of the WAC. At that time I had more than twenty-five thousand applicants for pilot training. They would be a fine addition to the WAC. Also there were some undercover politics at work. Colonel Smith was fostering the WAC idea but General Arnold was with me in opposition, although not openly. He called me to Washington and asked me to see Colonel Hobby. She opened the conversation by telling me she didn't know one end of a plane from another, but that if the pilots could be brought into the WAC, she would count on my direction of them. I told her that there was just about as much sense putting the women pilots under the WAC as putting the Air Force pilots back in the Army Signal Corps; that I was unalterably opposed to it and if the scheme were to mature, she would have to find another leader. I probably was not too diplomatic in my language and I think Colonel Hobby never liked me after that — which thought caused me to chuckle in the spring of 1954 when Secretary Hobby accepted the hospitality of my plane to fly her from Palm Springs, California, to Phoenix, Arizona. When I returned to General Arnold from this appointment with Colonel Hobby and reported the conversation, he had a good laugh and sent me back to Fort Worth with the assurance that the women pilots would remain a part of the Air Force. However, for some time I kept a suspicious eye on General Smith (by then he had received his star) and some of the others in the Ferry Command, who seemed to me willing to make a trade with Colonel Hobby.

The applicants for women pilots were screened on the same basis as the men applicants for cadet pilot training, except that I tried to keep a geographical balance to make the WASP representative of the country as a whole. After we settled down so that statistical conclusions could be drawn, it was found that in training and in operational work, the women and the men proved to be equal by practically every yardstick. By that I mean the eliminations through failure to pass tests were percentage-wise the same, the ability to fly various types of missions was the same, as well as the ability to carry on for long hours. Also the rate of accidents and deaths was the same for similar work. During the program thirty-eight girls lost their lives and it was pretty depressing to be able to forecast at the beginning of a month just how many would take their last flight during that month.

The first week the girls were at Sweetwater we had over one hundred men pilots make "forced landings" on the field. That was carrying things pretty far and the field was barred both by gate and from the air except in real emergency. They began calling it "Cochran's Convent."

More than eighteen hundred women entered that course and more than one thousand of them graduated and went to work flying with the air forces. The first graduating groups were sent to the Air Transport Command, then I tried groups, with great success, on target towing, on engineering flying, and in various other ways.

The troubles in the administrative end were plenty, all stemming from the fact that the girls were not militarized but had to be controlled and dealt with under Civil Service regulations. I had to get around the Pentagon building so fast and often to see all the generals and colonels I had to see on this, that and the other thing that I could have effectively used a motor scooter. Also I regularly flew back and forth from post to post where the WASPs were assigned for duty.

As soon as the graduates were being turned out from Sweetwater, the pilot training program and the ferrying work being done by the original twenty-five known as WAFs were combined into the over-all organization known as WASP and I was transferred to the general staff in Washington in charge of the whole, with title of Director of WASP. I reported to the Assistant Chief of Staff in charge of operations, commitments and requirements. My chief in turn reported to the Chief of Air Staff. The persons holding these offices changed often so I had many top generals to see and resell my plans to. General Arnold was over the whole and because he was keenly interested in the women pilots' program I had access to him when desired, but I took care not to abuse this privilege.

When it came time to select a uniform for the women pilots a drive was made to have them use the uniform which had been readied in quantity for the Nurses' Corps and then changed. Another drive was attempted to have me use an excess amount of material that had been bought for the WAC. In addition to the discarded uniform for the nurses and one I had made from the WAC excess material, I had one designed according to my own ideas with San Diego blue material which I knew was a favorite with the Air Force. I presented these three uniforms on live models to General Arnold. My choice was on a beautifully proportioned Greek professional model who had volunteered her services. The other two uniforms were on girls I had borrowed from the Quartermaster General's office and they did not have classical physical dimensions to say the least. There was no question of choice in General Arnold's mind and he was so intrigued with the fashion show and my technique of presentation that he took us all immediately to General George C. Marshall's office. General Marshall looked us over carefully and speaking very judiciously said he liked best the uniform I had on. I was not wearing a uniform but a regular suit and I tried to so explain. He still liked it best and I finally had to tell him how very much more uniforms like it would cost than the others. Economy won him over to his second choice which was on my Greek model and that was how the choice as to the WASP uniform was made. Before I got out of General Marshall's room I had his consent to use regular Air Force wings with a distinctive center as well as a small-sized eagle for the caps.

There were many amusing as well as pathetic incidents connected with the WASP program. Twins happened to be accepted for training. One was a good flyer while the other had failed her flight test. Before elimination the one who had failed was to receive the final check ride from independent officers. She did well; we then discovered her sister had substituted for her. They wanted to stay together and they did, but outside the program.

Three girls were eliminated from the first class for failure to pass tests. One happened to be a respected friend of mine. Another was a friend of General Smith's protégée who by this time was taking the training course herself. Pressure was brought on me through General Smith's office to have them reinstated. I refused. Two colonels came to Fort Worth from Washington to make me reverse my position. I told them they could issue the order which would also be my signal for resignation because, once the teachers at the school had passed on a girl's flying qualities, I would not interfere — and I did not propose to have others in the class feel that they could go around corners to exert pressure in order to undercut me.

Only once afterwards did I have anything resembling pressure brought to bear. Assistant Secretary of War for Air Lovett called me in one day and asked by what authority I was handling elimination of trainees from the training program. I explained the routine and that, while we were on Civil Service status, the right to eliminate was a part of a signed agreement by every applicant who had been accepted for training. He explained that it nevertheless might not be legal. It finally developed that a girl was about to be eliminated who was a daughter of an ex-partner of a Supreme Court Justice, and the Justice apparently had asked the Assistant Secretary of War for Air to intervene. Mr. Lovett was finally convinced that I was not only right but could not be swayed even to help him or the Justice out of embarrassment. He asked me to see the Justice. I did and as politely as possible said that, short of orders from the topside to me, the wheels of justice at the Sweetwater Court of Inquiry would grind on. Both Mr. Lovett and the Justice saw my point and left me alone with even the hint of a compliment for my willingness to stand up for what I was sure was necessary by way of controls and procedures.

I started a group of twenty-five girls in new work at Camp Davis, North Carolina. During the first week two were killed. The remaining girls at the base were in somewhat of a panic and the whole program in its broader than ferrying aspects was at stake. The girls claimed the planes being used were faulty with respect to maintenance and not fit for the night flying that was being done. My abdominal adhesions were giving me serious trouble at the time. I was in fact barely able to stay on my feet. An Air Force base doctor showed me how to get temporary relief by having someone hold on to my legs while I hung for a few minutes from a table with my head down to the floor. My friend, Dr. W. Randolph "Randy" Lovelace II, then in charge of Aviation Medicine at Wright Field, gave me a list of hospitals from which I should never be more than four hours distant by air in case of emergency (and the emergency did in fact develop later). However, I went on down to Camp Davis because of this crisis and flew every plane that was being used for the work. Most of the planes being used had plenty of faults needing correction.

The "squawk sheets" in each plane proved this. But what plane in those days didn't have such deficiencies? None of the deficiencies had really contributed to the accidents. Another girl crashed while I was there and had a fractured skull. I went into everything carefully and the answer was that there had been apparent sabotage. Sugar was found in some of the gasoline and sugar in gasoline stops the engine in no time at all. Two of the girls wanted to quit. I refused their request and placed them in quarters until final disposition of their cases. They then asked for transfer back to the Ferry Command which would have been ruinous to the effort to expand the operations of the WASP. I eliminated them from the WASP program. They appealed to the higher Civil Service authorities, but at last their case was thrown out. They spoke some about suing me personally, but that never happened.

Occasionally girls lost their nerve. Usually they would hide this fact under some alibi, but when they came to me with the honest admission I allowed them to resign or go into ground work. These same things happened to male pilots to the same degree.

When the B–26 came into service, it was known as the Baltimore prostitute because it was made in Baltimore and had no visible means of support, that is to say its wing area seemed too small for the weight of the plane. Many accidents occurred. Few planes returned from the first missions of B–26s that went out from England over Europe. The pilots generally feared the plane, but, because it was in quantity production, a great problem was presented to the General Staff. General Barney Giles, my chief at the time, went out and flew it time after time himself and would bring it in for landings at even less than the air speed indicated for safety in the manuals. He and others were sure the plane was all right. I then flew it and could find no serious fault.

I asked General Arnold to let me assign twenty-five girls right out of Sweetwater to the B–26 transitional training base and if they proved satisfactory to let them fly this plane in operations. The suggestion was approved. These girls did a fine job. They weren't afraid of the plane because they hadn't heard the underground rumors about it. They made the male pilots' faces red for a while and then the B–26 suddenly became accepted as a safe plane. (I see one flying around even today as an executive plane.) The only accident the girls had in the many thousands of hours in the B–26 was when two planes collided in the air. The B–26, with my WASP in it, made the airfield for a safe landing; the girl was so excited, however, that she left the plane while the propellers were still turning and walked into one of them. She was quite badly cut, but not killed as is usually the case when pilot and propeller meet.

Another time the men pilots were complaining that the B–29 would not safely fly on only two of the four engines as it was supposed to do. We sent two WASPs in a B–29 from base to base, flying back and forth on two engines. The obvious conclusion was that if a woman could do it, so could a man.

The so-called Negro question was laid on my doorstep in a very direct way early in the women pilots' training program. Several Negro girls applied for training but never more than one at a time out of the thousands of applicants. I interviewed these particular applicants in proper order without prejudice or preference, hardly knowing what I could do at that stage of my program if any one of them had passed the preliminaries. Fortunately for the formative stages of the work none met all of the specifications. Finally one, a New Jersey school teacher who was a pilot and a fine physical specimen, made application for acceptance as a student at Sweetwater. I asked her to join me for breakfast on a Sunday morning in my New York apartment and made a special trip to New York for the purpose. I told her the manifold troubles I was having getting the program started and ended by stating that I had no prejudice whatever with respect to the color or race of my candidates but that the complication she had brought up for decision might, for one reason or another, prove the straw that would break the camel's back. This fine young Negro girl recognized the force and honesty of my arguments, stated that first of all the women pilots' program should be stabilized and strengthened, and she withdrew her application. She also saw to it, I believe, that I was left alone thereafter so far as this particular issue was concerned. I appreciated her understanding and respected her as a person.

At the start of the program General Arnold and I agreed that militarization would be desirable and probably even necessary if the program were to be more than a short-lived experimental test. A few months would give the answer. The WASP never received later the militarization they deserved because a political situation arose which caused several civilian male pilot organizations to oppose the Militarization Bill which had been introduced in Congress. Their opposition was aided and abetted by some of the girls themselves who did not understand the problem and wished to retain their freedom of action about resigning.

As a result the WASPs did not get the benefits of the GI Bill nor did the injured get suitable compensation nor did those killed in service get proper recognition.

I did, however, get the Air Force to accept the WASP in the Air Force Reserve just as if they had served as enlisted officers. The only exception is that they are not yet on flying status, even for the short stretches needed to keep them in training. I hope to get that one bar removed before I consider my work as Director of the WASP really finished.

My final report to General Arnold with respect to the WASP program was accompanied by an official summary in which I said:

More than 25,000 women applied for women pilot training. Eighteen hundred and thirty (1,830) were accepted. 30.7% were eliminated during training for flying deficiency and another 2.2% for other reasons, with consequent lower elimination rate than among male cadet pilots. 8% of those accepted resigned and 1,074 graduated, or 58.7% of the total. Of the 1,074 who graduated, 900 remained at time of inactivation, or 83.6% of the graduates, to which should be added 16 of the original WAFs employed who were still with the program at time of inactivation.

The women pilots, subsequent to graduation from the training program, flew approximately 60 million miles for the Army Air Forces: the fatalities were 38, or one to about 16,000 hours of flying. Both the accident rate and the fatality rate compared favorably with the rates for male pilots in similar work.

The report among other things stated that women meeting the proper height and weight requirements could be trained as quickly and as economically as men in the same age group to fly all types of planes safely, efficiently and regularly, and therefore could be used, as they were in the WASP program, effectively to release male pilots for other duties; that physiology peculiar to women is not a handicap to flying or dependable performance of duty in a properly selected group; that the psychological, aptitude, and other tests used in the case of male pilots have approximately the same usefulness in the case of women pilots; that women pilots have as much stamina and endurance and are no more subject to operational or flying fatigue than male pilots doing similar work and can safely fly as many hours per month as male pilots; and that an effective women's air force of many scores of thousands of good dependable pilots could be built up in the case of need from the nearly thirteen million young women of our country between the ages of eighteen and twenty-eight.

I recommended that any future women pilots' program should be militarized from the beginning and that for general economy and efficiency, the upper age limit should be twenty-seven or twenty-eight years for women to be accepted for pilot training.

In November 1943 I spoke at the Herald-Tribune Annual Forum on women in the aviation industry. As a matter of fact, I was not as optimistic as most of the girls in the WASP program as to the future that they would carve out for themselves in flying. I had seen too much of the opposition and rough spots that women would encounter. What I said at that time was:

> I can see them in the cockpit of many small commercial planes. I can see them at the controls of some of the small feeder lines. I can see them in the traffic control towers and they are ideal in the training of air students. But it is my considered judgment that when all is said and done only about 25% of the WASPs will continue to earn their living in aviation.

I continue to keep in touch with the ex-WASPs. Hardly a week goes by that I am not called on to help one or more in some way — to get a reserve status straightened out, to get a transfer from an enlisted status in one branch of the service to the officer's status they have earned in the air branch even though it is to be for ground work only, or to help with advice some ex-WASP who has taken on supervision of a feeder line or an airport. Many, of course, have married. One has become a nun. The fact is, as stated in my forecast, that about a quarter of the number are still earning their living in the aviation field.

In the fall of 1952 I invited all the ex-WASPs in the Los Angeles area to a "wing ding" at my ranch. I thought about fifteen would show up but over eighty accepted. A chuck-wagon dinner was followed by singing of the old Sweetwater Base songs and much reminiscing. It so happened that General and Mrs. Carl "Tooey" Spaatz were visiting us at the time. The General had been in command of the Air Forces in Europe and North Africa while the WASPs were active here at home and consequently had not come into contact with them. He was much taken by their attitude that evening and equally amused by their direct, raucous songs. After the girls had departed, he said that the only difference he could see between them and his own fighter pilots was that the WASPs wore skirts. He added that, given a war, he would ask for nothing better than to have a few hundred such women under his command as fighter pilots.

During World War II the Air Force was a part of the Army. The women's part of the ground work was carried on, therefore, by the Army's WAC. Since the Air Force has become an independent branch of the armed services, the women in the Air Force are in a separate group known as WAF. But the WAF has never included pilots as such. The law creating the WAF is broad enough to include flying but specifically excludes combat flying.

The WAF has had its troubles too. Because I have grown up with many of the Air Force officers and have known many of the problems of organization and personnel confronting them, I have been consulted from time to time concerning the organization of the WAF.

In the summer of 1950 the late General Hoyt S. "Van" Vandenberg, then Chief of Staff, was dissatisfied with the standards of the WAF and asked me if I would become the Director even if only for one year. I had to refuse for many reasons. He then asked me, as special consultant, to check the various bases where WAFs were stationed and to make recommendations. After several weeks of work and consultation with the top Air Force officials, I submitted my recommendations. Prior to their formal submission I had them studied and approved by most of the top Air Force officers who had worked with WAFs in their commands.

There were a large number of recommendations dealing with physical standards, recruiting, age brackets, dress, promotions and reserve status.

Although the Air Force was a separate branch of the Armed

Services the recruiting of the WAFs was still being carried on through Army channels and according to standards and specifications that were below those set by the Navy for their WAVEs. I recommended that the Air Force should take over its own recruiting of WAFs; that the physcial standards for WAFs should be raised to Navy standards and furthermore that consideration should be given in selection of applicants to *proper distribution of weight* as well as to weight in relationship to height. Another recommendation was that there should be a careful medical screening by a woman doctor to eliminate those who appeared to be emotionally or hormonally maladjusted. Still another recommendation was that one hundred enlisted WAFs should be carefully selected and sent to secretarial schools — because among the more than five thousand who had come into the program, there were few well-qualified secretaries.

General Vandenberg felt the start had to be made in carrying out these recommendations by putting in a new head of the WAF, because Colonel Geraldine May was nearing the end of her term of duty. Again I was asked to take over but again I refused. Colonel May resigned. Colonel May considered that I was her undoing, which was farthest from the fact. She struck out at me in the press. Garbled and isolated parts of my report — particularly the ones referred to above — were allowed to leak in a way which gave a completely wrong impression. It was made to appear from these stories that I wanted to make the WAF a glamorous, kid glove, lily-fingered organization, composed mostly of beautiful girls who would act as companions for the top brass.

I was in Morocco at the time that Colonel May resigned. Word came to me from the Air Force Public Relations personnel that Colonel May was striking at me in the press; that if reached by reporters I should say nothing; and that the Air Force at the proper time in its own way would clear the matter up publicly.

What a punishment I took in silence! It was made to appear that my statement that weight should be properly distributed as well as being in proportion to height should be read with a lifting of the eyebrows. Drew Pearson had a field day in his column. Presumably there were some who thought or were being made to think the Air Force should fill its quota of WAFs by catering to the potbellied and bowlegged of our American womanhood. Oddly enough it was the Army and not the Air Force that eventually publicly supported my position. Given time enough everything seems to come out right. In August 1953 the Army issued a rule designed to keep the WACs "trim and fit" for duty which stated that "in the interests of efficiency and morale" weight must be "well distributed" and the posture and physical bearing must be "acceptable and free from obvious defects of appearance remediable by physical exercise and good health practices."

The WAFs have moved forward. They are a smarter group now. My recommendations have been put into effect for the most part. The public beating I took was not in vain. Whether Colonel May could have done the job or not, if given a higher place on the Table of Air Force Organization, I don't know. It was not my function to pass on this. But certain it is that she couldn't be effective tucked off in a corner room as she was — a point that I made in my report — and equally certain it is that I did not cause her resignation or want her job. I am a Lieutenant Colonel in the Civil Air Patrol which under the active direction of General Spaatz has grown into a large and effective organization. As the ex-head of the WASP, I also have the rank of Lieutenant Colonel in the Air Force Reserve. I would not have taken that job of head of the WAF if a full general's rank had been thrown in. If a fighting war should eventuate, I would, however, willingly lay aside my manifold civilian obligations, let my cosmetics business float again, and if necessary, in the lowest rank, crawl across the country on my hands and knees to be of aid to my country. I'll do this if I can't handle a fighter plane in combat. My inability to so fight in the last war was my great disappointment. A couple of times I thought I might get the opportunity to fly on a mission or two but nothing of this kind ever matured.

CHAPTER VIII

WHEN my work in the Pentagon with the WASP was completed, the war wasn't over but indications were that it wasn't going to last much longer. I wanted to manage, if possible, to do a little real fighting myself, either in a bomber or a fighter. And I wanted to get to the Orient and see what was going on there. I wanted to get the facts for myself. I have always been a factual glutton and I will go to a great extent to get some bit of factual information I want. For example, once just before the war I wanted to have an elephant on the ranch as a pet. Floyd said it would be a destructive and expensive hobby. I phoned the zoo to find out what the diet of an elephant was, the different intake for different sizes and breeds of elephants.

I didn't get that elephant, but on this later occasion I did get to the Orient. Military jobs that would take me there were slow in maturing and not too sure. So one day I chatted with the editor of *Liberty* magazine about the Pacific Theater and asked him to send me out there for his magazine. I admitted that I was an inexperienced writer but I pointed out that several hundred people had been sent out ostensibly as war correspondents who had never even turned in a story. I promised good copy would be forthcoming from me. I was hired. At the last minute I was given a Priority No. 1, an unusual rating for a correspondent, but General Arnold had signed orders making me a Special Consultant for the duration of my trip and had given me some specific assignments to perform while in the Pacific. I knew he had done this as a gesture of appreciation for my hard work during the war. I was very grateful for it.

The processing took practically no time at all because I was in a hurry to get to the Far East before the war's end. The preventive shots were a problem as I seemed to be allergic to most vaccines so I omitted them with the thought that probably the Orient had nothing worse for me than the branch water I had drunk in the South as a child.

The second atomic bomb was dropped just about the time I reached San Francisco. The Air Force had been alerted to send all available crews forward as fast as possible and that took precedence over practically all other priorities. All means of getting out of San Francisco seemed closed to me, but I had military friends there who believed I had a right to be in at the kill and thought they could get me on a plane as overload. I limited myself and my baggage to two hundred pounds and at the end of twenty-four hours, in the middle of the night, I was hoisted aboard a DC–4 just ready for the take-off. The captain of the plane turned out to be a friend of fifteen years' standing and I also knew several of the pilots aboard. So life for the moment was perfect. I was on my way.

The commanding officer of the base at Hickam Field in Hawaii had been one of my strongest opponents in my work with the WASP. He didn't like women very much and he didn't like women pilots in particular. He said I hadn't a chance of getting a plane out of Hawaii. I insisted on quarters near the field so I could be on hand in case someone didn't show up for a flight and he sent me to visitors' quarters there where he said some theatrical people were staying. They turned out to be camp followers but I was able to get a bath, press a uniform and pack. I was resting when I was told someone was there to see me. It was General Parker, one of the nicest, one of the kindest men I think I have ever known. He said he had just heard I was there. He wanted to take me to dinner and he wanted to move me to better quarters. I said I would stay right there and didn't plan to retire until someone offered me a ride to Guam. He asked if any place but Guam would do, and I said I would accept any place eastward but that my friend General Barney Giles was in Guam. I finally had dinner with General Parker at the Officers' Mess on the airfield. Before we finished dinner word came that I could leave immediately for Guam. Someone went for my bags and I raced to the end of the runway in my host's car and the General and several others made a sort of human ladder — someone held the pilot's feet as he leaned down from the plane entrance and took my hands, and together they pulled and pushed me up. Then they threw my bags in after me. At the last instant, another package came flying up through the door of the airplane and General Parker yelled above the roar of the motors that it was something that would come in very handy and would have to substitute for a better present.

That was the last time I ever saw this very likable man. General Parker was killed a few months later in an ocean flight when his plane hit almost the only piece of land sticking above the surface within several hundred miles.

The plane I was in was the first B–24 that was converted to passenger use. The so-called bucket seats were very small for men to sit in and so close together that the knees of the passengers would touch the seats in front of them. The boys presented a complete picture of misery and exhaustion.

I decided to find out what my present was from General Parker. It looked like an interesting little package, which I unbuckled and unrolled. It was rather limp-looking rubber. One of the boys said it was one of the fabulous rubber mattresses. By rolling it in the opposite direction, it automatically inflated itself. It was wide enough for one to lie down on with comfort. I put it down in the aisle. Some B–4 bags substituted for pillows and I started the boys, one at a time, having an hour rest. We set up a system of rotation but it was sometimes difficult to get the incumbent to move on schedule. The rubber mattress on the floor of the plane was extremely comfortable compared to the bucket seats and indeed was far more comfortable than the pallets I used in my childhood.

Finally, way in the night, we landed at Kwajalein for refueling. The island was bathed in the most enchanting moonlight I have ever seen and I was quite excited about it all. Commodore Ben H. Wyatt, who was Commanding Officer on the island, was at the airport to greet me. I was curious and asked how he knew I was on the airplane. His reply was that no woman could come through that island without his knowing about it and that in point of fact he got a cable, saying that a blond woman, under forty and attractive, was on the flight so he didn't intend missing the occasion even if it meant staying up all night.

We finally fetched up in Guam about two o'clock in the morning. I was the first one out of the airplane. General Giles was on hand to greet me and gave me a good hug, which caused much whistling and cheers from the other passengers. Barney said I had quarters at his home but informed me that sleep was not in the cards because General Spaatz wanted to take me fishing at daybreak. We didn't fish but we did cruise up and down, looking over the lovely island.

That night we played gin rummy and I was somewhat of a champion so my stock was above par. General Jimmy Doolittle was there and with the fighting war over he was about to leave for home and wanted me to pack his bag. Packing wasn't one of my specialties so I refused that job but cooked a meal for him and then sat and talked with him about our friends, the war and one thing or another. While he packed, out of his overflow of personal effects, he gave me two gifts which he said I would need badly in Japan — a suit of woolen underwear and a roll of toilet tissue.

Later that afternoon, I went next door to "Tooey" Spaatz's and we played poker. That is where I met for the first time that outstanding fighter and leader, General "Curt" LeMay. There was a very interesting group of people at that poker party besides General Giles and General Doolittle: General LeMay (now in charge of our Strategic Air Command), General Kenneth McNaughton (now in charge of our Air Forces in Japan), General Nathan F. Twining (now Chief of Staff of the Air Force), General Carl "Tooey" Spaatz (later Chief of Staff but now retired), General Tommy Power (now in charge of the Research and Development Command), and several other general officers. The civilians included Charles Murphy of *Time* magazine and Carl and Shelley Mydans of *Life*. The Mydans had been prisoners in Santo Tomos prison in the Philippines. I had had a couple of poker lessons from Floyd before I left because General Spaatz's weakness for poker was well known and I wanted to take him on — but I wasn't prepared for "spit in the eye," "spit in the ocean," "one-eyed Jacks" and everything under the sun, because it was always dealer's choice. They had table stakes, not too big but fairly healthy. I started winning and I became embarrassed because I won so much. I noticed that as each person lost his money, he quit. So pretty soon, I was just gambling with one person. The next night, I lost all of that and then some so they got square with me.

I was anxious to get on up to Manila because I knew that was the place for the arrival of the peace planes, bringing the people who were to make arrangements for the formal surrender of Japan which later took place on the battleship *Missouri*. Barney Giles said I should wait another few days and go with him. That delay gave me the great privilege of meeting Cardinal Spellman, then Archbishop.

The following day, very early, Colonel Harry Chesley, aide to

General Giles, knocked at my door and said that Archbishop Spellman was arriving and General Giles would like my advice as to
what should be done. They were surprised that I, a Catholic —
the only one in the group — didn't know what to do but even a
Catholic, particularly one from Sawdust Road, doesn't meet up
with an Archbishop every day. They made me an official one-man
reception committee for the Archbishop and I asked to have the
Chaplain brought over for a conference. He looked blank while
we discussed the Archbishop's visit. Somehow, I had assumed
that he would be a priest and would know what to do but he
turned out to be a Methodist minister. I learned from him that
there was a priest on the far end of the island — some fifty or sixty
miles away — so we had him driven down. It developed that this
priest had gone into the military service almost on the same day
he was ordained and the only Mass he had ever heard said by a
Bishop was when he was ordained. He was about as much in the
dark about the whole thing as the Methodist minister. I inspected the church which was in a Quonset hut. A puddle of
water from the constant rains was right in the middle of the hut
and it was there again within five minutes after a complete drying
operation. It was decided that Mass would be held at five-thirty
in the morning. General Giles and General Spaatz were to go to
the Mass, along with all the other General Officers. The Navy
being separate, it was decided that the Archbishop would say
Mass for the Air Force first and then go over to the Navy.

I was up that next morning very early. I was all shined up and
ready to go to Mass by three o'clock. Archbishop Spellman was
standing outside the Quonset hut when I arrived with General
Giles but minus General Spaatz, who had overslept. At Mass the
Archbishop read a prayer which he had composed. Around him
seemed to be an atmosphere of wonderful friendliness and hu-
manness. I think the prayer was one of the most enthralling
things I have ever listened to and while near the Archbishop I

sensed the presence of the truly great. I was the only Catholic among the VIPs present but none of us was sure just what to do. Fortunately, the puddle of water was right in front of us so the Archbishop omitted the kneeling for everyone. The building was uncomfortable and I was uncomfortable. The only thing I kept hanging on to as a bit of comfort was that I had well arranged the breakfast that would follow Mass. The day before, I had gone over and borrowed some special food from the Navy. We had a Mexican boy in the General's kitchen, although he was not really a cook. Before going to Mass I made the biscuits and got all the eggs prepared, ready to scramble, and told the boy just what to do with the bacon. Oranges were squeezed and put down in a container of ice to chill. I didn't know it at the time but the boy who was helping in the kitchen had been studying to be a priest before he was drafted. He was thrilled to be helping.

The Archbishop ate the food with gusto and took three servings. When he asked where all the good things came from, my reply was that in case of need for extra good things, the Air Force always goes to the Navy.

That was the end of a wonderful experience — awkward in parts but one that ripened into a warm friendship with Cardinal Spellman.

On my arrival in Manila arrangements were made for me to stay in one of the rooms at the bombed-out Manila Hotel. The room had no windowpanes and no door or furniture at first, but by afternoon a cot with a mosquito net was provided and the next day a door was put in place and I got a chair. Some Filipino girls cleaned the place up. When I came back in the late afternoon they were just finishing the shining job on the floor. They had cut coconuts open and put the husks on their feet. Patiently, using their feet so adorned as polishers, they had put an excellent sheen on every inch of the beautiful tile floor. (In the summer of 1953 I saw one of these same girls working as attendant in the ladies' room of the Beachcomber Restaurant in Los Angeles.) The plumbing in that hotel which had not been destroyed by bombs had been cut out by the Japs and taken away. The fixtures were gone. There was a hole in the middle of the bathroom floor that served as a drain. I took my baths by standing in the middle of the floor, first wetting myself with a bucket of water, and then, after the soaping routine, pouring more buckets of water over myself.

Admiral Frank Wagner gave me the use of his Catalina flying boat. On the side of the plane was a picture of a cat sitting on a cushion and its face had been made to look like the Admiral. In this "Cat" I flew over many of the islands. I also took motor trips with Admiral Turnbull through the little villages. The poverty was incredible.

Finally, the big day arrived when the peace planes were to arrive in Manila with the Japanese. There were two planes — painted snow white. On landing, the Japanese stepped out, dressed in high hats and striped trousers. That sight was ludicrous to me. Our military men didn't shake hands with the Japanese as they stepped from the planes, but walked up and gave a military salute. The Japs didn't know what to do — they looked very awkward and unhappy about the whole affair. The Japs were put in cars and immediately taken away to the most luxurious accommodations that could be provided. I talked to a sergeant who was on duty at these quarters — not as a guard, but to see to the needs of the Japs — and he said the first thing the chief Jap did was to give him a brand-new American five-dollar bill and ask him to procure some cigarettes.

Word came down from the hills that Yamashita would surrender and our military people were to go up to Baguio in Luzon to meet him. No newspaper woman was permitted to go. There were more than twenty-five newspaper women in Manila, all waiting and hoping — far too many for this ceremony — so only the men in the line services were to be present. Baguio was where the summer palace of the President of the Philippines was located. It was also the location of some of the worst action of the war and where the headquarters of the Japs had been. Our people consequently felt it would be a fitting place to have the surrender take place.

Major General E. H. Leavey had been chosen to accept the surrender. He had a lower rank than Yamashita. It was felt that only an officer of such lesser rank should participate in surrender proceedings. Much to my amazement General Leavey asked me if I would like to go to Baguio and see the surrender.

I was to go, he said, as his personal friend — nothing to do with the press — and in consequence for a period of time I must not write anything about the surrender and should avoid mentioning my trip to other correspondents. The General Officers, he said, considered me as a service woman and not of the press. After thinking things over I told him there was one woman who should by all means go to this surrender — even if it meant my staying away. I was referring to Mrs. Carl Mydans. She had been one of the prisoners there under Yamashita's rule and it seemed fitting and right that she should see his humbling even though she was one of the most famous and well known of all the women correspondents there. He finally permitted me to feel her out and if she would agree not to write anything, he would try to take her along. She agreed.

The great day came. It was arranged that Shelley Mydans and I would fly in one of the courier planes to an airstrip called Luna. The plane was a broken-down DC–3 with bucket seats. The pilot looked as if he hadn't been shaving too long. We taxied out without much of an inspection of the plane by the crew. When we got out on the end of the runway, I noticed the gustlocks were still on the controls. I rushed up front and told the pilot about this. He looked startled and then said he was about to remove them. (Failure to remove the gustlocks before the take-off caused the crash in which our great singer Grace Moore was killed in Belgium.) When we touched down on a wire matting which served as a landing strip on Luna beach, the three planes carrying Yamashita, General Robert S. Beightler and the remainder of the surrender party were about to land.

I've never seen such handsome specimens of manhood as our American M.P.'s that day. They were all six feet two inches or more in height. The Japs, by their actions with the prisoners during the war, proved that they hated tall people. Yamashita was getting plenty of them that day. Our men looked absolutely magnificent. They were turned out practically in full dress, with all of their decorations and with perhaps some decorations borrowed for the occasion. General Beightler told me how fascinating it had been when his group arrived in the mountains that morning and discovered that instead of forty thousand men, the enemy amounted to more than seventy thousand.

When the planes landed, carrying Admiral Arima, the top Japanese Navy man, in one and General Yamashita in the other, each with aides, servants and interpreters totaling about thirty people for the surrendering group, a search of the Japs was made and a hand grenade or small bomb was found on one of Yamashita's personal servants. One toss of that bomb and the surrender party would have been over.

Since Yamashita had brought more people out of the mountains with him than had been anticipated, our authorities had to requisition the room which Shelley Mydans and I were to have in the palace. So Shelley and I on arrival in Baguio were sent over to a field hospital which housed sick American soldiers. We were put on a sort of porch. It was bitterly cold. The place was all filled with a kind of green, slimy moss that grows in damp places. There was a trough where we washed our hands. The washroom was full of bloody cotton and was filthy. The big dank and depressing ward was filled with sick and restless men and it looked as bad as the washrooms. I was burned up thinking by contrast of our treatment of Yamashita, who "never had it so good."

The overcooked oatmeal and canned cream in the hospital's mess hall didn't attract me the next morning so I decided to go over to the palace and through applied resourcefulness obtain some good food. With Shelley in tow, I proceeded right around to the back door of the beautiful palace. The place was simply alive with military police, again handsome, tall and beautifully dressed. They all looked like my idea of Adonis. I smelled good cooking and went into the kitchen. There on the stove was the most appetizing food — eggs, bacon, rice, everything one could think of. After seeing what the American boys at the hospital were getting I was mad and sarcastically asked who the fancy breakfast was for. I was told that it was for Yamashita and his party because it had been decided to feed him well this once. I rejoined that they might add to that little gesture by also feeding a couple of Americans. There on the steps of the kitchen, Shelley and I sat and had a most delicious breakfast, while Yamashita rested in what were to have been our quarters.

In the meantime, word had come that the surrender wouldn't take place until sometime that afternoon because General Jonathan M. Wainwright and General A. E. Percival were in flight to be present. They had been on the U.S.S. *Missouri* the previous day for the big surrender. Wainwright had surrendered Bataan to Yamashita and had become a prisoner of war and Percival had surrendered Singapore with like results for himself. I was excited that I would get to see Wainwright and shined myself up to the last degree possible prior to the luncheon I was to have with Commodore Norman C. Gillette and General E. H. Leavey.

Right after lunch the surrender took place. In the surrender room, which had been the banquet hall of the palace, there was a long table. On one side of the table were some gaudy and ornate carved chairs for our people. On the other side of the table were some folding camp chairs for the Japs. It was a long, narrow room with a fireplace at one end and it was crowded. Shelley and I stationed ourselves at opposite ends of the room so we could between us see everything and compare notes. The little raised place in front of the fireplace gave me a good vantage point. Then in our people came — Generals Leavey, Styer, Wood, Wainwright and Percival. When they walked in, Percival had the faltering step of a completely broken man. Wainwright, although he was very, very thin and presented almost an emaciated appearance, came in with a buoyancy in his step. His head was high.

I was terribly lucky because the surrender party came in at the far end of the room, giving me a full view of Yamashita, Admiral Arima and the interpreter. As they sat in the low folding camp chairs they looked insignificant. Admiral Arima looked a bit bewildered by it all. But not so Yamashita at the start. Yamashita was fat, gross, vulgar-looking. His lips were thick. He just couldn't have been worse. Yamashita, after being seated, took one look around and realized when he saw Wainwright and Percival what was happening. I am not exaggerating when I say one could see the muscles sag all over his body, starting from the top of his head. I didn't believe it was possible to see a person change before one's eyes as I saw this man change. He turned into a pile of flabby flesh, all of a sudden, and his color changed along with his whole attitude. He was completely shocked to see these two men present because it was just so recently that the surrender had taken place in Japan. He probably thought they were still in prison.

The proceedings started. General Wood read the surrender conditions very, very slowly and, after he finished reading them, they were carefully translated and interpreted and then Yamashita's interpreter again interpreted them but with impatience. Finally, when this ceremony was over and all the papers were signed, Yamashita got up, as a prisoner. Of course, you know his fate. He was hanged, and I think rightly so, — in the same prison where he had permitted so many Americans and Filipinos to be tortured and starved.

I wish I could have been present when the rope tightened about Yamashita's neck. I thought of the lynching and the hanging I had seen as a small child in the South. They had left me with bad memories and bad dreams. I don't think I would have had any such aftermath from seeing the death of one of the most brutal men of modern times.

Following the surrender, it was announced that General Wainwright and General Percival would talk for five minutes or so to the assembled press without right on the part of the reporters to publish anything, or to ask questions. Shelley and I crowded into this small room and I was a little bit in front. General Percival got up to talk — he stammered and finally broke down. He was almost on the verge of sobbing, he was so emotional. General Wainwright's remarks will ever live in my memory. He said that almost up to that moment he had felt disgraced because he had surrendered his troops, but now his country was treating him with kindness and honor. There had been no choice for him but to surrender and, as he said, the people seemed to understand this. Now, he said, he fully knew what freedom and democracy really meant. I don't think there was a dry eye in the room when he got through talking. He turned to me and expressed the desire to kiss me. I was startled and didn't know for a moment to whom he was talking. I looked for Shelley but she wasn't visible. So I walked over and he kissed me soundly on both cheeks, put his arms around me very tenderly and walked out of the room. I stood there with tears rolling down my cheeks. It wasn't Jacqueline Cochran he was kissing — I was just a symbol of

American womanhood. It was a never-to-be-forgotten experience.

A few days after the surrender of Yamashita Admiral Barbey was giving a dinner for Manuel Roxas who would be the next President of the Republic of the Philippines. I was to be the only non-Filipino guest.

In the morning of the day of the dinner, I got a call from Admiral Kauffman, stating that Archbishop Spellman was arriving and asking me to act as his hostess. The plan was for the Archbishop to say a Mass about four o'clock in the afternoon and then Admiral Kauffman was going to have a reception in his house, followed by a buffet supper, all to be finished by ten o'clock, against the possibility that Archbishop Spellman would not want to stay up late. I was in a predicament because of these conflicting invitations, but Admiral Kauffman was Admiral Barbey's ranking officer so I asked Admiral Barbey to be excused under the circumstances. Admiral Barbey compromised by asking me to try to bring the Archbishop over to his party at ten o'clock. This was agreed to all around.

I was not sure of the proprieties. I had acquired a very pleasant friend, Commodore Sullivan, and I thought anyone by that name would be a Catholic. So I asked him to use his car to take us to Admiral Barbey's. We were riding along on the way to the Archbishop's quarters so he could say his office, when I heard Commodore Sullivan say he thought it would be wonderful if we could stop off at "Sugar Charlie's." I was completely startled by the thought but the Archbishop simply asked if we thought he should go. It was a question being asked almost at large — for anyone to answer, including the driver.

It turned out that "Sugar Charlie's" was one of the many Jap ships that Commodore Sullivan had lifted. He had done a fabulous, fantastic job — one of the most wonderful ever done by a human in this way. He had been salvaging ships from the time he was a child. He cleared the channels into the ports in the Philippines so that our ships could come in. He had made "Sugar Charlie's" ship into some sort of a night club and I was frightened to take the Archbishop there and said so during the Archbishop's absence. Indignantly, Commodore Sullivan stated that he had fixed the ship up for the noncommissioned officers and their girls and was very proud of it. If the noncommissioned officers at "Sugar Charlie's" were not behaving Commodore Sullivan thought it good for the Archbishop to have a chance to see and do something about it.

On a queer hunch, I asked Sullivan's religion, only to learn that he didn't have any. That name of Sullivan meant Irish and Catholic to me but he said his family was on the black side of the Irish which left me all the more aquiver about "Sugar Charlie's." However, we went aboard and there must have been about thirty noncommissioned officers and their girls, mostly Filipino, or rather *mestiza*, who are half and half, and to my way of thinking the most beautiful women as a group I have ever seen anywhere. One could have gone in to the best public places in America or Europe and not have seen better behavior. I was proud of these noncommissioned officers and their girl friends. I felt somehow or other mental telepathy had carried through. The Archbishop was delighted and Commodore Sullivan beamed.

When we arrived at Admiral Barbey's quarters, there were about thirty Filipinos there, lined up as if for inspection, waiting for the Archbishop. He mixed with all the people and had an hour's talk with the future President. That evening the Archbishop said he had a present for me and with that he opened his purse, took out the beautiful prayer he had read in Guam, and presented it to me.

Again, because the people in the Armed Services rated me as one of their members rather than a war correspondent, I was invited down with Generals Styer and Uhle to meet the first batch of repatriated prisoners.

Great preparations had been made for them. Temporary buildings had been fabricated for their occupancy, supplemented by individual tents. A large tent with real tablecloths on the tables was to serve as the dining tent. Advance information was that the prisoners were in bad shape. They were.

I could hardly believe that human beings could be in the condition I saw. Some broke down and cried, others were greedy for food, and still others just looked at the food with longing eyes but could not eat.

About a week later, I went back to the camp with all the news correspondents. Things were looking up. Some men had put on as much as three pounds per day. I saw again a tall Texas boy who had looked completely skin and bones when he got off the boat. He was in better condition physically but psychologically was a wreck. I saw him jump as if he had been hit when the camera's light bulb snapped for a picture. He had been badly beaten by the Japs and had scars over his entire back. I was again told that the tall people had extra bad treatment by the Japs, who apparently suffered from a Napoleonic complex.

CHAPTER IX

I WAS anxious to move on to Japan. General MacArthur's head-quarters answered my application for travel orders by saying there was not a chance of a woman's getting to Japan. So I went to my own people in the Air Force who took a different view. Shelley Mydans also got travel orders to Japan so all we needed after that was a method of transport. Afraid that her orders might be canceled, Shelley took her chance on the first bucket seat courier plane that showed up in its island-hopping work. I figured I might that way get stranded on Okinawa Island indefinitely and decided to wait for a "plush" ride. General Giles showed up the next day for a conference with General Kenney and I returned to Guam with him because he intended shortly thereafter to go to Tokyo. Instead he went directly to Hokkaido in northern Japan and from there led a nonstop flight of three B–29s to Washington, D.C.

All available planes at Guam were ordered to proceed to Japan immediately to evacuate the released American prisoners in bad health. In one of these planes, I became the first American woman to land in Japan after the war. Before we left the airport for Yokohama, fifteen miles distant, arrangements were made to load the same planes with very sick released prisoners for a fast return to the United States. One of these had been a co-worker of mine in the Pentagon and had become so restless that he asked for and was granted a second tour of duty. He was shot down over Japan on his first mission.

The docks and shipping facilities of Yokohama seemed almost intact, although I had understood they were destroyed. But the city itself, except for the concrete buildings like the hotel I used, had been completely leveled by fire bombs. Even so, it did not present the scene of complete destruction that I later saw in Tokyo and elsewhere.

I arrived at the hotel without advance notice and no rooms were available. I was trying to get through by U.S. field telephone to headquarters in Tokyo when a Japanese messenger brought me greetings from his industrial boss in Tokyo and offer of any needed assistance. The fact of my arrival was known to the Japanese quicker than to our own people. I guess the "thought police" were still at work and it was supersensory transmission. While I was still at the telephone an old friend of mine, Colonel Merian Cooper, the movie producer, came up and asked me to stay over and fly with him and General Paul B. Wurtsmith the following morning to the still-smouldering Hiroshima. He helped me get a room for the night where I had a supper consisting of canned scrambled eggs which I had brought along in my travel kit.

Next morning's take-off was General Wurtsmith's second unsuccessful attempt to get to Hiroshima. It was the first time I had flown a jeep. By that I mean a jeep was put inside the plane for our use after landing in Hiroshima, and because all the space in the plane was filled, I sat in the jeep. Bad weather always seemed to hover around the Hiroshima area in those days.

Soon I was invited by General Wurtsmith to go up forward and fly. The weather looked very bad ahead and kept getting worse. There were no radio facilities and, as a copilot, I asked the pilot what would be the procedure from there on. He suggested we go out to sea to avoid the mountains. The lava, which in its molten, moving state had formed these mountains, spread out into the sea like the scallops in a big shell, but the above-water parts of these shells were also sticking up into the overcast we had that day. We kept going lower and lower to keep under the overcast until we were but two or three hundred feet above the ocean's surface. It was evident even when I took the plane's controls that we could not get to Hiroshima but the pilot said that we should keep on going until receipt of the General's orders to return. The General was a fine pilot himself but he was dozing in the cabin and not paying attention to things outside the plane. I took things into my own hands after a while by surrendering the copilot's seat, waking the General and asking him to take a look at the weather and the flying maps. Immediately, he gave the order to turn back to the Atsugi Airport. General Wurtsmith was later killed in a similar flight over water. I hope he was not dozing while the pilot was just flying into trouble, awaiting orders. I made three subsequent flights to see Hiroshima, but all were aborted, due to foul weather.

The day was so little spent when we landed that I decided to push on to Tokyo and General Wurtsmith and Colonel Cooper joined me.

Nothing I can say would adequately describe the destruction and desolation I saw in the forty-mile trip to Toyko. Some salesman of safes must have experienced a field day in Japan and each home, it seemed, had had a safe, partly because of the losses of valuable papers that followed the earthquake and fire many years before, and partly because industry during the war had been so dispersed that each home was a factory for bits and pieces. These bits and pieces or the tools to make them were housed in the safe. On that automobile ride, I saw safes littering the landscape, but practically no buildings. The houses had been burned. An entire family would be living around a safe with a little lean-to of tin or thin board or even paper for shelter. The safes themselves were often used to house the babies.

General Kenney was expected in Toyko within a day or two.

Private quarters had been obtained for him. Some other General Officers were going to join up with General Kenney in this same home, which reputedly had about forty rooms, but General Wurtsmith had not seen the place and had agreed to see that it was in order before the arrival of General Kenney. The problem as to where I was to stay for one night was solved. General Wurtsmith asked me if I would give General Kenney's headquarters a "checkout," as we say in aviation.

It was a house that belonged to one of the princes of the royal family and it was quite fantastic. It was a complete mixture of Tudor, French, English, Spanish and American, all thrown together in hodgepodge fashion. This monstrosity was connected by a closed passageway with a most beautiful Japanese house that was completely intact. This Japanese house and the garden behind it were like a motion-picture set or a Japanese painting and the interior of the house was immaculate and furnished with the best according to Japanese custom. The monstrosity, on the contrary, had in it cheap copies of every kind of furniture one can imagine — from everywhere, including Grand Rapids. The bathroom had a long zinc trough over which were spaced five spigots. The bathtub looked as if it had not been used in years, with the encrustation of rust and dirt. The toilet was not too bad according to Western standards, which is astonishing when the toilet facilities of Japan are considered. There was also a Japanese bath, a box with waterproofed doors in which one sits encased up to the neck.

General Wurtsmith announced that if I would direct the cooking, a feast would be served that night as an opener of the house, because some frozen turkeys had been flown in.

The Japanese butler in his cutaway coat and striped trousers and speaking English with an Oxford accent carried me back in fancy to Merry Old England. The butler understood perfectly my instructions about cooking. It would take until nine o'clock according to my calculation to get that turkey properly cooked, so the officers and I played cards and talked about the war. At nine-thirty o'clock the turkey came in and it was a golden brown but underneath the skin it was raw. What the butler had done was deliberate, because the facilities for cooking were there. So out to the kitchen I went with him and recooked the turkey myself. We sat down after midnight to consume that bird.

A room in the Imperial Hotel was made available to me the next day. Many of my old friends were in that hotel, including Admiral John J. Ballentine, whom I knew when I was very young. The late Karl T. Compton also was there. True, the food in the dining room was the ten-in-one rations as usual but prepared in every imaginable form by the G.I.'s and more than excellent after the fare I had been getting in the Philippines. General Wurtsmith put a jeep which had extra gas tanks at my disposal and also an escort, Don Larabee, who was exceedingly pleasant, sensitive and intelligent. While Don was no physical giant, he carried sidearms and anyway I had no fear that we would have trouble with the Japs.

A half-Japanese, half-French boy, Eddie, worked at the hotel. His French father had been in an internment camp. Eddie spoke English with an American accent and even knew slang. When he was off duty, he accompanied us as guide and as additional protection, because I jeeped each day into sections where sometimes they did not even seem to know the war was over. The only restriction on my travel was that I had to be off the road by dark. I usually started at daybreak. On our entering a native village, the reaction of the people was astounding. First they would stare and then they would start bowing. We were never molested but were usually given wrong directions when we got lost which was frequently. This happened so often that I started carrying a compass to get us back in the general direction of Tokyo. We took our water and ten-in-one rations with us. It was quite usual, while passing by the small and mostly improvised shacks, with the windows wide open to the public, to see the women sitting nude, at least to the waist, bathing themselves. At the edge of one village, we found a large crowd talking excitedly and gesticulating. Eddie reported they were saying they knew now why they had lost the war. The "why" was not visible until we edged into the crowd. An enormous American bulldozer, the like of which the Japanese had never seen, was clearing a path almost as wide as a normal street. I still wonder how we got that mammoth bulldozer into Japan so soon.

I called on Eddie's mother and thus saw the interior of a middle-class Japanese home. There was no furniture. The stove top was only about eighteen inches above the floor. In Japanese fashion we exchanged presents.

The Japs everywhere were working awfully hard. I noticed they were very kind to their children, particularly the boy children. The only time I ever saw a mother do anything remotely naughty to her boy child was in front of the Emperor's Palace. Every time the Japanese passed any side of the Palace, they would stop, turn around solemnly toward the Palace, bow from the waist, touch their foreheads and, in the case of the men, replace their hats and then pass on. This particular five-year-old boy did not bow even when his mother instructed him to do so. After the third attempt, she grabbed him by one arm and gave him a healthy kick in the seat of his pants. He then bowed. I wondered if a kick in the seat of the pants was the way all Japanese learned to respect their ruler. Or maybe the boy was a democrat.

From Tokyo, General Wurtsmith and I made another attempt to visit Hiroshima but with the same results. Storms and a low ceiling drove us back but the day was not lost for I conceived the idea of seeing from the air the inside of the Imperial Palace grounds. These grounds are surrounded by two moats. The carp living in the outer moat were fed by the people, much as we see pigeons fed in some of our parks. The Palace had not been bombed at all. I was at the controls of the plane and took a slow, low bomb run over the Palace to within twenty feet of the roof and looked everything over. The next day, a notice went up that all planes must stay at least three miles away from the Palace grounds. I now confess that I was the culprit who caused this action. Figuratively, I had my fingers on the bomb controls and was settling the Pacific war right there and then.

General Kenney on arrival in Tokyo decided, and I think on the suggestion of the Japanese butler, to give a Japanese banquet in the Japanese house. When I had been in this dining room on my first inspection tour, it seemed rather small but this night of the banquet it was large enough for the entire party. The walls in the Japanese homes, or at least some of them, are movable. The partitions travel on ball bearings.

The tables for the banquet were about twenty inches above the floor. We sat on cushions on the floor. There were about a half-dozen Japanese girls to feed the ranking guests and there was one old lady in charge who seemed to have just stepped out of a Japanese picture.

There was a big brazier in the center of the table in which the main dish, sukiyaki, was cooked before our eyes. All sorts of meat and vegetables went into it and finally many spoonfuls of sugar. Each girl would break a raw egg in a dish and beat it up with her chopsticks. Then the girl would pick a choice morsel out of the brazier, dip it into the raw egg and plop it into the mouth of the guest being attended by her. One of these girls was kneeling between General Kenney and myself just before the food started to be served. Although dressed in Japanese style, her head-dress was Western and her lipstick also gave her a Western tinge. General Kenney had been under a long strain which had finally developed an eczema on his hands. I turned to him and inquired

if he were going to eat the food. I told him I would not and suggested he should follow my example and avoid the possibility of
dysentery. I carried on with my views to the effect that the whole
affair had been suggested by the butler in order to spy on us. I
stated my opinion that the girl kneeling between us could understand very well everything we were saying. He doubted this. I
said that if she could not understand, then what I was saying
didn't matter but if she could understand English my remarks
would serve her right.

The girl never changed expression but General Kenney and I
passed up the food and gave our attention to conversation and
to the weird stringed music that was being played. After the
banquet was over, I suggested to General Kenney that we might
find a can of corned beef in his Western-style building, so we
adjourned to his quarters. The Japanese girl who was assigned
to us went along and after she had some hot sake and some Western drinks, her tongue loosened at both ends and she broke into
English. General Kenney looked at me with astonishment and
asked how I knew she spoke English. My reply was that all the
servants and entertainers would naturally be on hand to find
out what the great generals who had beaten them were thinking.
General Kenney was insulted that the Japs would consider him
so dumb as to talk about important matters with any of their
people around. He added that they certainly had a clear idea
what I was thinking about the Japanese people.

I guess my bomb run over the Imperial Palace annoyed someone on General MacArthur's staff. In any event, General Mac-
Arthur's aide in charge of billeting told me the Imperial Hotel
was reserved for high-ranking officers of the Armed Services and
I would have to move. General Kenney and others in the Air
Force were doing what they could to let me stay on in the hotel
but I was the only woman there and not a high-ranking officer so
eventually the day arrived when an eviction was threatened. Ad-

miral Ballentine had told me that come the worst, he would close off from his combination office and living quarters one of the rooms for my use. Fortified with this knowledge, I called the billeting officer and told him not to worry any longer because I was moving in with the Admiral. The officer misunderstood me and mumbled something to the effect that for the sake of the reputation of the Navy, I could stay on in my original quarters.

At least, I had not lost character with the Navy by this maneuver which gave Admiral Ballentine a good laugh. The day following this housing crisis, Captain Eddison presented the card of Admiral Spruance along with an invitation to lunch on the flagship *New Jersey,* the largest battleship we owned at the time. There was a forty-five mile drive to the Jap Naval Base where the *New Jersey* was anchored. The trip was done in style with a guard of honor. The Admiral's barge, which was in fact more like a small, beautifully appointed yacht, was awaiting me and the trip out to the battleship was unbelievably beautiful. The lunch took me back in my mind to the Sundays on the *West Virginia* at San Diego and Long Beach.

Following lunch, I cruised about on the Admiral's barge, looking over the Japanese boats still afloat, including a number of the small two-man suicide submarines. Finally, I fetched up at the aircraft carrier *Shangri La* for tea with my very old friend, Admiral John Towers. It was only that day I learned that the *Shangri La,* used as the place for take-off by Jimmy Doolittle and his raiders, was not just a figure of speech by President Roosevelt in his announcement of the raid but a real aircraft carrier.

General Arnold had directed me to make an official investigation of what the Japanese women had done in the Imperial Air Force. This took me to the Dai-Ichi building which served as the General Headquarters. It was a magnificent building and most impressive but I will not forget my first entrance. Just as I walked to the door to pull it open toward me, a high-ranking Japanese officer pushed the door open in my face and almost pushed me down. He was a pretty haughty customer — still in uniform and carrying his sword — and his action was as startling to the military police on duty as to me. There was not the slightest doubt he had seen me through the glass door and that his action was premeditated. These Japs had a curious way of being officially polite while showing in small ways their displeasure, such as putting mosquitoes inside the bed netting and arranging the bed on a slant, which they did the night I "checked out" General Kenney's quarters.

My search of the records found no evidence that the Japanese women had participated in any active war effort beyond factory or home production. I did, however, find numerous clippings and photographs about Amelia Earhart and Jimmy Doolittle and other American pilots, including myself. There were several files on Amelia Earhart.

General F. L. Ankenbrandt and I occupied the city of Kyoto. I have a certificate from him to that effect. We did so by mistake.

Very few places outside of the Naval bases and Air Force bases had been occupied by our troops when I arrived in Japan.

Kyoto is the Japanese city of shrines. It is somewhat the same to the Japanese as Vatican City is to Catholics. Care had been taken not to bomb it during our air raids. General Ankenbrandt wanted to see it and so did I but we thought it already had been taken over by the American forces. We started for Kyoto in a C–47 (known in civilian work as a DC–3) plane with a jeep parked inside. On arrival, we were startled by the appearance of the airport. It was a grass field with one runway and a small hangar. A few dilapidated, small planes were on the field but it was questionable whether the C–47 could land on the short runway. After circling for a while, we decided to chance a landing. Everything was fine. There was a hard-surfaced runway hidden by the grass. An old man greeted us by sign language. We let him know we wanted to go into town and expected him to guard the plane during our absence. He pointed the way to the city, brought an old-fashioned American variety of rocking chair from the hangar, placed it under the wing of the plane, sat down and proceeded to rock. He was the only person we saw at the airport but through caution we decided that the three enlisted men who had accompanied us should stay with the plane. General Ankenbrandt and I set out for the city in our jeep. We saw no one en route. We saw no smoke rising from the city and we saw no one as we entered the city. The General concluded that the occupation, which was to have taken place two days earlier by General Robert Eichelberger's forces, had not taken place but I persuaded him to go on and see what we could turn up. It was a dead city so far as we were concerned. We reached the heart of it without seeing any sign of life. We had parked our jeep and were walking about considering whether we would go to a temple we saw a short distance away when I noticed the flutter of a window curtain. I peered into the window with my eyes shaded by my hands but could see nothing. But when I turned away I noticed again the flutter of the curtain so was sure someone was inside. I tapped on the window. By this time, General Ankenbrandt was becoming quite concerned and suggested we should return immediately to Tokyo. He was afraid he could be criticized as a military man for going into Kyoto ahead of the occupation forces. But I prevailed on him to let me stay a little longer and I repeated my window tapping. This time I saw a face and I smiled broadly. While we were looking at the window, someone spoke behind us and in the most perfect English asked if there was anything he could do for us. We turned and faced a Jap with top hat and striped trousers and a cutaway coat. When we asked where all the people were he explained that the city was due to be occupied by the American forces and the whole population was staying indoors waiting to determine what the occupying authorities wished them to do.

I told this formally attired gentleman that we were the advance guard of the occupation forces and wished to have a look around. I asked to be shown the inside of what clearly was a department store with the windows and doors all boarded up. What was going on inside was amazing. They were hauling in for display carts full of cheap goods which had been repriced upward. The ink was not yet dry on some of the price tags. Obviously the word had been passed around that the American soldier would buy everything in sight irrespective of price or quality. I reprimanded the store manager for this sort of conduct, told him I was there to see whether this sort of thing was going on and that I would make a report to General Eichelberger. He tried to square himself but without success.

The gentleman in the striped trousers then accompanied us up the hill to the temple. After taking our shoes off we went inside. It was exceedingly beautiful. One of the priests wrote a little prayer on parchment and gave it to us. In all we spent about eight hours in Kyoto. The women who lived in the house where I tapped on the window invited us in and offered us tea and gave me some little squares of silk they use for tea napkins on special occasions. The store manager brought gifts which I refused but I did buy for a fair price some fine silk.

All the General Officers who were scheduled to go home wanted to go by way of China. But General Wedemeyer had closed the Chinese war theater to everyone on account of lack of food and housing. A few who were bold enough to fly into China were allowed to gas up and turn back to the island of Okinawa, which was a stopping place between Japan and the Philippines.

I wanted to see China and to visit Floyd's cousin, General

Victor Odlum, who was the Canadian Ambassador to China. I talked the question of transportation over with General Kenney, who said he had "kids" on Okinawa who had never had leave since they arrived — in some cases their tours of duty had lasted for three years — and he would be delighted to fix me up with a plane and crew. So I wired my friend, General George E. Stratemeyer, in Shanghai that I wanted to come to China, throwing in for good measure my wish to call on the Canadian Ambassador. There was a prompt reply from "Strat" and also from General Odlum, making me welcome.

General Kenney had left Japan so I showed the cables to General Wurtsmith with a request for travel orders and transportation. Four days later Colonel Murray Bywater reported to me. He was a very clean, wholesome and distinguished-looking individual. He had a large crew, he stated, and they were prepared to leave immediately. I discovered none of them had seen Japan, so I put the start of the trip off four days so they could look around.

Carl and Shelley Mydans were trying to get orders to go to China and so I managed to get them included in my trip.

Imagine my surprise when I got to the airport and discovered that my crew consisted of three colonels, three lieutenant colonels, three majors and two captains as well as enlisted men. I doubt if any plane was ever crewed with so much rank. It was General Kenney's way of giving a leave to these particular people, who had done so well for so long. On the first leg of the flight to China, we tried to pass over Hiroshima but again for weather reasons my third attempt to see this place, which had been destroyed by the atomic bomb, failed. Our pilot was the first to make a reconnaissance flight over Hiroshima after the explosion. We stopped at Okinawa but hurried on to get ahead of a hurricane which was moving in and which hit with very destructive force shortly after our departure.

The seven-hour ride from Okinawa to Shanghai with no sanitary facilities in the plane presented problems. But the troubles en route were minor compared to the barriers I had to cross on arrival. General Stratemeyer was away in Chungking. General Kennedy met me with the news that while he had very nice accommodations for me at the hotel, he also had instructions that anyone else on the plane would have to stay on the airbase overnight and return to Okinawa or Japan the following morning. After about an hour and much telephoning the military capitulated as to the Mydans and the officers and I arranged complete liberty passes for the enlisted men who were given billets on the airbase.

My superfine accommodations in the Imperial Hotel overlooked the Yangtze River and I spent many hours entranced by the movement of humanity on that river. I had heard many times about life on the sampans. Here it was before my eyes. Boats by the thousands. They were scurrying at the time of my arrival to get shelter under the bridge for the night. Generations had lived on these sampans with little knowledge of any other kind of life.

A new crisis arose before I had been in Shanghai twelve hours. Carl Mydans laid before me the plight of the war correspondents in China. A notice had been filed that thirty days later every war correspondent in China would revert to the status of an ordinary private citizen in the Orient, and that was no status at all. Many of these writers were out in the field or in the interior of China and would have no way to protect their interests. Carl Mydans felt that with Communism already being fought in China it was important to keep the war correspondents on the ground. If they were all to be sent home at least they should have longer than thirty days to communicate with their home offices and to make arrangements for the transportation back to the States. Through him, the correspondents in Shanghai were requesting me to go to Chungking to see General Stratemeyer and get the order canceled or at least to get a sixty-day extension with passage furnished back as far as Hawaii where accommodations on commercial boats could be obtained.

I agreed to go but put off for one day that trip across China in order to see and participate in the "Double Ten" celebration which is the biggest celebration of the year for the Chinese.

General C. B. Stone met my plane on arrival in Chungking after nine hours of flying. He reported that General Stratemeyer was at a reception being given by Madame Chiang Kai-shek and that I was requested to go there immediately. I said that I had been up since four o'clock that morning, was very tired, was in slacks, and to go to the reception seemed impossible. General Stone brushed all these reasons aside saying it would be very wise for me to be at the reception and I should change clothes if necessary in the plane. I did just that and also asked Colonel Bywater to brush himself up. Soon the Colonel and I were off in General Stone's car for Madame Chiang's country residence. The reception was for the Tenth Air Force which was being moved to Shanghai. I took it for granted that Colonel Bywater would be invited in. But not at all. He was left sitting in the car. When I got beyond hearing distance from the car I asked General Stone if he was not going to take Colonel Bywater along. He replied to the effect that no one could be taken into Madame Chiang's house unless specifically invited. It made me very mad to think that an Air Force man who had done so much in the war would be left sitting in a car and I very nearly turned back myself, but knowing that Floyd's cousin, General Victor Odlum, the Canadian Ambassador, was inside as well as General Stratemeyer I decided to go in, say hello to them and then disappear. The home was much like any country house in Connecticut with clapboard exterior and with a New England type of furniture for the most part. It was surrounded by spacious beautiful gardens. The reception was fine in every way but I could only think of Colonel Bywater sitting in the car. I said hello to General Odlum and General Stratemeyer who said Madame Chiang had especially asked to meet me. I paid my respects and left the house after finding out that I had quarters at the Canadian Embassy.

I had been at the Canadian Embassy perhaps an hour, being ministered to by a Chinese girl and another who was half Chinese and half Russian, when the phone rang and General Stratemeyer wanted me to come to his home.

He was most cordial and apparently had no idea of the purpose of my hop to Chungking. I chose the most severe-looking chair in his room and said that before carrying on the pleasantries of conversation any further I had better get the purpose of my mission out on the table so he could determine whether or not he wished to remain on speaking terms with me. I had been well briefed by the correspondents in Shanghai and felt that all the justice was on their side. I pleaded the case in the strongest of terms and finally pointed out that the American correspondents were very important to the Air Force at a time when a strong independent Air Force was wanted.

His chief, General Wedemeyer, had issued the order and General Wedemeyer was now in Washington. General Stratemeyer admitted that the order probably came as a result of a story which got through without being censored and which, while it did not violate security, was a personal attack to some extent on General Wedemeyer. General Stratemeyer stated that he was not going to rescind the order.

The argument became heated. In anticipation of his attitude I had drafted a cable to Robert Patterson, Secretary of War, and this I showed to General Stratemeyer. General Stratemeyer replied that I would be disappointed to learn that that cable would not go through because it would be stopped by the censorship. I rejoined that it would go out if necessary in the diplomatic pouch of the Canadian Ambassador and be sent to Washington from Canada. Strat said he thought he could even stop that and in any event the order with respect to the war correspondents would be carried through. I then drew my last card. In addition to being an accredited war correspondent I was still on orders from General Arnold as a Special Consultant to the Commanding General. The orders had a catch-all phrase that I should report on anything I considered of benefit or interest to the United States Air Force. I told General Stratemeyer I would, if necessary, report this treatment of the war correspondents to General Arnold as a matter of great importance to the Air Force. He suggested that we think the matter over for a day and meet again. I pressed for an immediate cancellation of the order. He then agreed to go to Shanghai the next day to talk to the people but would not commit himself as to what his action would be. I told him in that case I would be in Shanghai and at the meeting. He was surprised to learn that I had a plane in Chungking at my disposal which had been assigned to me by General Kenney, top air chief in the Far East. Strat finally said he would like to put the return to Shanghai off another day and agreed that if I would wait and go along with him he would as a minimum extend the effective date of the expulsion order for another sixty days.

The war correspondents in China — and the order applied to all nationals, not only Americans — were most grateful to me. I was elected an active member of the American War Correspondents' Association even though it was recognized by all, including myself, that as a correspondent I was a fake. Indeed *Liberty* magazine had a representative in China so while there whatever I dug up for a story I sent to that representative with my supporting material and he got the credit and the money for the story. It was because of my membership in this writers' association that I first met General Dwight D. Eisenhower. The association gave a dinner for him in New York and I was seated beside him at the table and personal friendship grew on a foundation of respect. Thus an argument over war correspondents in China had something to do with the election of General Eisenhower as President, as you will realize after reading subsequent parts of this book.

I noticed one thing on my trips from the Banshi Airport near Chungking to the Canadian Embassy. In an area of just ordinary pasture land at least fifteen miles from the airport were parked many American-built fighter planes, known as Mustangs, Lightnings, and Thunderbolts. They were new but had been stripped of various parts, such as tires and instruments and in some cases even engines and propellers. It looked like a terrible waste to me and I suspected these usable planes had been put in an inaccessible spot and had been made nonflyable through some dirty work at the political crossroads. I had heard it said that Generalissimo Chiang had been laying aside all the equipment he could to carry on his fight with his political opponents (now the Communists) after the war with Japan was over.

I had been back in Shanghai only two days when I received an invitation to lunch with Madame Chiang Kai-shek. That meant going all the way across China again to Chungking and I wanted to send my regrets but General Stratemeyer told me that in the interests of the American forces in China I should go. I arrived at Madame Chiang's same Connecticut-style country house just a little before lunch hour and was given a guest cottage in which to rest and freshen up. General Odlum was at the lunch as well as the British Ambassador, the Commanding General of the Chinese Air Force, and three Chinese gentlemen. Madame Chiang, the hostess, was the only other woman present. Madame Chiang told me she was giving me a very plebeian Chinese luncheon because so many Americans preferred it, although she herself preferred the American food. Most of the home was furnished American style but one room was bare of decoration except for a most lovely piece of jade on a mantel.

The first order of business at the table was for Madame Chiang to prepare the soup. A tureen was brought in and plates of various pieces of meat and vegetables. Madame inspected each piece carefully before it was put into the boiler, which was then put over the heater on the table.

Pork spareribs and many dishes of Chinese meats and vegetables appeared. I was given the choice of a knife and fork or chopsticks and chose the latter. Some of the pieces of meat were too large to take into the mouth so I watched Madame Chiang. She would raise the piece to her mouth with her chopsticks and bite off a morsel. She then explained some of the chopsticks etiquette. The Japanese in such a case would break the piece apart with their chopsticks.

I did not expect Madame Chiang to converse with me about state secrets. She didn't. But I did learn something about Chinese customs and where I might buy some fine silks in Chungking and also about the early history of the Siccawei Convent near Shanghai.

The Chinese do not have dessert as we understand it but serve cookies instead. When we got down to the cookies, the chief of the Chinese Air Force made a long speech in Chinese and handed some Chinese Air Wings to Madame, who in turn pinned them on me as an acknowledgment on behalf of China of the war work I had done with the Air Force.

Back at the Canadian Embassy I asked General Odlum why Generalissimo Chiang Kai-shek was not at the luncheon. He told me that during the luncheon hour General Chiang and Mao Tse-tung, the Communist leader, were having a conference trying to see whether an agreement could be arranged for the splitting of China, with the north to be controlled by Mao and the south by Chiang. General Odlum arranged for me to meet Mao Tse-tung, the Communist rival of Chiang, and I spent a very interesting two hours with him. He gave the impression of being

an intensely serious, forceful and honest man. I asked him if he
had ever spent time in Russia. That one he did not answer at the
time but about a half hour later he came back to it on his own
accord and stated that he had spent about three years in Moscow
going to school. My sympathy had been all with him up until then
but it suddenly cooled down. I realized that he was a part of the
machine working out of Moscow and I also sensed that he would
be the ruler of all China. But he spoke on and on, explaining his
views, ideals and philosophy. He said that his desire was to do
something for the common people of China — the ones who like
animals in harness had to push and pull heavy loads all day over
the cobblestone roads. He said he was not foolish enough to think
that there would not still be coolies and carts and plenty of hard
work but he hoped that they would at least have shoes and a little
more to eat. He also said that he was not foolish enough to believe
that China would become a great mechanized or commercial nation or that riches should be eliminated, but that he felt there
should not be such a wide gulf between the few very rich and the
many very poor. He explained to me that no place in the world
was there such wealth in a few hands — Chinese merchants rolling in luxury with many concubines. Inasmuch as Madame
Chiang's family was the Soong family, reputed to be the wealth-
iest and most powerful in China, I thought he was taking a particular crack at my luncheon hostess of two days before.

His talk was the kind that appeals to the have-nots. The
Chinese coolie wants just a little more rice in his belly and some
shoes on his feet. He has been promised that by Moscow through
Mao, and has swallowed the bait. Now we will see if the promise
is made good. Certainly China needs more food or less people.
Maybe the aggressions she has embarked on under the Russian
banner will give her fewer people to feed and in consequence
the balance can have a few more grains of rice a day.

Madame Chiang Kai-shek, through her secretary, had notified

the best local store to get their best silks out for me and I had a wonderful time shopping. The curtains in my guest room in New York came from this store in Chungking. As I started to leave this store, I noticed a man across the street either dead or very seriously injured and unconscious. He had been washing windows and had fallen from the rickety ladder. But no one had gone near him. I tried to get help but was prevented and was informed that the official people would eventually come and pick him up but that no one else would be willing to assist in the meantime for several reasons including the liability that would be assumed by the person going to the rescue for the support of the man's entire family. All over China I noticed this same thing happening. It was a clear case of man's inhumanity to man. Life was pretty cheap in China during the time of my trip and I guess it has always been so. Any early morning in Shanghai one could see the wagon going around picking up the bodies of people who had died in streets and doorways overnight. The wagon was drawn not by horses but by coolies. There were dozens of such bodies picked up every day with no apparent attempt at identification.

In spite of all their poverty and lack of education, the Chinese people are fundamentally clean and kind and I like them. Given a chance at education and at forms of activity to support themselves, I believe China could once again become a great nation.

Girl children are usually not wanted in this desolate land, for each girl baby provides one more mouth to feed. Many a newborn baby girl is drowned in the river. But for those children who are on hand for rearing, the love of parents is manifest. One night I watched one very poor coolie attempting to provide a meal for his small child. On the street corners here and there are people who will serve a little rice and water for a small coin. This father, with bowl in hand, went to one of these wayside cooks. The coin was passed and the dab of rice and water delivered. The father tasted of the water and then threw the rice and water to the ground and spat in the cook's face. The water had not been boiled and the father was protecting his child against the diseases of the raw river water, even if it meant starvation. I never saw such a woebegone look on this father's face as he walked away without food. It was apparently his only coin. I followed him and gave him in Chinese money the equivalent of about one dollar. He seemed transfixed with joy, bowed and bowed to me, and then took the boy in his arms and ran to another, higher-class rice cookery. I guess that dollar would be as much as he would earn by several days of hard work.

While in Shanghai, I spent a day at the famous Siccawei Convent. Catholicism had about seven hundred thousand followers in all of China. The convent has a little revolving gate where unwanted infants can be left for care. And all so left are cared for and raised and taught a trade. The little girls are taught to do needlework. I brought home a lovely table service from this Chinese convent and some years later saw its duplicate on the table during a formal dinner at the American Embassy in Switzerland. Ambassador Richard Patterson and his charming wife Shelley had also been in China years before. I also brought home for my namesake, Jackie Lovelace, a bedspread with Snow White and the Seven Dwarfs beautifully embroidered on it.

I had one experience with the very rich whom Mao Tse-tung mentioned. A Chinese merchant sent his emissary to me, asking for an appointment. He wished to invite me to his home. I granted the request for an appointment and he showed up at my hotel with two servants laden with gifts for me. They had the finest of jade and silk and embroidery, the whole having a value in my opinion of several thousand dollars.

I told this Chinese that I could not accept gifts but did select one small piece of jade by way of expressing appreciation of his graciousness.

His home, where I went to dinner, was not a house but rather a large group of houses called a compound. Each house had dozens of people. How many wives and concubines he had I do not know, but I saw two or three of his wives.

It turned out that he was an operator of cotton mills and, while I did not go through any of them, I had a description of working conditions and concluded that the mills back in Alabama where I pushed the cart and mended the warp were models of virtue compared to these Chinese mills, where for their long hours of work the laborers got a bowl of rice and a few cents. General Stratemeyer cautioned me that this cotton merchant belonged to a class that was causing much discontent in China and I should be careful about becoming friendly with him. I never saw him again and have often wondered why he went to such trouble to be nice to me. I concluded he wanted to put some deal over with the American forces and thought I might be helpful. The five-per-centers are not an exclusive product of Washington. They are not unknown in China and many other parts of the world.

One could not tell from day to day the value of Chinese money. It was not all the same currency. When our United States Tenth Air Force moved northward to Peking to take over that area from the Japanese, I went up in one of the first planes. It had several bales of goods covered with a sort of tinfoil. We were curious as to what was in those bales and took a look. They contained Chinese money. The story is told that an engine quit on a plane one day and it had to lighten its load either in food or money to get over the last mountain for a safe landing beyond. The crew chose to toss the bales of money out instead of the canned vegetables. Whether this is just a story, I do not know, but it could well be true. The Chinese money was printed by a bank note firm in Philadelphia and I am told that the entire issue eventually went to a value below the cost of its printing.

Peking was still controlled by the Japs. The war was over but there had still been no disarmament or surrender of these particular Japanese troops.

My first day in Peking I went to the Peking Club for tea and found it crowded with German and Japanese officers. This I did not like and said so in strong language to the club management. The next day, on returning to the club, I noticed a sign reading: "Will the Japanese and Germans kindly refrain from using the club as it gives offense to our American allies." There were no enemy patrons there that day.

The following day I received an invitation from the Commanding General of the Japanese forces in that area to visit him at his headquarters. I had about a two-hour interview with him and was given a tour of inspection. This general, at the end of the visit, presented me with his samurai sword. He said that he would be surrendering it anyway in a matter of days and he would prefer that I have it.

The substance of his talk with me was that his forces had been pitted against the Chinese Communist troops, that he was organized and manned to fight Communism and such fight should be carried on or otherwise Communism would conquer all of China. He was making a plea that his army should not be disbanded but should be kept intact in place and under arms but responsible to the American Army. In such a cooperative way he said the Orient could be saved from Russia. How true his words were, measured in the light of subsequent events! Some weeks later, back home, I was recounting this experience to a General Huang of the Chinese Nationalist Army. He knew this Japanese general well and said he had been educated at Princeton University.

With this Japanese general's plea and forecast ringing in my ears I set out for Europe, where the war had come to an end and Hitler's cohorts were to go on trial. I wanted to see them in the prisoners' dock as I had seen Yamashita.

I flew from China over India to Egypt. To say more about what I saw in these places would be merely to repeat what any travelogue presents.

General Ben Giles was in command of the general area at the time of my visit to Egypt, with headquarters in Cairo. I expressed the desire to see Palestine, now known as Israel, and the next day he put a Beechcraft at my disposal. I thought it impossible to get lost because the Suez Canal had to be crossed at a certain point and I assumed it would look something like the Hudson River. But I found no such canal. Finally, after flying up and down what looked to me like an oversized irrigation ditch, I concluded it must be the canal, notwithstanding no boats were in sight, and I went on my way, soon to pick up the radio beam into Jerusalem. In flying over Israel I saw the great changes due to erosion which have taken place during the last two thousand years because it is now an arid, unfertile country and not the land of milk and honey I had read about in the Bible.

My first surprise was to discover that the building housing the Holy Sepulchre belongs to the Arabs who guard the door with great ceremony. Without being charged a fee (which seemed to me rather un-Arabic) one is let inside the fabulous building with a key about two feet long. Inside there are many chapels, including about seven that are Catholic.

I visited the place where Christ was born but it was not the stable and the manger I had pictured in my mind, primarily, I guess, because all around were commercial establishments which to me seemed a disgrace to the Christian world.

I left Jerusalem before I wanted to, because I had an appointment elsewhere with "Mohammed."

Persia, now known as Iran, was where I went to keep that appointment. The young Shah of Iran, Reza Pahlevi, is gentle and somewhat shy and rather friendly toward the Western world. He married the sister of the King of Egypt, became an amateur pilot, and tried to avoid dictatorial methods. Young Reza Pahlevi's first name was Mohammed — and it was with this Mohammed I had the appointment. Mohammed seems to be a first name in common use in these Arabic countries just as Jesus is a given name in great use in Latin-American Catholic countries.

Our Ambassador to Iran, Wallace Murray, took General Giles and me to the Shah's palace. The Shah received us in the mosaic-decorated parlor of a most beautiful jewel-box palace right in the center of the city. The walls of the palace grounds were about sixty feet high and surrounded four main buildings, two of which were for the Shah's use, one for his mother, I was told, and the other for distinguished official visitors. The palace we entered was built of huge blocks of pale green alabaster and inside the building all the walls and floor were of mosaic made with gold and lapis lazuli and other semiprecious stones. We were received in a room on the second floor. The furniture consisted of a couch on which the Shah sat, a desk with a chair behind it and three other chairs for our use. The Shah had on a military uniform which set off his tiny, beautifully shod feet. The Shah, in perfect English, discussed my flying, which as a pilot he knew about, and told about his interest in America, about his two brothers, who were in American schools, and about how his country had cooperated with us during the war and had served as a bridge for the transport of goods to Russia. He pointed out that his country was having its troubles and he hoped America would find a way to be helpful. He pointed out that Russia was then occupying a very important area in Iran, into which even his own countrymen could not go without Russian permit. He continually interrupted his flow of conversation to say he must not be quoted and I must not write about what he was saying. But it was clear that he wanted the American people to know things were developing in Iran not good for the Western world.

Ambassador Murray had briefed us that following tea we

should wait about five minutes and then take our leave without turning our backs on the Shah. Tea serving was delayed for well over an hour, so there was much talk.

Then, in came a golden teapot and one cup and saucer. The Shah turned to me and said that I might serve him his tea, so the service was placed in front of me. While I was pouring the Shah's tea, in came a silver tea service with three cups and saucers. So I poured from the silver teapot for the Ambassador and the General. The cups were finally sipped dry and I was keeping an eye on the Ambassador for a signal to rise and depart when the Shah said I might pour him another cup of tea. That meant we had to carry on with another cup ourselves, for it was protocol to sip tea so long as the Shah was sipping. He then asked me to pay a visit to the Premier, which he would arrange for later that same day. The Premier, His Excellency D. E. Ebrahim Hakimi, had the same story to tell me as the Shah and again with the admonitions not to quote him.

During the years following my visit while so much trouble was building up in Iran over oil, I thought a great deal about my tea in that jeweled palace with the very attractive Shah, who later discarded his Egyptian wife and made an Iranian girl of commoner background — Soraya — his Queen. And I have thought about the day following the tea when the Royal Princess, dressed in peasant attire, took me down through the bazaar and haggled over prices with the best of the haggling merchants.

In the midst of the rioting in 1953, while Premier Mossadegh was for a time moving things rapidly in his own direction, I thought of the advice the Shah was given as a boy when his roughneck, hard-riding, hard-drinking, dictatorial father (who had made himself Shah of Iran by force of arms) found him in contemplative mood by a pool of water. The Shah asked his son, Reza Pahlevi, what he was doing standing there, looking into the water. The reply by the son was that he was thinking. Whereupon his father kicked him into the water with the advice to act rather than think. And I also thought of the time the Shah was in America and in the New York Hospital for diagnosis of what proved to be chronic appendicitis. The nurse who attended him told me that the Shah's nightly drink was a cup of Ovaltine. The sight of the Shah sipping Ovaltine would probably have caused his cursing and carousing father to turn over in his grave.

I hope the Shah retains his throne and that for the sake of his people agreements between his government and others will be worked out whereby everyone will get a fair share of the oil that has not been pumped since Mossadegh fouled up the lines. It does no one any good just remaining underground where it has lain for ages while soldiers tramped overhead creating and losing empires.

The day after I returned to Cairo from Teheran the peripatetic General Gross arrived and indicated that he could set up a flight for me to Paris if I so desired. I said I would rather go to Rome. He and his aide decided to join me and a B–25 was made ready and on we went.

Though it was getting late when we arrived in Rome I called my friend, Mrs. Carlo Ciulli Ruggieri, to say that I would be in Rome for not more than two days and to ask about the possibility of an audience with His Holiness the Pope. She called me back the following morning to say that twenty-four hours later His Holiness would receive me in private audience but it would have to be sandwiched in and I might have to wait for several hours after my arrival at the Vatican.

The landing and trip to the hotel the night before in the moonlight had intrigued me. I decided to sleep the afternoon through and go out and tramp about Rome late at night by moonlight. There were no street lights that soon after hostilities. I put on my long woolen underwear and slacks and an extra sweater and then my trench coat because of the cold night air. I took my pistol and a piece of stationery from the hotel on which I had the concierge write in Italian a request I could present for help in case I became lost.

I tramped about that immortal city alone from fairly early evening until two o'clock in the morning, when the moon started to fall below the horizon. It was an unforgettable and enchanting experience. I say I was alone but in my mind I saw the emperor and his subjects in the stands of the Coliseum and the gladiators and lions and Christian captives in the arena. I saw Nero's golden palace where I suppose he did his fiddling act while Rome was burning. The Forum was not a mass of broken marble that night but a beautiful square surrounded by arches and columns and temples and peopled with white-robed aristocrats and vestal virgins. Paganism had returned to show its best in art. The statuary on the bridges seemed shimmery. I turned toward St. Peter's Cathedral, and its dome, like an angel dancing in the sky, signified that Christianity, in winning out over paganism, had also absorbed and carried forward the beauties of pre-Christian art. I located the fountain where if one throws in a coin and makes a wish to return to Rome the wish will be fulfilled. Mine has already been fulfilled three times.

I saw few people during this nocturnal excursion. I was not molested. But I became thoroughly lost. Finally, I saw what looked like a little coffee room and walked in. The waiter could speak no English but my piece of paper was being put to use when out of the shadows an American appeared, prefaced his question by stating the answer was none of his business and then asked what I was doing out alone at such an hour. I told him he had answered his own question by stating it was none of his business. No conveyance was available. The American's offer to accompany me back to the hotel was refused, and after directions and a cup of coffee I started the long trek back. The trouble was that I got sidetracked in attempting to follow directions and ended up a street away from the hotel and far below it because the hotel was almost on a cliff. There were about seventy-five steps to climb — the famous Spanish Steps — and I was thoroughly exhausted. I did not climb those stairs. I crawled up a few steps at a time with a rest in between. My wish had been fulfilled. I had seen Rome by moonlight. But I hope not to see it that way again because the blacking out of windows and street lights would mean another war.

I had arranged through Mrs. Ruggieri to have General Gross and his aide included in the audience with His Holiness, and the three of us, without any preliminary briefing as to formalities to be observed, arrived at the Vatican at eleven o'clock the morning following my moonlight excursion.

We were met by one of the papal chamberlains and before we reached the audience chamber we waited in many different rooms. In each there was a new Chamberlain of the Vatican to meet and to take care of us. I enjoyed each room and would have been content to wait all day. In the final waiting room we were greeted by Count Pacelli, whom I knew to be a nephew of the Pope because the Count and I have mutual friends. From Count Pacelli I learned that the private audiences that day were lasting only two or three minutes because of the pressure of appointments and that the signal to leave would be when His Holiness offered me the choice of a medal or a rosary blessed by him. From the Count I also learned the history of the Noble Guard and the Swiss Guard who way back in the past had saved the Pope's life at the loss of their own almost to the last man.

On entering the audience room, which was small and simple, we knelt and received the papal blessing. I thought that might be all but we were asked to sit down. The Pope said he had learned that I had just returned from China and he wanted my impressions. I told him conditions were bad and that I thought the Communists would be in control within five years; that the

Nationalist Government was weak, that Mao Tse-tung, trained in Russia for his job, was strong and probably could take over South China at any chosen time. I also said that I believed there would be similar trouble in Iran. I told him of my talk with the Japanese general at Peking and of my talks with the Shah of Iran.

Finally the time came when the medal or rosary was offered. I decided that if I had to back out when leaving the presence of the Shah, I would do the same when leaving the papal audience room. But this was impossible because His Holiness walked to the door with us and on our knees we there received a final blessing. The audience had taken twenty-eight minutes. I have lived that wonderful experience over in memory thousands of times since and always with a feeling of uplift.

CHAPTER X

THE trials in Nuremberg of the German high officials who had been accused as war criminals were starting and I hurried on my way to attend that historic event.

The travel order that came through was for Frankfurt only and I went there from Paris by train operated by the American Armed Services. A clean bed and an excellent breakfast en route served as the background for the constant sight of wretchedly poor and starving people as I watched out of my car window. So, during breakfast, I took some of the lovely white rolls from the table and put them away in my catch-all bag. Also I had fortified myself for this trip into Germany with about thirty pounds of candy and a quantity of cigarettes.

Off the train, I immediately started giving the rolls and some candy to the bedraggled children who crowded about. Most of the children secreted the bread or candy in their clothes and started running as though they were going to share the windfall with others.

The population seemed to be roaming the streets and all seemed prepared to barter anything for cigarettes or candy.

In the Visitors' Bureau at Frankfurt I was having no luck with the colonel in charge in getting the right to go on to Nuremberg. During the presentation of my arguments, in walked my old friend General Gross, but he sadly told me he could be of no help. He said that United States Supreme Court Justice Robert

H. Jackson, in charge of the trials, controlled the area and only he could permit entry. That news was like a ray of light from my standpoint, because the Jacksons have been the close friends of Floyd and myself for many years.

I learned that the Nuremberg trials recessed for lunch precisely at twelve o'clock noon each day and therefore I arranged for a private wire at this time. I had Justice Jackson on the line almost immediately and he was enthusiastic about my coming to the trials. I asked him to tell the colonel in command of the Visitors' Bureau in Frankfurt that I was to have immediate orders to go to Nuremberg and I added that if he would have orders issued also for General Gross and his aide, they would produce a military car and bring me through. I learned that Justice Jackson obtained my accommodations by saying that if they were not provided elsewhere he would give up his own to me and use an army cot in his study.

Justice Jackson celebrated our arrival in Nuremberg by taking us to dinner in the Marble Room of the Grand Hotel where Hitler had often entertained guests and by postponing curfew for an extra hour.

This was in November 1945. The trials had been on for four days. It is symbolic that the Palace of Justice, while bombed, had been spared sufficiently so that it could accommodate these trials. The cathedral had also been bombed but still stood fairly intact. Justice Jackson gave me an autographed copy of his opening statement and for me it is a highly prized historical document.

The following morning I attended the trials. I watched the defendants carefully. Goering, always the extrovert, was brash and quite boastful of his part in the Hitler regime. Most of the others were sullen and glum. One of the defendants had indicated he would testify against some of the others in return for a sentence of shooting rather than hanging. Shooting was regarded as a soldier's death, not without honor. There was considerable doubt whether Hess was actually out of his mind or merely playing a part. Our own psychiatrists thought his memory block real. Before the start of the trials Goering, who was disgusted with Hess, said if Hess could be left alone with him, he would make Hess remember and talk. They were given most of one day together, but Goering failed. Then our people tried another angle to enable themselves to reach a conclusion concerning Hess. A combined motion picture of the worst of the German atrocities was shown to the prisoners in a group and their faces were watched carefully. Hess never changed expression and seemed not to know what was going on. Finally, later during the trials, Hess and his lawyer were held back after the other prisoners had been returned to their cells. A hearing was to be held on the motion by the lawyer for Hess to have Hess discharged as a prisoner because of his mental condition. Hess indicated during this hearing that he wanted to say something and was given the microphone. Hess completely startled the court by then stating that his loss of memory was nothing more than carefully planned tactics on his part; that he remembered everything perfectly. His tactics, even to this change in midstream, worked fairly well for he is alive today while most of the others were hanged. I do not believe this interesting story about the "insanity" of Hess has ever been told publicly. Goering, somewhat true to form, beat the noose by use of poison at the last minute. It was generally thought at the time that he had the vial previously secreted under his skin in his navel. I am reliably informed that this was not the case. His lawyers could pass papers to him and it is almost certain the vial of poison was attached to the back of one of these documents.

One piece of testimony caught my eye particularly. Field Marshal Erhard Milch was testifying on behalf of Goering. The testimony made it clear that on two occasions — once when Milch wanted to warn Hitler of Russia's air strength and to advise against making war against Russia and once when Milch reported to Goering that American and British fighter planes had been seen accompanying our Allied bombers as far as Lüttich — Goering had forbidden Milch from reporting these things to Hitler lest the Air Force be looked upon as defeatist. The conclusion was clear that Goering preferred to deceive Hitler than to take a chance on losing Hitler's confidence by reporting bad news. Goering, shortly after his arrest, told our General Vandenberg he knew the collapse was at hand when he personally saw our Thunderbolt and Mustang fighter planes over Berlin. As I read this testimony I thought back to Sasha Seversky's efforts to put long range into our fighter planes and to my own 2000-kilometer flight in his pursuit plane to support these efforts.

Justice Jackson said that for me to see the document room would be more important than to attend all the sessions of the trial. I spent many hours poring over the documents and photographs with the help of a German-speaking captain who had been assigned to me.

I saw the pictures taken at Buchenwald and Dachau. I saw pictures of people in Poland lined up against a wall for mass shooting and of others trying to escape out of windows while the trucks that were to take them away were being loaded with family and friends. In these trucks the occupants were asphyxiated en route, and then buried without trace, if possible. And I saw the opened graves of some of these people. The routine seemed to be to tell these people that the inhabitants of the entire village were being moved elsewhere for military reasons. But the destination for them was death.

What was most important, I saw many documents signed or initialed by Hitler, Goering, Keitel or Jodl approving these atrocities. Each of these top people used a different colored ink. I recollect that Goering used green ink. Hitler used red ink and his signature on these documents reminded me of blood. These documents showed beyond doubt that the military leaders knew about and formally, officially approved these atrocities. In fact they ordered them. For this reason, if for no other, I believe their trial and punishment were justified. Most of these documents were signed in triplicate. The Germans were orderly and had Teutonic passion for putting things on paper, even to the gory details of the extermination of whole villages and millions of people who were in the way of the leaders for one reason or another. I saw one document signed or initialed by Hitler and several of the defendants which provided for the killing of every one of the twenty-five thousand people in a Polish town, and several orders, similarly approved, for the extermination of all Jews.

A press conference — the first one — with the lawyers for the defendants was arranged and I attended. One distinguished German lawyer spoke through an interpreter for all the defendants, who had been sent back by that time to their cells. The usual questions were being asked, which I thought were getting nowhere, and I decided to have a fling. I asked the lawyer if he felt the defendants were receiving a fair and judicious trial. His answer was that there could be no such trial without a German sitting on the tribunal. A pin could have been heard drop when I asked the question. A clamor started when it was answered. Then I asked this lawyer if he had been a member of the Nazi Party. He threw his shoulders back in an attitude of defiance and said that he had not only been a Party member but a prominent one. Thereupon a number of the correspondents present wanted to know why he was not on trial rather than serving as a lawyer for the defendants. Bedlam broke loose and they had to call in the military police to clear the courtroom. That ended the press conference — just two simple questions.

Over the week end Justice Jackson took me to see Buchenwald. There was plenty of evidence left of the executions. We saw where the bodies after gassing had been stacked up against the wall like cordwood awaiting their turn in the incinerators, several of which were kept busy around the clock. We saw the prints of feet on the wall, plenty of bloodstains, and the large "shower room" where the people in large groups were sent in naked to be killed by gas. This was all reported in fair detail at the time but I refer to it now lest we forget — just as I often repeat "Remember Pearl Harbor," an expression coined by Floyd in a speech he made the day following that sneak Japanese bombing of our fleet in Hawaii.

My orders permitting me to go direct to Berlin from Nuremberg arrived and I decided to be on my way.

The people in Frankfurt had seemed poverty-stricken to me but they were quite well off compared to the Berliners. Everything had been pretty well devastated in the German capital city. Women with their feet wrapped in rags were cleaning brick rubble from the streets. Women and children were living in basements and sometimes just holes in the walls. Misery crowded in on us from all sides.

I drove around Berlin and handed out here and there bits of food. It was getting dark when a little boy who seemed to belong to no one looked so miserably cold I took him into the car for a while and cuddled him and fed him a chocolate bar. It then started to snow and a woman came along, with one child on a sort of a wagon she was pulling and with four more children at her side. She looked harassed and nearly starved. General Bob Harper, then quartered in Berlin, was away at the time and his medical officer was accompanying me on this trip. He spoke German so I tried to get the woman's story. Her husband had disappeared during the war. She did not know whether he had been killed or captured. She had no food and wanted to know if I could give her some. I thought I had distributed all I had. We therefore drove on and in the darkness I watched the street fill up with people from their underground rooms, people who searched even the garbage cans of the military for scraps of food. The hunger I so often experienced as a child on Sawdust Road came back to me with sharp vividness. I knew better than most observers what were the inner feelings of these unfortunate people and what a terrific lift just a little food can give to a hungry person. Suddenly I realized that I had a considerable quantity of food packed away in the baggage compartment of the car. I determined to turn back and try to find that woman and her children. General Gross said it would be like trying to find a needle in a haystack there on the big main square, half on the Russian side and half on the American side. Luck was with us. We found her. I gave her a half pound of sugar, some cocoa, some hard-boiled eggs, a can of fruit juice and some big lumps of bread. She seemed terrified that someone would take it away from her. The last sight I had was of her standing there in the crowded street with tears welling out of her eyes and freezing on her cheeks because the air was so cold; and I had a very satisfactory cry myself.

I made several attempts in company with my friends to get into the bunkers of the Reichschancellery where Hitler was supposed to have ended his career. They were guarded by the Russians and we were politely turned back each time. I finally went back on my own and offered one of the outpost guards a couple of cigarettes and by signs explained what I wanted to see. He took me to his captain. The captain cost me a package of cigarettes and approximately ten dollars in money. But as a result I had a special guard to show me through the Reichschancellery and through the bunkers, as well as a full description on the spot of the final burning of Hitler's body outside the door. The captain spoke English and liked American cigarettes very much.

I believe I was about the last person to get into the bunkers, which were in reality a fabulous underground home. The rooms had been flooded and in some places about a foot of water remained on the floors, but boards had been put here and there to serve as foot bridges. I saw a library beautifully done and the beds where the six Goebbels children slept during the last few days before their deaths. The rooms were air-conditioned. I looked at the spot where Hitler's body, after his suicide, was supposed to have been burned to nothing. I saw no evidence of fire. I also saw in the grounds of the Reichschancellery, close by the bunkers, a long paved strip where even a fairly good-sized airplane could have managed a landing and take-off. I think the strip was there for that very purpose. The Reichschancellery — a large and architecturally beautiful structure which served as headquarters, like our Pentagon building — had been gutted and looted. The looting was still going on. I got a doorknob which cost me two cigarettes. For a few more cigarettes I also bought a medal which Hitler had on hand to give to a woman for bearing sixteen children. These and the right to see the bunkers were the only things I bartered for. All else I had by way of food or money I gave away.

One interesting fact I learned years later about the looting of the Reichschancellery which has never been published. The Russians were allowed to occupy Berlin first. When our people first entered the Reichschancellery offices, books and papers were still scattered all over the floors of Hitler's private offices. One of our people found an index to Hitler's private files and there was a file so indexed for Hitler's personal foreign exchange accounts. There was another file apparently dealing with sums spent for propaganda in the United States. But the files themselves were gone and never showed up. The one about Hitler's holding of foreign funds would have been invaluable at the trials and to track down Hitler if he had made his escape. Was it carelessly destroyed or carried away or did it get into the hands of the Russian authorities, who, for reasons of their own, failed to turn it over?

Hanna Reitsch was my opposite number in Germany. I had watched her do a brilliant job of soaring and gliding at our National Air Races in Cleveland just before the start of the war.

Hanna Reitsch spent those last days in the bunker with Hitler and his associates. I have her complete statement of what took place and it is fascinating to me.

On April 24, 1945, when Berlin was practically encircled by the Russians, General von Greim — by Hitler's orders — was flown to Berlin. Hanna Reitsch was to have been his pilot because she was skilled with helicopters but at the last moment a standard-type plane and another pilot were chosen. Hanna Reitsch begged to be taken along and was stuffed into the tail of the plane through an emergency opening. Most of the forty German fighters used as cover were destroyed but the plane bearing the pilot, von Greim and Hanna Reitsch got through to the Gatow Airport, where they changed planes and later made a landing on a street near Hitler's bunker. During this last flight von Greim's leg was badly injured by shrapnel.

Hitler had called von Greim to the bunker to tell him in a dramatic way, with sagging head, pallid face and trembling hands, that Goering at Berchtesgaden had sent word he was taking over successorship to Hitler because Hitler was no longer able to rule from Berlin. This was treachery of the worst sort, said Hitler, for which he had caused Goering to be arrested as a traitor and von Greim was now to be Goering's successor as head of the Air Force.

But things were getting worse by the minute. General von Greim and Hanna Reitsch begged to stay on with Hitler to the end. Hitler consented and then passed poison vials to everyone, saying that if Berlin could not be saved no one was to be taken alive and each was to find his own way to have his body destroyed after death. Hitler at this moment still thought an army — which

THE STARS AT NOON

days before had been destroyed — was trying to come to his rescue. His attitude and actions, however, showed doubt and despair.

The commander in charge of the defense of Berlin apparently tried to escape to the enemy on the afternoon of the 27th. This caused Hitler almost a total mental breakdown. Goebbels, according to Hanna Reitsch, kept cursing Goering and making speeches to all and everyone, even to empty rooms, about the example the people in the bunker were about to show the world by dying for honor. Frau Goebbels asked Hanna Reitsch to do away with her children in case she herself at the last could not go through with this duty. Eva Braun occupied her time polishing her finger nails and changing her clothes and cursing the deserters. Bormann kept to his desk, writing down every word, every action, for posterity. If preserved, it must be a pretty miserable recording of a Hitler fast crumbling physically and mentally. By the 29th Hitler was striding about the rooms with a crumpled map in his hands directing in a maniacal way a nonexistent battle for the defense of Berlin. On the 29th Hitler had to place Himmler with Goering on his list of traitors. On the morning of the 30th, Hitler said the one hope left was to get air coverage for the ground forces which he thought were trying to break through to his rescue; and he ordered von Greim to leave the bunkers for that purpose, as well as to arrest Himmler. Thirty minutes later Hanna Reitsch and von Greim were on their way. An armored car took them to a nearby hidden plane. They took off from a short stretch of undamaged street. From an altitude of 20,000 feet they watched Berlin by night as a sea of flames. From Keitel they learned that the army counted upon by Hitler had been destroyed or captured and that Keitel had sent this word to Hitler. That meant to Hanna Reitsch that the people in the bunker had already carried out their suicide pact. On May 8 the general capitulation came. A few days later von Greim committed suicide with the poison vial he took with him from the bunker.

Hanna Reitsch says that Hitler was physically and mentally incapable of leaving the bunker at the last even if a wide path had been cleared to his door. I doubt that. It may be true that he died by his own hand. But even that takes courage, when it is claimed he had neither courage nor initiative left. One plane hidden near the bunker was used for a getaway by von Greim and Hanna. There could have been another plane hidden. The foreign-exchange accounts of Hitler's indicate a plan to get abroad under certain circumstances. Of course, even if he did leave the bunkers, he could have died in the air over Berlin, for it was filled at that time with Russian aircraft and ground fire.

Since the days of the Nuremberg trials I have gone to Germany three times. One of the trips coincided with the airlift into Berlin known as "Operation Vittles" and I had the experience of riding and working with the crew of one of the airlift planes carrying sacks of coal from Frankfurt. These planes were moving on such a close schedule that if a plane missed its final approach, it had to return to Frankfurt rather than snarl up the traffic behind. My next trip to Germany was on active duty with General Vandenberg to study the problem relating to the WAF abroad.

My last trip into Germany was with Floyd after we left Spain on that sunshine-studded trip told about later on in this book. Our landing was in Munich. Things were hot and hysterical in Western Europe at that particular time because the push had started by the North Koreans which brought us into war in that area and the question was whether there would be a similar push into Western Germany. If so, we were to have a grandstand seat for we were the guests of Lieutenant General John K. Cannon, then in charge of all the air defense of Western Europe.

This was my first trip into Bavaria except for the days spent at the trials in Nuremberg. At Garmisch, where we stopped for four days in a modern and luxurious house being leased as the guest house of the American High Command, things seemed to be going as they had for centuries. The quaint Bavarian costumes with the short leather breeches that are handed down from father to son and the Tyrolean hat with the feathers sticking out to show the owner's accomplishment in mountain climbing, the Tyrolean Alps just off to the east, the Swiss Alps in the distance and the Austrian Alps all about with their old castles, their ski runs in mothballs for the summer, and their cable cars up to the peaks — all this presented a diversified and lovely picture.

I remarked to Mrs. Cannon on the third day that someone from the spirit world seemed to come to my bedroom toward dawn each night and to be quite active and disturbed. I then learned that the woman who had owned the house had been questioned by the de-Nazification authorities as to her Party activities and had chosen suicide as the way out. I was told that she snuffed out her life in another of her homes. But I think she did so in the very bedroom I occupied. I was glad to move on to Berchtesgaden.

But even at Berchtesgaden we had the shades of the dead for company, for there we occupied the home of Field Marshal Keitel, Hitler's Chief of Staff. I used his bedroom. Keitel was among those tried at Nuremberg and subsequently hung. His house servants were still on hand attending to us and seemed not to resent our presence.

Off at the edge of this small city of about ten thousand people, about halfway up the mountainside, Hitler had his home which was given to him by Martin Bormann, who was the custodian of Party funds, and it came from levies on "grateful" Party members. It has since been razed. I have a small piece of marble from the

fireplace of that home to go along with the doorknob from the
Reichschancellery and a bit of gold-inlaid marble from Nero's
golden palace.

A road led from Hitler's home up the mountain to its very
peaks, where was built the "Eagle's Nest," also by levies on
grateful Party members. Many have in mind that this was Hitler's mountain home and hideaway. It was not.

In point of fact, I am told Hitler was in the Eagle's Nest only
five times. On one of these occasions, he gave a reception in connection with the marriage of one of his top generals to Eva
Braun's sister. These five tea parties were rather expensive because it took in the neighborhood of seven million dollars to build
the Eagle's Nest, and the road to it. That made each cup of tea
almost as expensive as at the "21" Club in New York City.

We also attended the Passion play at Oberammergau.

One of the highlights to me of this dramatic presentation of
the last days of Christ on earth was the sequence of scenes in
which the high priest worked his followers up to such a pitch of
frenzy that en masse they demanded the Crucifixion. As I saw
this example of leadership and mass psychology, I could not help
thinking of the concentration camp at Dachau, just a few miles
away, where the followers of Hitler, through a similar use of leadership and mass psychology, exterminated more than two hundred thousand people, a great portion of whom were Jews. I
wondered if those simple Bavarian folk gave thought, while
they were acting out their roles, to this repetition of history. In
one case a man, who was a symbol, was being crucified by the
Jews — one of their own. In the other case, Hitler had turned the
wrath of the Nazis on the whole mass of Jews and then, for good
measure, on other "enemies."

Floyd and Mrs. Cannon went through Dachau without me. I
had had more than enough of such things at Buchenwald. They
reported that at the entrance to Dachau there was a large sign

reading "Drive Carefully — Children at Play." That represented a lot of progress from the days of the gas chambers.

The two weeks just prior to the outbreak of war in Korea I spent in Russia. I believe I was the only American who in years, up until then, had crossed the border into Russia traveling on a nondiplomatic passport. My friend Admiral Alan Kirk, Ambassador to Russia (who was on the battleship *West Virginia* in those flying days of mine in San Diego), asked Mrs. Cannon and me to be his guests at the Embassy in Moscow.

From Helsinki to Moscow by direct airline is approximately five hundred miles, or about a two-hour flight by plane. We were two days and two nights on the train. On this first leg of the trip, the train felt as if there were no rails underneath and that it was bumping along on the ties. The windowpanes were so full of faults and distortions that one could scarcely see out, but I found one panel that gave me a good vantage point.

Just over the border and early in the morning, we were awakened by a woman who spoke English as if she had been raised in New York. It was indicated that I should pull all my bags down from the various racks in the compartment and carry them to the customs office. I informed this Russian lady that if the authorities wanted to see the contents of my baggage they would have to find their own way of doing so. She disappeared and showed up with a man who put all the bags on the floor where the customs lady examined them one by one. I had several party dresses along and considerable finery. I noticed out of the corner of my eye how she fondled them and rubbed her cheek on my mink coat. She even looked up at me with a smile and uttered the word "lovely." Then it came to jewelry. I listed it all and there was considerable — enough to make her eyes bulge when she looked it over. She asked us to step out of the compartment and while we were in the corridor, she searched

every crack and cranny of our room. Finally, she asked me if I
had any reading material and I gave her two fashion magazines
I was taking through to the womenfolk in the Embassy. She disappeared with them for about an hour and then returned them.
I hope she enjoyed reading about American fashions for I'm
sure that's what she did.

The train service was terrible almost beyond description. Mrs.
Cannon and I carried our own food and water along. The food,
except for bread and some fruit, was canned and we had the
water for our trip in a small-sized milk can in our compartment.

The first thing that struck me as I looked out of the railroad
car window on the way through Russia was that all the railroad
and road workers were women and children. The children ranged
from age ten upward. Most of the women were powerful looking and they all were working just like section hands in the
United States. I learned while in Moscow the secret of the child
labor. When a boy fails to pass his tests in the equivalent of our
fifth grade he ends up in the "trade school," which means labor.

Russia seemed to me a land of contradictions with a broad foundation through it all of fear, work and poverty. I put fear first
because it seems basic in everyone from the highest I met to the
lowest. They tried to hide it, but unsuccessfully. The customs
girl had looked up and down the corridor of the train before she
felt of the fine silks and dresses with a smile. The man in the state
store who was showing us some fine antique art and jewelry
lost himself for a moment in his enthusiasm but suddenly stepped
back and finished the monologue about three paces away in a
fairly loud voice. I was later told by those who should know that
he was afraid not to let the others in the store hear what he was
saying lest they report him for secret conversations with for-
eigners.

As for poverty, the average person on the streets of Moscow
was more poorly dressed than our lower-grade tramps in New

York. Shoes, according to our conception of shoes, were almost nonexistent, and the same was true as to women's hats. The majority of the houses in Moscow were what we know as log cabins and this was true even right up close to Red Square and the Kremlin. But I was struck by the carved window frames in these log cabins. Apparently the inhabitants take pride in this decorative touch.

The streets, except for a few of the main highways, were paved not at all or with rough cobblestones that would jar you loose from your eyeteeth if you rode over them in a bus. And yet Red Square is as wide as a city block in New York and has several lanes side by side of fine highways. The center lanes are reserved for the high governmental officials whose cars usually were seen rolling along at certain hours of each day with all window curtains drawn. Was it fear from within the car or outside? Or were the cars sometimes empty?

But on even the terrible highways I saw fine buses — finer than our Fifth Avenue buses. And working on the roads I saw steam rollers fantastically large and manned by women.

Along Avenue Gorki there were some wonderful façades of buildings that clearly had the modern Russian touch. But I walked down a side block and discovered that only the street sides of the buildings were up. The building part itself was hardly twenty feet deep behind the walls and the back side unfinished. It reminded me of the story of early days in Russia when "stage" cities and the like were put up along the river while the Empress and her entourage and foreign diplomats were passing by boat. These "sets" were moved by night and set up again ahead of the boat. It looked wonderful from the boat deck but got no one any place. Why a wonderful front for a building and no substance or usefulness behind?

There was a twenty-two-story office building being built of steel construction in Moscow. Although it had been under construction for three years, all the steel girders were not yet in place. No paint had been put on the steel already up and it was rusting. Furthermore, the steel pillars were so out of line that I wondered if the elevators would work.

On the other hand, the subway system in Moscow is something great to behold. The stations are far larger than the New York City stations, with the walls and ceilings decorated beautifully. Also there is much fine statuary. There are five levels of subway lines with double rows of escalators leading up and down. The escalators from the bottom level to the surface are so long that when halfway up one can see neither end.

I walked the first day to Red Square with Mrs. Kirk. It was only a few blocks. She had a set path she traveled each day. I prevailed on her that day to make a foray for another block or two, but we became objects of curiosity or worse from the passers-by and soon turned back. One woman who was cleaning the street tried to wet our dresses. Each householder must keep the street clean in front of the house to the street center.

One day I covered several of the state stores. In addition to the run-of-the-mill goods for the householder they had some fine antiques in those stores but priced so high in rubles at four to the dollar that one could not think of buying. The wonderful-looking breads and meats in the windows of these stores were all painted wood, but exceedingly well done.

Another day I covered the few churches that were open. They were filled with a constant stream of worshipers and with numerous beggars. The great mass of beggars with distortion of limbs and sometimes open sores presented a pitiful sight. Apparently the Soviet system did not have a plan for taking care of the crippled and nonworkers.

Religion was having a hard time in Russia except as it consisted of worship of the State. The Roman Catholic Church was having particularly hard sledding. Father P. Jean de Matha-

Thomas, a French priest, was, until some time back, in charge of the old Catholic "Church of Saint Louis." But a Polish priest about two years before my trip to Moscow took over from Father Thomas the keys and the maintenance of the church and the spiritual welfare of the congregation. Father Thomas thereafter could say Mass only for the foreign diplomatic people.

Father John Brassard, an American priest, had been sent to Moscow several years before by Cardinal Spellman, but he had not been permitted to exercise the duties of his office. In civilian garb, as an honorary member of the diplomatic staff, he sang in the choir on Sunday morning while Father Thomas was saying Mass. But betweentimes in his tiny rooms, where a small altar had been improvised, at so-called cocktails, he managed to give spiritual consolation to the many who chose to come. The Russian neighbors must have thought Americans steady and heavy cocktail sippers. Father Brassard is now back home. More than eighty per cent of all the diplomatic personnel in Moscow were Catholic by faith. The British Ambassador was Catholic.

On the second Sunday I was in Moscow I went to the Mass celebrated by Father Thomas. I arrived at the church early to observe. It was filled with Russians, but a Polish priest was going around telling them that these services were not for them and they should leave. Some left. Some changed their seats and stayed. The diplomatic corps sat in the first few rows, and soon Father Thomas, a benign, elderly man with a long white beard like a patriarch, started Mass. I could not be too devout in my external actions that morning because of the strange proceedings. During the forepart of the Mass the Polish priest walked out and across in front of the altar with a bottle in his hand. It looked like a bottle of vodka to me. His apparent objective was to disrupt the Mass but Father Thomas seemed not to see him at all. Then the Polish priest four times walked out past the altar, down through the swinging door between the altar and the congregation, and around the congregation. He was clearly checking up to see who was there from among the Russians. Some elderly Russian women were crawling down the aisle on their knees to take Communion when the Polish priest made his fourth foray and as he opened the gate he nearly bowled one of these women over. The whole thing seemed unnecessary and obnoxious. The collections were taken over by the Polish priest even at this Mass for the diplomatic corps. Father Thomas and Father Brassard got along as best they could with help from the larders of the Embassies. Apparently the rulers of Russia believe their form of government and their continuance of power cannot endure side by side with established religions. I'll place my bet in the long run on religion. Faith will always conquer fear, and faith among the Russians has not been stamped out.

We obtained permission to drive in the Embassy car with a Russian chauffeur to the home and grave of the great Russian writer, Tolstoy, a distance of about one hundred and fifty miles from Moscow. The permission was conditioned. We could not stop in any village. We could not tarry. We could only stop in the woods by the roadside for a picnic lunch. The woods also served as our powder room and because on our first stop we noticed row on row of barbed-wire barricades back in the woods running parallel to the highway, we stopped often to see what we could see. Always there was the barbed wire. Once through a clearing I glimpsed the runway of an airport. It was a long one — about ten thousand feet. And while we were riding along in the car a group of jet planes flew overhead where we got a good view. It's interesting that those jets should have been there just that day. They were the only ones I saw the whole time in Russia. However, I did drive out to the main Moscow airport the following day where I saw fine administration buildings and through the high wire fence many transport planes that looked very modern.

Tolstoy's home was as interesting as it was modest. It housed the writer's library, including *Riders of the Purple Sage* by Zane Grey, and on the wall was an autographed photograph of William Jennings Bryan. I thought of how small the world was growing with age — my age — because Zane Grey lived and wrote that book in the Coachella Desert just a few miles from our ranch house. As a youngster when I read the book, I thought the purple sage was in a faraway enchanted dreamland.

On the way back to Moscow, at the foot of a hill, our car had to dodge quickly around a badly wounded peasant on the road. He had apparently been struck by an automobile while riding on his bicycle with his scythe over his shoulder. The bicycle had become twisted about him and had torn his body. The scythe had cut him badly. The Russian chauffeur would not stop on our first request but we insisted and he backed up to the body lying there in a pool of blood. The man was alive but in shock. It was apparent he had been there for some time, which means that many trucks had passed him up. We stopped truck after truck but with no help. The drivers all said the same thing and went on, "We cannot stop and help. We will be involved." We pulled the bicycle out of the man's body and put blankets from our car around him and under his head. Two of us stayed with him while the chauffeur took the rest of the group back to the nearby village. Our car stopped outside the village while the chauffeur and one of the Russian-speaking members of the Embassy staff, who was with us, went into the village to find the village commissar. Finally, after a few unsuccessful tries, this local official got a truck to stop and take the unconscious man away.

I attended the Russian Ballet which was as wonderful in every way as I had hoped. I went to see the preserved body of Lenin and I wondered if the body would last longer than Communism.

I did not get into the Kremlin because they were having sessions — but I tried. I went near the gate and smiled my sweetest at the guard. He smiled back, but when I took a step forward toward the open gate, he cocked his gun and got ready for action. I decided that it would be better to see the inside of the Kremlin grounds from the roof of the nearby British Embassy which I did.

From Moscow we went to Leningrad, where we were not given a key to our hotel room. A policeman sat outside our door at all times while we were there.

An old prewar Baedeker guide I had studied in the Embassy told me about the beauties of the palace and grounds at Peterhof, about three and one half hours by boat from Leningrad. It also told me that the ideal way to go to Peterhof was by boat down the waterway. I told the woman at Inturist I wanted to go to Peterhof by the boat. She tried to dissuade me. The fountains would not be running that day, the river trip was really not interesting, the boat was uncomfortable. I was adamant and finally, after a long delay she took us to the dock and we embarked. We were taken down to the small cabin and given chairs in the center of the room where we were so surrounded by people we could not see out. I insisted on going on deck and had my way. Whether that girl made a mistake I do not know. Floyd says such mistakes do not happen in Russia with Americans. Anyway, we were entering and during the next several minutes passed through the largest naval base I have ever seen. It was bigger than the Brooklyn Navy Yard, the Norfolk base, the San Diego base and the Long Beach base all combined. We counted some sixty completed submarines close at hand. Back of them on ways and slips and channels were many others in some state of completion. If the Soviets wanted to show the Americans that they had the biggest submarine fleet in the world they succeeded. If you take a map of Russia and study the coast line, you will conclude that these submarines are not for defense of that coast line. They are either for attack or to keep ships from traveling the open ocean highways.

Peterhof is an extravagantly gorgeous spot. An early emperor — the first I am told who traveled outside Russia — saw Versailles Palace in France and decided to model after it, but outdo it, at Peterhof. The palace is large but visitors were not allowed inside because it was under repairs. The grounds are larger and more magnificent than the gardens at Versailles. The fountains were throwing their water high into the air, the Inturist girl to the contrary notwithstanding. The water is brought under pressure from the mountains, some miles distant. Off to one side of the gardens I saw some large posters that I wanted to examine. I used a nonfunctioning fountain under repair as my excuse. The Inturist girl tried to stop me, giving various reasons, but she finally tramped along. The posters were propaganda against the United States and England. The people of Russia apparently had not been informed that President Roosevelt had died and Churchill was then out of power. The whole thing was pretty disgusting and in a burst of anger I told the girl guide so. She apparently did not appreciate my remarks for when we went to a restaurant she first would not accept our invitation to join us and then on our insistence took a chair placed about three feet away from the table.

Finally we left Russia. We were tired after two weeks of constant daylight and at least eighteen hours a day of moving about. I think Mrs. Cannon was greatly relieved. I have a hunch she was afraid I would get us both into trouble with my curiosity and determination to see things.

There is nothing wrong with the Russian people as a whole that a higher standard of living and the truth won't cure. They work hard. Perhaps we could take a small page from their book in this respect. The Russian rulers have publicly stated that their system and ours cannot live side by side. One must perish. And the Soviets are moving forward in the machine age. Conditions in Russia for the common man are such that there would be no more perfect cure for those few in the United States with Communistic leanings than to send them to Russia to taste it firsthand without flavor or the hues that distance lends.

From Russia I went almost immediately to Spain, stopping only a while in Norway and long enough in Paris to meet Floyd. The contrast between Russia and other lands became greatly highlighted as I traveled. Spain reminded me constantly of Russia, but only because it was so different. It was like going from a stale cellar into sunlight. Spain is in truth a land of sunshine and smiles, castles and flowers.

At the Madrid airport, we were met by a customs official who whisked our many pieces of baggage through customs in the space of five minutes. We were also met by a high-placed representative of the Ministry of Foreign Affairs and his wife, who took us to our hotel in a government car and then to lunch.

Floyd and I had a forty-five-minute audience with the Chief of State, Generalissimo Franco, at the small palace about nine miles northwest of Madrid that serves as the executive seat of government. The coloring, military bearing and straight arm-across-the-chest salute of the Moorish guard seemed to me exotic and even more impressive in a simpler way than the picture presented by palace guards at Buckingham Palace in London. Franco's palace is rather small, but all the rooms I saw were elegantly furnished. The walls were covered with various tapestries, mostly from Goya paintings, the originals of which are in the exquisite Prado Art Museum in Madrid. The clocks, chandeliers and furnishings seemed to me to be more French than Spanish, and as we sat there in one of the outer chambers, waiting our turn with groups of laymen, churchmen and military men also waiting their turn, I was reminded of the stories I had read about audience day at Versailles before the French Revolution. But here there was an air of democracy about the whole thing, an atmosphere of friendliness. Smiles were the order of the day, as they were in all parts of Spain we saw.

We moved from the one big waiting room to another and finally to a smaller one before being taken into Franco's chamber.

The title "Dictator" should really be forgotten in connection with Franco. He is not in the category of Mussolini or Hitler or Stalin. True it is that the Spanish form of government is not just like ours but, by the same token, ours is not just like theirs. When Franco came into power, it was a case of either Franco and his conservative followers taking over or of Communism. There was no third choice. All people in every social level in Spain told me the same thing. The government of Spain is much like the government in many of the Latin-American republics that we completely recognize and have political and business relations with. A tighter central control seems more suited to the Latin temperament. But whatever it is, it gives considerable freedom to the people of Spain. I heard much good-natured grumbling about the government, its Ministry and its Chief of State, which I thought was a purely American habit.

Franco himself is on the smallish side physically, quiet but friendly in his expression and attitudes. His whole tenor of conversation indicated that the lot of the ordinary man in Spain was much on his mind. He spoke of projects to increase the productivity of the land and to increase the standard of living. When I mentioned the idea most Americans have of dictators, Franco smiled. His rounded face and soft expression seemed better suited for smiles than for harshness.

From this audience in the palace, we were driven to a ranch south of Madrid in the vicinity of Toledo, where a fiesta was given in our honor. It was preceded by a "small" bullfight, which is not fought with bulls at all but with heifers and then only with sticks. The bull is never trained or aggravated in any way before going to the ring. His aggressiveness and fighting characteristics are determined by these play skirmishes with the female side of the herd. The mother will pass on her characteristics to the son and this can be proved by the sisters.

The house where this fiesta was held embraces the original quarters given by King Ferdinand and Queen Isabella to Columbus in appreciation of his discovery of America. A few of us were served dinner in the one room that is intact from the time of Columbus. The setting made me keenly alive to the shortness of time between the days of our Indian tribes and today's most powerful nation on the face of the earth.

A group of flamenco singers and dancers entertained the group of about forty guests who were present. Flamenco music was something new to me. No one among my Spanish friends had quite the same story as to its origin. Some gave credit to the gypsies but it is not at all like the gypsy music I know. Others said it came from the Moors. The strange rhythm put it back in my mind to the Near or Far East. In a sense, it bears the same relationship to standard Spanish music as cowboy songs do to standard American music.

I finally was pressed into seeing all the processes of a bullfight from start to finish. By this I mean from the boxing of the bulls on the ranch two days before the fight to the skinning and quartering of the bulls for meat back of the arena immediately after the fight. The fact that the *torero* was making beautiful *serpentina,* butterfly and *verónica* passes with his magenta fighting cape did not distract my mind from the blood flowing from wounds made in the bull's shoulder by the picador, in order to weaken the bull and make it more nearly a setup for the matador.

Littre was the chief matador that day at Toledo and at that

time was Spain's leading matador. Because he got his start on Señor Thiebaut's ranch where these particular bulls were boxed for shipment to the Plaza de Toros, Littre gave us, that afternoon on the ranch, a private exhibition and had dinner with us afterwards followed by jovial dancing and singing. Littre was a mild-mannered shy boy hardly in his twenties.

Floyd was the first American to try to be helpful in the economic recovery of Spain. He sold planes to Spain for pesetas and agreed to leave the pesetas in Spain for investment. Floyd conceived the idea that if Spain could get more rain its people would have greater abundance even without large expenditures for fertilization and farm equipment. So he decided to try rain-making in a test area with the help of Dr. Irving Krick, our foremost American rain-making meteorologist. This technical and comparatively inexpensive project may mean more in time to Spain than all the money our government has granted for bases and the like.

For my part I took to my heart three very poor Spanish boys whom I am raising in a home I have provided for them in Madrid. Handicapped by complete lack of schooling until I took them over, they are already up with the classes of their same ages. They are my insurance that I will return to Madrid often. So sure am I of this that I leave a set of golf clubs there rather than tote them back and forth.

My wanderlust took me from Spain to Morocco. The Sultan of Morocco and the Shah of Iran had much in common during the summer of 1953. They were both being evicted from their palaces at the same time. The Shah returned shortly under his own power to take up residence again. The Sultan was whisked away under guard in a plane to the island of Corsica — Napoleon's birthplace — and there his loneliness was softened by the presence of his two wives and a couple of dozen concubines although his splendor was limited to one entire hotel. The Sultan, his wives and concubines have since moved to a "safe" spot elsewhere.

There is nothing more effective in bringing about disastrous results than doing the wrong thing at the right time. The Sultan's daughter was photographed in a Bikini bathing suit when even the face of a Moslem woman should be covered in public. And Papa at the time was not only temporal head of Morocco but spiritual leader of the Moslems as well. Not that the bathing suit would have mattered so much given the right time; but at this particular time Sidi Mohammed Ben Youssef, the Sultan, was in wrong with the French and one of his most powerful pashas, Si Hadj Thami el Glaoui, the Pasha of Marrakech, was both pro-French and ambitious. So the strip-tease act was built into heroic proportions and into a mosaic that added up to a "vote" of no confidence in the Sultan.

The Pasha of Marrakech ruled over the four million Berber tribesmen who have occupied from almost time immemorial that section of Morocco which lies mostly between the Atlas Mountains and the Sahara Desert.

The Berbers I wanted to see, and see them I did in the early summer of 1951. That was before the Sultan got his political views straightened out. I had no friends or personal contacts in Morocco but an American friend had wired ahead to the hotel at Marrakech and to his representative there. The season was ended but the wire had been effective and quarters in the hotel were held open for the benefit of myself and Mrs. Strauss, who was my traveling companion, and Ellen, my maid.

The Pasha of Marrakech was in France but I and my traveling companions were invited over to the palace for tea presided over by the Pasha's secretary. It was mint tea and not good according to American taste, but many a mint tea I had to sip before I left Morocco. The Pasha really had two palaces, facing each other.

One was furnished Western style and in it I was told he housed the many "femmes" he would bring down from Paris — a sort of transient harem, I guess. These girls must have been a chummy group, for each bathroom had two tubs and two toilets.

I was informed by the Pasha's secretary that on my proposed trip through the Atlas Mountains and to the Sahara I would be under the patronage of the Pasha. A driver of his choice was sent along. At the Casbah de Telouet, just before the entrance to the pass through the mountains, we were to have lunch presided over by the Kaliffa, who was the Pasha's representative in that area.

Most of the population turned out to greet us on the narrow passage leading to the Casbah. It seemed a gala occasion for them. And down to this roadside came the reception committee from the Pasha's quarters led by a finely robed person whose garment was kissed by the multitude as he passed along.

We were shown about the quarters, which were in fine taste — finer than the Pasha's palace in Marrakech. Before we were seated on our floor cushions in the dining chamber two attendants brought in beautiful trays laden with bowls, kettles, soap and towels. Etiquette required that we eat with the thumb and two first fingers of our right hands and all out of the same portion of food. Cleanliness, therefore, is of concern to all and not only to one's self. The cleansing process becomes an important ritual.

Following the luncheon of fourteen courses and coffee made from acorns, dances were put on for us in the inner courtyard, which we viewed from a balcony strewn with fine Persian rugs. To the rhythm of drums played by a group of ancient-looking men sitting in the center of the court, the women did a long series of stately dances. After an hour of this dancing the girls started their routine all over again. I suggested it might be time to be on our way and that perhaps they were supposed to keep on dancing until some signal of departure from us. Not so! The guide informed us that the dances would have to be seen at least twice and probably three times, and three times we saw them.

We headed south toward the Sahara and until we arrived at Meknès and Fèz fifteen days later, we were like nomads mounted on an iron horse rather than a camel.

We drove southward until the road ended and then we followed the camel trail until we could go no farther. The wastes of the desert stretched before us. The sands were not as white as I had expected. A French military outpost, manned at the time entirely by Arabs, with a small mud-hut Berber village close by, marked this "no farther" point. How these villagers managed to grow food in that barren soil I could not realize until I was shown a river coursing by in the sands. Not a growing thing was on either bank. The river came from the mountains and carried on through the desert for hundreds of miles until it reached the ocean.

CHAPTER XI

ALL that I had seen in my travels made me more aware of how precious what we have here in America is. We must keep it. So it was that I found myself becoming more and more interested in politics.

My activity in the political field, to date, has been like the setting up of a new air speed record — brief, exciting, and successful. It all started with an ambition I developed to become a congresswoman and ended with the election of General Eisenhower as President.

Back during World War II, while I was on the General Staff of the Air Force in Washington, I had much need and also constant opportunity to work with senators and congressmen. I was in uniform and completely nonpartisan, so had plenty of chance, through official friendships and otherwise, to peek behind the scenes and to see democracy at work in both its good and its bad aspects. I learned greatly to respect that group of honest even though not always brilliant men and women who were faithfully doing their best. The demigods and nitwits I thoroughly despised and am afraid that I sometimes threw discretion to the winds and told them off.

Shortly thereafter I had the opportunity, and what I considered need, to engage actively in a political campaign in California, but not in my own Congressional district. We were successful.

This taste of home-front politics led me to believe that I might be successful in getting nominated and elected to Congress from my own Congressional district. But there were plenty of hurdles. Congressman Phillips, Republican, had obtained both the Republican and Democratic nomination for several elections. To get to Congress, I would, as a Democrat, have to beat him in the primaries because in California they have the quaint custom known as cross filing, which means that a candidate must name his party but can then run on both tickets. If he wins on both tickets, the primary serves as the final election, but if he names himself as a Democrat and does not win on that ticket in the primaries, he is out of the running altogether, even though he has won on the Republican ticket. Congressman Phillips had no opponent in the finals.

I was quietly studying the situation in the fall of 1951, without anyone beyond my own immediate family knowing what was going on in my mind, when out of the blue I received a telephone call in New York from the head of the Indio district organization of the Democratic party, asking if I would permit them to advance my name for the primaries to take place in the spring of 1952. I referred them to Floyd who was in Indio at the time. Floyd was noncommittal but met for discussion with the leaders of the organization in the entire Congressional district. His noncommittal attitude with these people was not a pose. He was the same way with me. He kept pointing out to me that chucking babies under their chins and backslapping housewives was not particularly my kettle of fish and, also, that to have any hope of success, I would have to run as a Democrat, but that in his opinion, the Democratic party had slowly changed its ways until it probably no longer stood for the things that I considered sound. This line of reasoning from a man who had been identified with the Democratic party since 1932 only fortified the growing feeling I had that I could not honestly at that time take office as a Democrat and would have to be a Republican — win, lose or draw.

Finally, the top leaders of the Democratic party in our Congressional district waited on me and tendered me the unanimous nomination of the party as congresswoman. This was something I had dreamed about. But it was coming from the wrong party at the right time, or vice versa. I asked for time. This was in December, 1951. It was arranged that the key personnel in the party organization would meet at my ranch on January 13 to receive my reply. I had made up my mind definitely by New Year's Day. On January 4, I wrote a letter to the chairman of the district organization in which I said:

"This is an exceedingly critical year for our nation. Our district cannot be sound unless our nation is sound. Therefore, I think the national issues will be of paramount importance in the coming election. As a candidate in a political campaign, I could not be true to myself and remain silent on these national issues. My basic views on these issues are independent and do not follow party lines. I see courses being charted, or at least being followed, in our national affairs that, in my opinion, lead away from the kind of democracy I want toward a kind of social and political structure I don't want. I see too much of a tendency towards unnecessarily increasing the public payroll and towards wastage. I see what I believe to be too much government in business and too little business in government. I see inflation creeping on with what I believe to be too little effective effort towards stopping it; and, unless stopped, inflation will eventually end in the collapse of our national economy, which I believe is the real objective of our communistic enemies. Also, I see provisions in our tax laws that tend to stifle private initiative and enterprise which together have served as the keystone of our American structure — provisions which must have been put into the tax laws either thoughtlessly or primarily for their social and political impacts, rather than to raise funds for they have very little tax raising effect.

I would be compelled publicly and repeatedly to express

my views about these and similar important national issues, if I were a candidate.

It is, therefore, with regret that I must decline the nomination and keep myself classified for the time being as a private citizen."

I got this letter into the hands of the chairman well in advance of the meeting scheduled at my ranch and asked him to distribute copies to all local committees. The meeting at the ranch was not called off. The reason was apparent when the more than one hundred people arrived. The letter had not been sent to them. The chairman thought he could change my mind. After lunch, the letter was read, followed by silence. Then a series of group meetings were held, followed by an announcement which gave me great faith in the soundness of our people at the grassroots level. The organization still wished me to be their candidate because what I had said in my letter expressed their own views. I was extremely complimented but said there was a chance, in my opinion, that General Eisenhower might be persuaded to run on the Republican ticket, and, if so, I would be out shouting for him, morning, noon and night, which would not be very consistent action for a Democratic candidate for Congress. They accepted my point of view. All this convinced me that loyalty to an emblem does not have such a hold on the thinking and actions of most people as to becloud real issues when they arise. It is evident that my own neighbors will go for a person, or a principle, irrespective of party label. When Congressman Phillips — a good man — decides to retire I may have the chance to fill his shoes. That is my smoldering hope.

No sooner was this political meeting over than I headed eastward, determined that if I had given up my personal ambition in the hope of a Republican victory headed by General Eisenhower, I should not let any grass grow under my feet in an effort to make this hope come true.

The opportunity to become active was presented almost immediately.

"Ike" had been prominently mentioned as a possible candidate but this was always from some high political level. The people had not spoken, and "Ike" had not given the faintest indication that he had heard the call.

Tex McCrary and his wife Jinx Falkenberg, who are both long-standing friends of mine, Jock Whitney and I got together and decided we were plain citizens for Eisenhower and as such we would do something about it.

The Madison Square Garden rally was the result, with Tex McCrary and I as cochairmen. In the meetings in my apartment preparing for this rally the slogan "I LIKE IKE" was adopted and the early buttons and banners were ordered.

A public rally is not too hard to swing during a campaign when there is an avowed candidate who is fighting hard for himself and party, an organization and money. But here we were planning a rally entirely outside the circles of a political party, without organization or money and with the "Ike whom we liked" completely silent as to what he would do.

We signed up Madison Square Garden at our own risk. But we got it cheap because we agreed to hold the rally at eleven o'clock at night after the conclusion of a prize fight. Therefore, the Garden would be already warm and staffed, with the "ring" in place as a platform. We hoped there would be no count of ten in that ring for us as there had been for some of the boxers.

Jinx and I went to Texas to get a big delegation from that state where "Ike" was born. We got three special train loads from all over the state, including bands and Texas Rangers on horseback. We covered other states with similar success, notably New Hampshire which was to be the next rallying ground for our Citizens for Eisenhower. I got a long-range weather forecast for the time and place of the rally from Dr. Irving Krick whose forecast was completely accurate.

A few whom we hoped would participate in our rally failed to show up, presumably because they feared the rally would be a failure and they did not want to be tarnished. This was understandable and we forgave them.

The show that we put on from the elevated prize ring was pretty much of a second-rate performance. It lacked sparkle, except in spots; there were no political big shots to speak; we kept to no semblance of schedule. It was strictly an amateur production, that rally. The columnists for the most part said so over the next few days. And they were right. But the rally was a five-star smash hit considering our objectives. The audience was marvelous. It was made up of the amateur voter, the first voters and Democrats who were for "Ike." They filled the Garden to its capacity and spilled over into the neighboring streets by the several thousands. It was all that we had hoped for.

Moving pictures were taken of the milling crowds in the streets and of the activities in the Garden — particularly the offstage activities of the people present. The film was developed overnight and I left with it by air the next day to give it to General Eisenhower at his headquarters in Paris. A half-hour had been allotted to me for the purpose. I knew General Eisenhower, having met him on several occasions during and just after the war and having been his dinner-table companion at a couple of large dinner parties.

When one has something awfully important to say and a very little time to say it in, one sometimes fares better than if given hours to ramble on. When I was taken into General Eisenhower's office, I told him that I believed I was carrying a message of utmost importance to our country from the common people of America and that with but a half-hour at my disposal I was going to start talking and would ask for no interruption. My words seemed effective. They kept rolling off my tongue, out of my heart. At the end of the half-hour, "Ike" asked me to continue while he arranged to have the film set up for showing at least in part. "Ike" watched that film for about ten minutes and I watched him. He had it stopped and asked me if I would take it out to his home and he and Mamie and associates would look at it in full at the close of the day's work. And there at his home I watched emotions grip General Eisenhower as he realized fully for the first time as he watched the film that he was receiving a call to duty from the people, and not just an invitation from public leaders and politicians. After we stopped the film, I sat talking to "Ike." His whole outlook had changed. I saw tears. It was apparent that he had taken a decision. He talked about his childhood and about the honors and duties he had had. He asked me to get in touch with certain people immediately on my return to New York, telling them what had happened during my visit and asking them to come over to see him immediately.

The next week end one of these men spent with "Ike." On his return from seeing "Ike," he reported to our group that my trip to Paris and the pictures had accomplished what no one else had succeeded in doing and that "Ike" was ready to run and give his all to the cause.

That meant our work had only started. New Hampshire was the first battleground. Money was needed there and our little group turned to fund raising. New Hampshire proved an outstanding victory and "Ike" was well on his way.

Then came the Republican convention in Chicago. I was not a delegate, or for that matter even a Republican. But out to Chicago I went, determined to get on to the floor of the convention hall. Through an old Chicago friend of John Hertz, I wangled a badge as a deputy. I sat at times with the California delegation and at other times with the Massachusetts, New Hampshire and Connecticut delegates. I carried cola bottles and helped keep order and was pretty well on the inside of every-thing that was going on.

When that famous first-ballot victory came through by a switch in votes, I asked Sherman Adams to arrange if he could for me to be on the podium while General Eisenhower was making his acceptance speech. And I was there. After the speech when "Ike" and Mamie turned to leave, she spotted me in the aisle near her, leaned over and planted a kiss on my cheek with the remark, "Now see what you have done." At the Inaugural Ball in Wash-ington I went into the gallery to say hello to President Eisen-hower and our First Lady. Again, I received a kiss from Mamie. This time she said, "When you start something, you certainly see it through to the finish." Again she made a similar remark to me when I was at a state dinner in the White House in the spring of 1954. These were nice things to hear and made me exceedingly happy but it was even nicer to know that a great group effort in which I had a major part at the very start and a small part throughout had ended with a six-million-vote popu-lar majority and a new "new deal" for our country.

Between the Chicago convention and that Inaugural Ball, I had flown here and there about the country making speeches, raising money and helping, as I did in Los Angeles, in organiz-ing the rally that was put on for "Ike" when he made his political speech in that city.

One of the nicest things that stands out in my memory in connection with the campaign was what the Walt Disney or-ganization did. I had approached Roy Disney to see how much a three-minute cartoon would cost. It was prohibitive but he spoke to some of the members of the organization who were for "Ike" and they all agreed on their own time at night and without any cost to us to make a cartoon with song. It was done within a week. It was shown over television more than any other cam-paign picture. The song was a good marching tune called "Ike for President" and the cartoon showed butcher, baker, candle-stick maker, and all their friends and relatives marching to Washington, led by an elephant which was beating the drum, while Adlai Stevenson on a donkey was headed in the other direction.

By the time Election Day neared, Floyd and I had done all we could, and we decided to forego the formalities and festivities at Republican Headquarters in New York City and go to the ranch. There we installed a television set but it would not work. When Adlai Stevenson in Springfield acknowledged the Eisenhower victory, which we heard by radio, Floyd and I went out on the lawn and by ourselves whooped and cheered into the night air.

We took in the Inaugural festivities. They were colorful like the ones four years before which Floyd and I also attended as special guests of President Truman.

But the high spot for me, not excluding the swearing-in ceremony, was in the home of "Ike" and Mamie in the suburbs of Paris on February 11, 1952, when I watched the tears well up in the General's eyes and saw the transformation of a great general into our next President. I knew pretty well the type of man I was trying to get into the White House; and I had great faith.

I started in politics to get myself into Congress. I got out of politics all I ended up wanting — at least for the present — that is, the election of General Eisenhower as President.

My friendship with the President resulted in a wonderful experience in the spring of 1954. He came out to our Coachella Desert for a few days of rest and exercise on the golf course. Floyd, by long-standing appointment, had gone into the Methodist Hospital near the Lovelace Clinic in Albuquerque, New Mexico, to have "Randy" Lovelace perform, in one "sitting," operations for gall bladder stones, double hernia, and chronic appendicitis. In a telephone conversation at the hospital I learned from Paul Hoffman that President Eisenhower intended to call on us at our ranch home. So Floyd sent me immediately back to the ranch to be on hand.

Floyd, accompanied by "Randy," came home from the hospital in my plane on the eighth day after the operation. Three hours later, the President honored us with his call and visited with us for an hour about the growing of dates and ranching generally, golf and hunting and other homey down-to-earth things. After the departure of the President, "Randy" took Floyd to his bedroom and removed the stitches from his two incisions. Floyd, in keeping with modern surgical techniques, walked on the day of operation. I think he would have come home right then if not doing so would have caused him to miss greeting as host President Eisenhower.

CHAPTER XII

ON June 2, 1953, I had every intention of being in London to see a charming princess being turned into a queen. But Fate had other plans for me. While Queen Elizabeth was riding back from Westminster Abbey to Buckingham Palace in the royal carriage, flanked on either side by crowds of loving subjects, I was having a memorable day of my own. Just two hundred feet above a dry alkaline lake bed in the California desert at a speed of about seven hundred miles an hour I was piloting a Sabre-jet plane back and forth over a measured course in an attempt to set a new all-out speed record. Except for the official timers and a half-dozen friends, desert rats and prairie dogs constituted my only audience. I completed the necessary four runs that morning and returned to the airport only to learn that the timing equipment on the ground had failed to function and all my efforts had been for naught.

Since I started flying in 1932 until the jet phase came along, I had been in the center of aviation. But the jet phase was threatening to pass me by. I wanted a real touch of it. I had searched around the corners for some way to get my hands on the controls of a jet plane for some speed flights. This is the story of how I succeeded and why I was on the California desert on the day Elizabeth was crowned Queen.

A short flight in a jet plane back in 1944 had convinced me that new horizons had been opened. But for a woman to get a good fast jet plane was a difficult business. All jet planes in this country are owned by the military forces. I am a pilot in the Air Force Reserve but women are not on flying status. I have been a close friend of every Chief of Staff of the Air Force to date, but for that reason would not ask them for a personal favor.

I first approached the head of Lockheed Aircraft Company, who appeared sympathetic but said every jet in that company's possession was government property and therefore Air Force consent would be necessary.

A Canadian group of acrobatic jet pilots attending the Cleveland Air Show offered to let me fly of an early morning one of their Vampire jet planes, but after deliberation I concluded I could possibly get them into serious trouble with their top brass, so declined with thanks. The head of the French Air Force, also a good friend of mine, invited me to come to France and fly one of their British-built jet Vampires. I was all set to go when Floyd stopped me for the reasons that I would be flying during winter season in a strange country and the instruments and controls in the plane would be strange and my advisers would be speaking either in my language, which they might not speak accurately when accuracy was essential, or in a language I understood hardly at all. He was right but I was disappointed. Madame Jacqueline Auriol, daughter-in-law of the then President of France, was later allowed to fly that Vampire and with it established a women's record for the 100-kilometer closed course. Madame Auriol is a friend of mine, and a good pilot who has stayed with flying, notwithstanding a horrible crash (not with herself at the controls) which necessitated many plastic-surgery operations to restore her facial beauty. We each call the other "Jackie." Madame Auriol came to this country in the early spring of 1952 and visited us at our ranch. While in this country she was given a flight in a Lockheed T33 two-place jet training plane. I thought to myself that somehow that would open the door to me, for, courtesy or not, it was an open flight by a nonmilitary woman in a military plane. But nothing happened. So I turned my eyes to other countries.

Canadair, Ltd., was making Sabre-jet planes in Montreal for the United States, British and Canadian Air Forces. It was the fastest model of the Sabre-jet, the only one that could pass the sonic barrier even in a full-power dive. The Canadian authorities were about to try out a Canadian-designed and built Orenda engine in the Sabre-jet. I was present at Detroit in 1951 when Colonel Fred Ascani of our Air Force broke the previous 100-kilometer speed record with a speed of 635 miles per hour. After his flight he told me that if I could get the Canadian-built Sabre-jet with the Orenda engine he thought I could beat his record by fifteen miles an hour and he would help me do so. That was a sportsmanlike gesture from a great pilot and a fine soldier and gentleman. And it energized me into action.

I wrote a long letter to Mr. John Jay Hopkins, head of General Dynamics, American owner of all the stock of Canadair. I did not mention my desire to beat the speed of sound or to better Colonel Ascani's record. That might sound too fantastic. So I put it on the ground that I had much experience in high-speed flying, I could probably be of help to them in testing out the Orenda-powered job, and in the process perhaps I could be clocked for a women's record or two with some resulting benefit to the Canadian firms involved. If he had checked my activities he would have learned that I was opposed to women's records as such and had not tried for one in several years. I wanted to break men's records only. Mr. John Hertz, owner of such famous race horses as Reigh Count and Count Fleet, is one of my closest and most valued friends and a friend of Mr. Hopkins as well. So I induced Mr. Hertz to speak a helpful word for me. That was all back in the spring of 1952.

The net result of these efforts and a trip or two to Montreal was that I was hired by Canadair as a flight consultant. It was agreed that when the Sabre-jet with Orenda engine was ready I could put it through some speed tests in Montreal. By way of planning I could survey and have a 100-kilometer course certified by the Fédération Aéronautique Internationale. I went to Montreal and put in some flight time. I arranged for representatives of the National Aeronautic Association to go to Montreal and have the course surveyed.

Those representatives reported to me that, because of lack of tie-points, the survey would be expensive, and also that the winter weather in Canada would be tough to buck. The general public does not realize that warm air temperature gives increased speed. This is because heat increases the speed of sound and the actual performance of a plane is related to the speed of sound, known as Mach 1. The speed of sound can get down as low as 660 miles per hour in very cold air and up close to 800 miles an hour in very hot weather.

These American timing officials asked why I did not do the records where a course was already established, with warmer air available.

About this same time I learned that Canadair wanted to send the plane to Edwards Air Force Base in California to have some calibration and other tests done that could not be done in Canada. I had courses already surveyed in the desert near our ranch about one hundred and sixty miles south of Edwards Air Force Base, so it seemed a great opportunity. I asked that I be allowed to do my speed tests in the plane while it was in California rather than after it had been returned to Montreal.

Canadair agreed. But I subsequently wished many times that I had never thought of this because a simple test arrangement then developed into an international problem and a major project.

First of all, there were two facts which prevented my own courses in the desert being used. The available airports for these courses had runways too short for Sabre-jet operation and these airports were also too far away from the measured courses, because the fuel-carrying capacity of the plane would be a limiting factor on speed. In addition, the range of mountains around our valley would prevent the necessary low-altitude high "G" turns on the 100-kilometer and 500-kilometer courses. One "G" is the force of gravity. When a plane is pulled out of a dive or put into a sharp bank it builds up Gs. The plane is built to stand a certain number of Gs, above which it will pull apart. A pilot without a G-suit is likely to be in trouble with more than four Gs, even for short periods and with even less if long continued. My flights would call for turns involving about three Gs.

Rogers and Rosamond dry lake beds adjoin the Edwards Air Force Base in the California desert area and provide ideal emergency landing facilities. These lakes are wet during the winter months but as dry and almost as hard and smooth as a billiard table during late spring and summer months. I approached General Vandenberg to see if the Air Force would permit me to lay out measured courses over these lakes, which courses would be available thereafter to the Air Force. They were needed. He agreed and confirmed that as a pilot in the employ of Canadair I could fly a Canadair plane at Edwards just like any other Canadair pilot, and that Canadair, by previously existing arrangement, had the privilege on request of calibrating and testing its new Sabre-jet with the Orenda engine at Edwards.

With this everything seemed set except the consent of the Canadian Air Force authorities to let me serve as one of the test pilots. They finally gave approval to Canadair.

The request to have the plane sent to Edwards Air Force Base came through from Canada to the general staff of our Air Force in Washington. General Vandenberg was in Europe at the time. No one else knew anything about it. My name as one of the pilots was set forth in the papers. Drew Pearson got wind of this request, presumably from someone in the Pentagon, and published a story which built a large structure of wrong implications on a small foundation of fact.

The Canadian authorities did not want this sort of publicity and started to back away from my right to fly the plane at all anywhere. They thought the American authorities were opposed. General Vandenberg, on return home, cleared their minds on this point. If there was any opposition to the breaking of established records by a woman in a Canadian-built plane with a Canadian engine — and there seemed to be — it stemmed from other than the top officials of the Air Force.

The day before the plane was to leave Canada for California, the Canadian authorities received word "from the United States Air Secretary's Office" that "the project was frowned upon." The Canadians believed from this wire that even the usual calibration tests in California were not desired by the American authorities. They canceled the trip of the plane.

This wire presented a serious mystery because I knew that General Vandenberg and Secretary Finletter did not feel this way about the project. I had never discussed the matter with the Secretary but only a week before I had met him in the White House Executive Office, while we were both there in connection with the presentation of the Harmon Trophy, and he had asked me how my flying was getting along at Edwards Air Force Base and had stated that if time permitted he would like to be present when the timed speed flights were run. That meant he knew I was getting in some practice in Air Force equipment. I told him that to date it all had been dual time because regulations prohibited me from flying solo.

So this time, when things had gone seriously wrong, I sent a wire from California to Secretary Finletter, stating that someone had undertaken to misrepresent his attitude to the Canadians. As a result, he sent the following telegram to me:

I THINK YOU HAVE BEEN MISINFORMED ABOUT THE ATTITUDE OF
THE AIR FORCE. MY OFFICE HAS HAD NOTHING TO DO WITH THE
PROPOSED USE OF MUROC FOR THE TESTS AND SPEED RUNS OF THE
CANADIAN F-86 WITH THE ORENDA ENGINE AND WITH YOU AS
PILOT. GENERAL VANDENBERG HAS DISCUSSED THE MATTER WITH
WHICH I AGREE AND WHICH I HAVE TRANSMITTED BY TELEPHONE
TO THE HONORABLE BROOKE-CLAXTON. THE AIR FORCE HAS NO
OBJECTION TO THE CANADIAN GOVERNMENT USING THE FACIL-
ITIES AT LAKE MUROC FOR CALIBRATING THE CANADIAN F-86
TESTING ITS RATE OF CLIMB AND FOR USE OF MUROC FIELD BY A
TEST PILOT DESIGNATED BY THE CANADIAN GOVERNMENT WHICH
DEFINITELY INCLUDES YOU IF YOU ARE SO DESIGNATED BY THE
CANADIAN GOVERNMENT. THE AIR FORCE WILL BE GLAD TO
MAKE THE FACILITIES AT MUROC AVAILABLE AT A TIME MUTU-
ALLY SATISFACTORY TO THE AF AND THE CANADIAN GOVERNMENT
UNDER CONDITIONS WHICH WOULD NOT INTEFERE WITH AF
OPERATIONS AT LAKE MUROC.

Finally, everything seemed jelled. The Canadian authorities,
after all this hubbub, counted themselves out in any official way
but stated to Canadair that the plane was in its possession and
control for a period of ninety days.

I held my breath until the plane left for Edwards. I continued
thereafter on the anxious seat because everything seemed so mar-
ginal and teetering that I could count on nothing for sure until
the flight was back of me.

The preliminary tests by the Canadian pilot were finally completed and the following day I was to fly the plane. The weather
right then was very good for speed tests. It was discovered, however, that the photographic film used to record the instruments
during these preliminary calibration tests, for some unaccount-
able reason, had turned out unexposed. All the tests had to be run
over. A valuable week was lost. Then bad weather set in. Two
weeks more passed before I could get into that Sabre-jet plane.
A part of the engine time I had counted on had been used in the
retesting. And the three months' period, at the end of which the

plane had to be turned over to the Canadian Government, was fast drawing to a close. A newspaper or two learned about my flying plans and I practically begged them on my knees not to publish a story. Publicity would have been fatal to my program.

I had five short flights in that Sabre-jet plane before I flew it around the 100-kilometer course for a new world's record — for man as well as woman. But the timers and judges had been sitting around waiting for days and I could not let pass by the first morning when the air conditions were even moderately satisfactory.

The 100-kilometer course was circular and around twelve pylons. The course, for purpose of measurement, was in a series of straight lines from pylon to pylon to aggregate 100-kilometers, which is about sixty-three miles. The circumference of the circle was therefore necessarily longer than the series of straight lines and also each pylon had to be passed on the outside, all of which added to the flight course. The height of flight above the course was three hundred feet — this low in order that the photographic timing device would catch me accurately as I passed the start and the finish points of the circuit. But there were hills at one side of the course which I had to skim over by rising a bit at that point. Two observers were at each pylon. Two sets of judges were on hand, each with an automatic electric timer, accurate to one ten thousandth of a second, and with cameras that allowed even this timing to be corrected by fixing the position of the plane with respect to the start and finish line at instant of timing. Official observation planes were in the air with barographs. There was a sealed barograph in my plane. "Chuck" Yeager was in a chase plane to act as observer around the course. I had fuel enough at full power to fly the course twice, provided I would turn onto course promptly after take-off and land immediately after completion of the speed run. That would give me a margin of two minutes of fuel.

The plane in its calibration and other tests showed that at full power it had a top speed of 675 miles per hour. But this was in a straight line over a short distance. What could it do in a banked position of thirty degrees over a sixty-three-mile circular distance? There were varying opinions among the Edwards test pilots. They varied from 630 miles per hour to a maximum of 650 miles per hour.

On my first run I obtained 652 and a fraction miles per hour. On my second run I was a mile per hour slower. The first run was naturally taken for certification of record to the Fédération Aéronautique Internationale in Paris. Their representative in the United States is the National Aeronautic Association and Mr. Charles S. Logsdon, Chairman of the Contest Committee, was on hand as chief judge. All in all there were about forty judges, timers and observers.

The first to congratulate me was Colonel Ascani, whose record I had broken and the following day he sent me the following letter:

21 May 1953

DEAR JACKIE,

Even though you visit us here at Edwards almost daily, I feel the need of writing these few lines to offer my sincerest and warmest congratulations on your new record. I genuinely am tickled pink that it was you who broke my record and know of no more emphatic way to convince you other than this simple statement. Naturally, we have been a little concerned about the 100 km, not about your ability or capabilities, but about the possibility of any little thing going wrong.

I realize that Chuck Yeager has been of considerable assistance, but I want you to know that I feel very strongly you did this all by yourself and all the credit is yours. This proves you don't have to take a back seat to anyone, male or female.

I have missed the television newscasts, Jackie, but I have heard that you said some nice things about me. I appreciate it and again would like to say that the credit all belongs to you. You have done a tremendous thing with your many accomplishments in a jet airplane, *including* your high Mach dives, and I rank you on a par with our best Air Force pilots. There still are literally hundreds of our own jet pilots who haven't dived through Mach 1. In my book, you have accomplished the impossible and have shown what a little determination can do.

Hats off to a wonderful pilot and I'll pray for your continued success.

Sincerely,
(signed) FRED

The telegrams started pouring in from Air Force people and other friends abroad and at home. Letters of congratulations were received from President Eisenhower and Cardinal Spellman. But I appreciated the Ascani letter most because he knew what I had gone through; and next in line was the telegram I received from General Al Boyd, who is an outstanding test pilot and in charge of experimental flying at the government's Wright-Patterson Air Force Base. Formerly he had been in charge of Edwards Air Force Base and I had sought and obtained his advice about the Sabre-jet with the Orenda engine. General Boyd said:

THE MORNING PAPER CARRIED A REPORT OF YOUR 100 KILOMETER RECORD FLIGHT. YOUR SPEED WAS TWO MILES BETTER THAN I HAD CONSIDERED POSSIBLE. THIS REQUIRED PRECISION FLYING. MY HEARTIEST CONGRATULATIONS. THE COUNTRY CAN WELL BE PROUD OF YOU. BEST WISHES FOR CONTINUED SUCCESS

The following week a morning opened up with conditions satisfactory, except for a fifteen-knot wind, and I went around the course five times for a 500-kilometer record of 590 miles per hour. The plane, without the carrying of external tanks, had fuel for only seventeen minutes of full-power low-altitude flying, so for this longer run I had to carry the external tanks, which slowed the plane down by about 40 miles per hour. Even so, I had only fuel for twenty-seven minutes of full-power flying, which was insufficient, so had to make the runs pulling 94 per cent of full power rather than full power. I landed on the dry lake bed just as I did after the 100-kilometer run and again with two minutes of fuel remaining.

There were two more records I wanted to try for — the 15-kilometer straightaway and the 3-kilometer straightaway. The first was important to me; the second was comparatively unimportant because I doubted that the plane for this distance could beat Captain Slade Nash's record of 699 miles per hour made in December 1952 in a similar Sabre-jet but equipped with an after burner to give it more power.

Edwards Air Force Base is in the desert where the nights are cold and the days hot. With the rising sun the heat thermals started up from the desert terrain, causing by noon air turbulence to such a degree as to make full-out close-to-earth speed flying dangerous.

Record speed runs therefore had to be made in the late morning after air temperatures had risen to give better speed but before excessive turbulence had set in. But day after day passed with unsatisfactory conditions. Finally June 2 opened up with weather that was not good but was flyable. I had intended, as I have said, to be in London that day for the Coronation. I decided to do both runs this morning because only four days were left before the plane had to be returned to Canada.

At ten o'clock in the morning I started the 3-kilometer run. The passes were at two hundred feet above the course and all the turns had to be made at low altitude and high speed, either to meet the rules or to keep up high-speed momentum. I did the 3-kilometer first because I could take a little more turbulence on the 15-kilometer later in the day. I could make that later run at five hundred feet and also I could rise higher during the longer turns. Back and forth I went over the 3-kilometer course four times, having the greatest difficulty in holding the plane on course in level flight, due to a wing roll tendency at top speed, aided and abetted by turbulence. To get even two hundred feet on one side of the course or the other meant that the cameras could not clock me. I had made the record and landed, only to learn that the timing equipment had broken down. The four supplemental stop watches had timed me at about 690 miles per hour but stop watches are only accurate to one tenth of a second and are not officially accepted. The air was already too rough to try the 15-kilometer that day so I was pretty disheartened. Furthermore, the rough air had tossed me so badly on the first pass over the course that the connection between my G-suit and the plane's pressure system was jerked loose and in consequence I felt rather pulled apart after the flight.

That 690 miles per hour, which could have been as much as 697 miles per hour with accurate timing, led me to believe I had at least a chance to beat Captain Nash's record. So up the next morning I went for another try. I made two passes, under very trying conditions, and when it was evident that I could not better the 699-mile-an-hour mark, I aborted the flight and returned to base. I did not want a women's record, which I could easily have had, mixed in with the men's records I was after.

The plane was immediately refueled and the timing devices were shifted to the 15-kilometer course. That took about two hours and the roughness in the air was building up by the minute. A pass in each direction over the 15-kilometer course was needed for an average speed, as against four passes over the 3-kilometer course. I had fuel enough for four passes. The average of any two consecutive passes could be taken. The first pass from south to north was at a speed of 680 miles per hour. That result was relayed to me by air from my own Lodestar, which was parked on the lake bed near the judges' equipment. The second pass from north to south, with the wind against me, was at a speed of 670 miles per hour. I determined to make a third pass, even though the plane had developed a bad left-wing down roll at high speed and was in consequence next to unmanageable over the level flight course and its approaches. On this third pass I decided to take a long dive at the conclusion of which I would level out before reaching the approach to the course. I did this but, on leveling out, the controls again "froze" on me with the plane determined to roll over to the left. I used both arms to pull on the controls and one knee as well for leverage but with no effect. Another second or two and the plane would have been over on its back and into the ground. I prevented this only by slowing it down. At the moment I pulled back on the power there was an automatic temporary overcompensation of the direction of the plane to the right of the course and, as a result, the timing camera did not catch me on that third pass. That ended the flight. I made the long turn for a landing and "Chuck" Yeager, in his chase plane, closed in behind me. He instructed me to leave the throttle untouched as much as possible and to land on the lake bed. I wanted to put the plane down on the runway where the ground crew was waiting but "Chuck" insisted that I put it down on the lake bed where I could take a high-speed landing and long roll. I took off my oxygen mask and smelled fuel in the cockpit. When the wheels touched ground and the roll had about stopped, "Chuck" told me to cut the throttle and switches and get out as quickly as possible because I had a bad fuel leak which he had seen from his plane. A stream of fuel about the size of one's thumb was gushing out of the bottom of the main section of the left wing. A sergeant ran up just as I was about to jump (a short stepladder would ordinarily be used) and I asked him to come close and break my fall. He replied he was not going to get near a hot plane with that much fuel gushing out of it. But I finally convinced him the greatest danger had passed. Just as the sergeant helped me down from the wing a National Broadcasting Company camera truck drove up. I moved around to the nose of the plane and let them photograph and interview me without limitation so that their attention would be diverted from the leak.

It looked as if a fuel line had given way or a tank had cracked open. That would mean a repair job taking several days and a delay in delivery of the plane to Montreal. Therefore I immediately released the plane to the Canadian Chief of Crew. A close inspection in the hangar disclosed that the continual vibration caused by the high speed in rough air had opened a wing fuel tank. It was a close call for me. If that loose fuel had gotten back into parts of the fuselage behind me, where an engine was turning out in thrust the equivalent of 12,000 horsepower, there would have been a violent explosion. That would have been the end of the plane and the end of me. Someone would probably have blamed it on the fact that a woman was doing the flying.

The Sabre-jet is a good plane. The Orenda engine is a fine engine and one of the smoothest jet engines I have ever flown. The things that happened in my flights by way of wing roll and frozen controls were the direct result of trying to push the plane beyond its design limits.

The timed flights by me in that plane took a total of about one hour. For these flights the insurance on the plane cost $10,000. Had I embarked on these flights as a considered risk? I certainly had. I knew that Lloyds were pretty accurate in figuring risks. I knew that statistically I had fifty thousand times the chance of a mishap in every flight of that plane that I would have in every flight of a Convair Liner or Constellation. I knew that at two or three hundred feet above the ground, if anything happened it would be next to impossible to get out through the explosive ejection of the canopy and seat. One considers these things and prepares ahead for emergencies, but getting on with the flying is more satisfying than contemplation of risks.

For every hour in the air I have put in at least two hours on the ground in preparation. In this case the ratio of ground hours to air hours was nearer one hundred to one. It took two years of planning and work to make thirteen flights in that jet for a total of six hours' flying time, during which I established three men's speed records, tried for a fourth, and dived three times past the sonic barrier to beat the speed of sound. But I flew at least ten thousand miles back and forth across the country, to Washington, to Montreal and to New York, to make these few short flights possible. And then I had to put in weeks of study of the pilots' operating manual to familiarize myself in advance with every detail of that complicated piece of fine precision mechanism known as a Sabre-jet. What the test pilots at Edwards Air Force Base had well absorbed over years of jet flights I had to absorb, at least to a workable degree, in a very short time. These pilots were extremely helpful to me. Without their help it would have taken much longer to carry out my program. They are the greatest pilots in the world, in my opinion, and do the most difficult test flying of new experimental aircraft as a part of the day's routine.

I am often asked what sensation of speed one gets in fast, low flights. It is terrific. Consider yourself in an automobile going not eighty miles per hour but about seven hundred miles per hour and you will have a fairly good idea of the flight sensation, particularly if you lift the automobile off the road and hold it level about two hundred feet high above the ground. Now tip the automobile into about a thirty-degree bank and hold it there for a number of minutes while flying a perfect circle. In these maneuvers you have duplicated the flight pattern of the closed circuit flights discussed above. Don't think that your automobile is too heavy to fly as I have suggested. Even your heaviest car, say a Cadillac limousine, has a lighter wing loading — that is to say, number of pounds of weight per square foot of flying surfaces — than the Sabre-jet. The flying surfaces of the Cadillac consist of the underside of the body and the mudguards. Give that automobile power enough and structural strength enough and it would fly. Of course the underside would be smoothed out a bit and a part of it pressed out at the sides as wings and another little part extended at the back as a tail. Thus the car would be given control surfaces as well as lifting surfaces.

I have had my fling in the jet phase of aviation. The rocket is just around the corner. Will Father Time let me wait for this? I hope so. Flying has been my pleasure. It has given me memories and many friends all over the world. These memories will remain vivid and the friendships will improve with age even though the flying ceases. Two of my three jet records have already been beaten. That is the way it should be. It means progress in the air and progress is necessary.

Passing the sonic barrier to beat the speed of sound was a spiritual and emotional experience for me more than a physical one. "Chuck" Yeager was the first person to go through the barrier and live to tell about it. I wanted to have the experience — to move that barrier away and to prove to myself that it was also a scared calf rather than a ghost — and "Chuck" sympathized with me in my desire.

He acted as my mentor. No one else was to know about the plan. Time enough to talk about it when it was over because dozens of experienced and accomplished pilots had tried — some many times — to dive through that zone of shock waves and had failed. Besides I did not have much time available for the effort.

I have already stated that Mach 1 is the speed of sound and that such speed varies with temperature, like the stretching and shrinking of a rubber band. But so far as plane and pilot are concerned, Mach 1, no matter what the so-called "true" air speed at the given place and temperature, brings with it the same shock waves and problems.

On my first flight in the Canadian Sabre-jet I took it up to 30,000 feet and by putting it into a gentle dive I registered .97 of Mach 1 which is on the edge of trouble. For this kind of flying there is about one hour's fuel supply. The next day I went to .99 of Mach 1. "Chuck" was flying not too far away and asked me to look at him and tell him what I was seeing. I could see the shock waves actually rolling off my canopy like a fine film of water on a window. The atmospheric conditions have to be just right to see as well as to feel the shock waves and they were right that day. On the climb to high altitude, which is a fairly slow process, I went down to the Mexican border and back and showed the plane's contrail over our ranch as greeting to Floyd. This contrail is really a trail of ice crystals formed when the hot exhaust gas strikes the cool air at altitude and forms water vapor, which then freezes if the conditions are right.

There was nothing left for me to do now on the third flight in that Sabre-jet except to pass Mach 1. Because no one on the ground knew our plan the explosions would give them a surprise. I climbed to about 45,000 feet. Then I did a "split S" to start the full-power and almost vertical dive and headed straight down for the airport as my target. I counted aloud the changing readings on the Mach meter so "Chuck" could hear them. Mach .97, Mach .98, Mach .99, Mach 1, Mach 1.01. At Mach .98 the wing suddenly dipped. Then it overcorrected and the right wing dipped. Then the nose tried to tuck under which means that the plane wanted to fly on its back in the first phase of an outside loop. The turbulence was great and the shock waves violent. Then I started to pull out of the dive gently so as to level off before getting below 18,000 feet altitude. Down there, in that heavy air, a pull-out might tear the plane apart; also below 18,000 feet a flight under certain conditions can result in a compressor stall in the engine. The pull-out causes a slow-up of speed which means coming back past the sonic barrier again with a repetition of the shocks and the turbulence and the strange antics of the plane.

As I climbed for this dive past the barrier, I noticed that the sky above was growing darker until it became a dark blue. The sun is a bright globe up there above but there are no dust particles at that height to catch and reflect the sun's rays, so there is not what we know as "sunshine" down on the surface. Yellow has given way to blue. The gates of heaven are not brilliantly lighted. The stars can be seen at noon.

I landed with one more barrier behind me and was much pleased. As my friends congratulated me I felt as if I were walking about ten feet above the ground. The men on the flight line heard the two explosions but they had not been recorded in the control tower. What should be done about that? The answer was easy. I would do it over again.

So, at the end of an hour, I went up once more, only this time I wanted to do a little better so I climbed to 46,000 feet. Up there I felt as if I were teetering on the top of a rubber ball just before I did that split S to start the dive. A split S maneuver keeps a positive force related to air and the pull of gravity working on the plane toward its underside at all times. A negative force could result from just pointing the nose of the plane over into a dive and such negative G might disrupt the fuel and hydraulic systems, apart from its possible serious effect on the pilot. It is being found out that a pilot can stand little more than three negative Gs and then only for a few seconds. Blood is forced into the head and what is known as a red-out results with almost immediate occurrence of numerous small hemorrhages in the whites of the eyes. There is also such a thing as a "zero gravity" and when in that state the pilot just floats in the air with no weight whatsoever. How long a pilot could carry on with zero gravity is not known. It has been done by "Chuck" Yeager for forty-five seconds as an experiment. That is about as long as it is possible for even a great expert to hold a plane in the exact flying attitude that will give zero gravity.

This time I stayed with the dive until I registered well above Mach 1 on the plane's Mach meter. This time the tower reported it recorded the explosions and heard me counting the progress of the needle on the Mach meter. So I was highly satisfied.

I was a part of the plane in these flights. I was, in fact, attached to it ten different ways, for strapping on of the parachute, for strapping of myself to the seat, for oxygen and for listening and speaking. If something had gone wrong, it would have been impossible to open the canopy manually and bail out. The speeds are too great for this. So in such an emergency there is a lever to pull which sets off an explosive charge and blows the canopy off. Then another lever is pulled and pilot, seat and parachute are exploded out of the plane upward and toward the rear. All the pilot has to do after that is to maintain his composure and count to a certain number while falling and disengaging himself from the seat. Then he can open the parachute and start a slower drop to earth. That is, he can if he has taken his small bail-out bottle of oxygen with him for the air up there is too rare to maintain consciousness. But the pilot won't have use for the bail-out bottle unless, before pulling the trigger that sets off the explosive charge, he has propped his head back against the head rest and propped his feet into special bail-out pedals because the force of ejection would otherwise injure him severely. Furthermore, if the parachute is opened at high altitude, quick freezing will be the result to any part of the body not well protected. It is best to make a "free" fall until close to 15,000 feet of altitude.

Short of a bail-out, the pressurization in the cockpit can be lost due to a break in the canopy or otherwise. Then it is necessary to dive fast to lower altitude because it takes both oxygen and pressurization to keep one going very long above 30,000 feet.

240 THE STARS AT NOON

I said I was attached to the plane in ten different ways. But, when one is hanging face downward in the dive, it does not matter. I should have said eleven ways but I neglected to put on my G-suit in all these power dives. But "Chuck" Yeager was not wearing a G-suit even though he takes, in the course of the usual day's work, up to three or more Gs. Neither do most of the other test pilots wear such suits except under extraordinary conditions. I had my G-suit available but I thought I would follow the practice of the oldsters at the game. I had been tested years before at Mayo's and knew I could take more than four Gs without blacking out. But there was one difference between myself and the others which I did not take into account and which had nothing to do with the fact that I was a woman and they were men. I had abdominal adhesions from earlier operations. If all parts of the "innards" are thrown down in a freely moving mass, maybe nothing serious happens. But if one part is hung up by adhesions and the whole is jerked violently, there is a kinking both painful and dangerous.

And that's what happened to me on those two early flights past the barrier. Two days later, I was in the hospital at Albuquerque, New Mexico. By the grace of God and a rough air trip there, the kinks loosened en route. When I told "Randy" Lovelace of my flights, he knew exactly what had happened because he was aware of my adhesions. For several days thereafter I slept with the foot of my bed raised fifteen inches and breathed pure oxygen for three hours each night. Then I was back at the flying again, somewhat shaken up physically, but fortified by the protecting armor of my G-suit. I noticed that one of the test pilots always wore his G-suit and I learned that he found it necessary following an appendectomy two years before. He had a few adhesions also.

I am convinced that those pilots who take several Gs fairly regularly without wearing a G-suit will regret it. Blood cannot be constantly surged out of place that fast without causing something acute to happen eventually or something chronic to develop. A pull of four Gs will throw up to a gallon of blood from the upper part of the body into the abdominal cavity and legs. This is no proper experience for one who has less than perfect arteries. The G-suit is uncomfortable while on and time consuming to put on and take off several times a day, but it is a necessity, I feel sure.

I have given you my experience up to and through two dives past the speed of sound. A number of men have done it after "Chuck" Yeager. Some have done it often. But the entire lot constitute but a handful and it seemed inevitable that I should have the same experience and as the first woman. We know now that the troubles are not over when Mach 1 has been passed. "Chuck" in a Bell rocket plane, some months after these experiences of mine in the jet, went to about two and one half times Mach 1. There are other barriers to pass up there.

Twice past the sonic barrier should have satisfied me, but Paramount Pictures and *Life* magazine had gotten wind of my proposed record speed flights and wanted their cameramen to be present. I could never tell how long I would have to wait for proper weather conditions and didn't want them around because I was wary of any publicity. Nor did I want to get cameras mixed up with military bases and procedures. So, finally I agreed, after talking to "Chuck," that if they would come up to the dry lake bed, off the military base, the next Sunday while General Operations was closed down, "Chuck" as the first man to go past the barrier and I as the first woman would do it together for them in separate planes flying a sort of supersonic duet.

A camera plane followed us into the air. The take-off, an accommodation dive around an altitude of 20,000 feet for benefit of the camera plane, and the landing were photographed and the sound recorder picked up the explosions. We went to 48,000 feet this time and I put the Canadian Sabre-jet plane well above Mach 1 to give right good explosions. Seemingly to round out my experience, while climbing at about 30,000 feet, we suddenly bumped into a jet stream of air that was apparently traveling eastward at high speed. The plane was violently jerked and thrown about. Then all was quiet again because I was riding in that new wind. But it was a shallow jet stream and soon I passed out of it again on my way up to the diving point where the outside temperature was 35° below zero. Incidentally this climb established a new women's international altitude record.

I do not believe these explosions on the ground have been completely analyzed. There are two clear ones in sharp succession and usually a third that is sometimes referred to as an echo of one of the others. In effect, one is flying inside an explosion at Mach 1 or above and when the plane is slowed down and pulled out of the dive this explosive shock wave carries on to hit the ground in what had been the line of supersonic flight of the plane. These explosions rattle windows and sometimes break them and have been known to knock down porches. A number of planes all diving past the speed of sound at the same time and headed for the same ground point would set up the equivalent of bombardment on the ground at that point. More than once the people in an area have been frightened by these loud explosions. No one is permitted to make such a dive now without notice to the authorities. The day following my first flight past the barrier, one of the Edwards pilots dived at our ranch through the barrier as a salute to my accomplishment. It was without notice. I was on the golf course and was able to tell the startled players around me what had happened. But in nearby Indio, all the inhabitants thought a serious explosion had taken place and, in each case, just next door. Quite apart from the explosions, there is the noise of the jet engine in flight. It represents wasted power that will be harnessed in time. The blast of a fair-sized jet engine is roughly ten thousand times louder than a full symphony orchestra. That blast is no place to be for a human with ears and a nervous system. But the pilot in the cockpit gets none of this. He is ahead of the blast and running away from it. The cockpit of the noisiest jet plane is therefore silent while in speedy flight.

I am often asked what my sensations were while passing the barrier. I was too intent on the job to have any particular impressions of those moments. There was no fear. There was confidence. And there was a great alertness to what was happening to the plane and what had to be done about it. At sonic speed it takes less than a minute to reach the ground from the start of the vertical power dive. That means the earth was moving up toward the nose of the plane very fast. Finally there was that warm feeling of accomplishment when the dive was over. I wanted to get on the ground as quickly as possible and tell Floyd.

And there was another feeling — one of humility and trust. I am a strong believer in God and Divine Providence. But I am not a fatalist. God helps those who help themselves. Way up there, about ten miles above the earth's surface, things come into proportion. The people on the ground have disappeared. You have left them behind and are on your own and impressed with the immensity of space, reaching out between and beyond those noonday stars, and the divine order of things, which makes you realize with a feeling of comfort that you are not alone, that God is everywhere working in many ways His wonders to perform. That was why I had no fear and had confidence.

CHAPTER XIII

〰〰〰〰〰〰〰〰〰〰〰〰〰〰〰〰〰〰〰〰〰〰〰〰〰〰〰〰〰

FROM the beginning I knew that this book would have to be limited as to pages. But I am not too good at arithmetic and when I finished dictating the first draft to a recording machine it was found that my story, as it then was in the rough, would fill between four and five books the size of this one. From that point on it became a problem of elimination and concentration.

I wanted to tell in detail about some of the many unforgettable characters I have met in the hangars and along the sky lanes. There is, for example, an oil company executive and consultant to the Air Force whose hair is now on the thin side and gray. He is General James Doolittle, remembered mostly by people for his organization and leadership of the famous Tokyo air raid. For this dangerous and intrepid feat he received the Congressional Medal of Honor. To me he is "Jimmy" and I have heard from him the story of this raid in detail. When some of the men and all the planes were lost and Jimmy was sitting disconsolately on the wreckage of his own lead plane, he really thought the world had come to an end for him and that he would probably be court-martialed. I heard another Medal of Honor hero — General Wainwright — say about the same thing. Heroes are oftentimes not heroic to themselves. Back in 1950 Floyd and I had Jimmy Doolittle and most of the still-living Tokyo raiders at our ranch for a wing ding. Lowell Thomas broadcast the festivities from a ringside seat on the lawn. It was a great chance to talk to heroes en masse. These heroes were on the shy side and from the Main

Streets of America. They were running automobile agencies, stores and the like back home and looking for autographs from heroes or personalities. As a souvenir I have a map of the raid signed by most of the raiders. One of the raiders who was at the wing ding wanted more action and he got it. He lost his life in air combat in Korea. As for Jimmy Doolittle, I knew him as a natural pilot and a perfect speed pilot who oftentimes did things the wild and dangerous way.

Howard Hughes I know in quite a different way from the way he is known to the general public. It is true that he has personal peculiarities. But he is one of the most polite and thoughtful men I know. Time and again he has sent me congratulatory messages or helpful suggestions. Although weighted down with millions, he runs around most of the time looking like a tramp, without coat or tie or belt or hat and, because of preoccupation, he forgets to shave for a day or longer. But he was — and is — a great pilot. He has also done some outstanding designing of planes, including, according to my best knowledge, the prototype of the Constellation, and the racing plane built by him in 1937, which was way ahead of its time, and the mammoth six-engine plywood flying boat concerning which we have heard so much. This boat may have passed its usefulness. It was designed to keep our ocean lanes open at a time when metals were in short supply and Japan at Pearl Harbor had shown us how the surface lanes might be closed. But there is no doubt in my mind that this plywood plane can fly. Howard Hughes doesn't design planes not to fly. People wonder why, having so much money, he drives himself so hard. I happen to know that he is planning to establish and endow a medical center. He has, as his motivation for ceaseless work, the desire to make that center as big and fine as possible.

Frank Hawks also stands out in my memory as a fearless racing pilot in the days when I was learning to fly. Once, much later on, while Frank and I were flying across the continent together in an overpowered Beechcraft, we had a running argument as to the best way to land it. Frank insisted that if I did not stop bringing it in so fast I would kill myself. Finally, in exasperation, I told him I would send roses to his funeral. I did that very thing within a matter of months. A great pilot should have the right to go to the happy land of beautiful skys and everlasting airways in a fast new plane that has become unmanageable for reasons beyond his control. Frank Hawks had no such luck after all his outstanding flights. He hit a power line while taking off from a friend's front yard in a new-type private plane that was almost a midget.

Tex Rankin, the greatest stunt flyer this country ever produced, went in about the same way. He was taking three passengers up on a demonstration flight in a small plane suitable almost for a novice. But Tex had the plane a little overloaded that day and hit the wires at the end of the field. Most airports in those days had a habit of having wires at the end of the field and usually there was a cemetery just beyond. Tex Rankin wrapped up his dry spontaneous humor in a slow Texas drawl and was the Will Rogers of the air. He was always cleverly getting out of tight spots in the air but forever getting wound up in tight financial spots on the ground. Tex never learned to fly on instruments (called "blind flying" in the early days), having graduated from the old barnstorming school. I never could stunt very well. Tex proposed to me that we jointly buy an aerobatics plane and he would give me lessons in aerobatics in return for lessons in blind flying from me. We bought the plane and Tex used it in his exhibitions during the last two or three years of his life but I never found time to get or give that first lesson. Tex crashed once in the Rocky Mountains during a fog but did it so cleverly that he was unhurt and his plane not too badly damaged. But he was arrested by the forest ranger for entering the forest reserve without a permit. Once I got Tex a stunting job at the National Air Races on condition he would do something new. He agreed to do his entire exhibition upside down and to have colored exhaust to make it appear the plane was on fire. Only after he had finished his exhibition and was back on the ground did I learn from him that the flat upside-down spin he was in until he nearly touched ground was not a part of his repertoire. He had gone into this spin, which was something new, and did not know how to get out of it. Fortunately he learned how by trial and error just before it was too late. Thereafter he added that flat upside-down spin to his daily exhibition.

I would like to keep on telling about these early and great airmen with special anecdotes about Sasha Seversky, a great show-off in the air besides being a great pilot and a great plane designer. He lost one of his legs during World War I but did not let that ground him. Benny Howard was another who flew well with one wooden leg. This loss was the result of a crash while he and his wife "Mike" were flying in the Bendix Race in 1936. Thereafter Benny went on to his greatest accomplishments as a pilot, doing testing before and during World War II for Douglas Aircraft Company and others. Benny was one of the few early birds who taught themselves to fly. He was one of the great to whom I went when I needed sound advice and wanted peculiarities or possibilities of a plane figured down to the fineness of a gnat's eyebrow.

A book could be written about each of the pilots I have mentioned and others. What they did with antiquated equipment built in the back yard cannot be measured by what the pilot does today in multimillion-dollar equipment which has been double and triple checked. They and their buddies are why we are where we are today in the air age. But we had better keep alert for things are moving fast. Yesterday's equipment and procedures are obsolete by today. We are as safe in America today as the air above us, but that air is being supercharged with danger.

Yes, I wanted to talk about pilots but also of many other things.

I wanted to tell about my trip to Greece in 1950 and my visit with Queen Frederica in the palace in Athens. I would not have dwelt much on her beauty and youth and charm for she has since been to the United States and we all now know she has these graces in abundance. But I certainly would have told of my two-hour gossipy talk with her about people and charities and wars and cabbages and kings. Queen Frederica dropped her glass of sherry on the floor while we were chatting and she seemed quite embarrassed over the incident. I told her if she would wet her finger in the spilled sherry and then rub a bit of it behind her left ear it would bring her good luck. She followed my suggestion and I certainly hope she has luck in abundance.

I saw South Korea just at the end of the war and must bring out a few high points connected with this visit. Korea had an old civilization long before the time of Christ. We in America who can date our history back only a few hundred years must constantly remind ourselves of this difference between the Orient and our own country in order to keep a semblance of bearings.

Korea when I saw it was as shabby as it was old. Pusan was the filthiest city I have seen any place at any time. The conditions of the population as to dirt, lack of clothing, lack of housing and lack of food were almost indescribable. The third of our nation referred to by President Roosevelt as underfed, underclothed and underhoused rolled in the lap of luxury compared with these Koreans. Seoul, the capital of South Korea, was clean and attractive by comparison to Pusan. As we moved from airbase to airbase and I watched from the air the terrain with its mountainous barricades, I was struck by the difficulty our troops must have had in offensive operations. At the bases themselves I was impressed by the fact that our Air Force was still on continuous alert notwithstanding the fighting was supposed to be at an end. The pilots were on duty four hours and off duty four hours. The planes had pilots sitting in them or standing beside them twenty-four hours a day.

At one base General Cannon was reviewing the pilots on duty standing stiffly at attention at their various fighter planes. I was beside him and in slacks. In a joking sort of way he asked one pilot if he had ever seen a woman on the base. The pilot was looking straight at me and without changing his expression or "at attention" attitude answered in the negative. Later on I told General Cannon I had a hunch he was making a mistake when he told me that morning to be sure to wear slacks.

President Syngman Rhee, head of the Republic of Korea, which apparently we Americans pledged ourselves to support soon after its establishment in 1946, invited our party to his headquarters. President Rhee spent many years in Washington. Before this political representation he studied at Princeton under Professor Woodrow Wilson. He speaks English perfectly and for an Oriental should know well the processes of the Western mind. His headquarters consisted of a well-constructed and spacious Western-style house furnished with American furniture and surrounded by a fine flower garden. President Rhee during his youth and while working for the freedom of his country as a republic was imprisoned for a long time and was tortured by his enemies. He is the George Washington of South Korea.

The visit with President Rhee lasted about forty-five minutes. General John K. Cannon, General Anderson, who was heading our Korean forces, American Ambassador Murphy and I were the guests. President Rhee also had present his Minister of Defense. President Rhee delivered a monologue directed at me. The three high-ranking American officials present were almost bypassed. The gist of President Rhee's remarks was that Americans from the top down had shown themselves to be stupid and cowardly in their approach to the problem of Communism. He asked me to say this to the American people as a quote from him on my return to the States. I was asked afterward by my own people not to increase tension at the time by repeating the remarks. They thought the old gentleman was just irritable and perhaps doing a bit of high-class Oriental trading on his own account. Enough time has passed since this conversation that I now feel free to refer to it. I hope he meant to say we were stupid as meaning ignorant in ways Oriental and therefore inclined to give the erroneous impression of weakness to the Russians and Chinese at times when appearance of strength is needed.

After this very surprising visit with Syngman Rhee I was anxious to be on my way to Formosa where our group would have the opportunity of conferring with Chiang Kai-shek and Madame Chiang. We were given the full red-carpet treatment including reviews of the troops, a trip around several of Formosa's military bases, a dinner by the Chief of Staff of the Chinese Nationalist Army and a dinner by General and Madame Chiang.

I saw here pretty much the same Chinese I had seen in the United States and in China during the war. I was happy to have this additional meeting with Madame Chiang Kai-shek. There is no doubt in my mind that the Nationalist organization on the island of Formosa represents the greatest pro-Western influence today in the affairs of China and Indochina. General Chiang's forces are well trained according to all information I have but are getting old for soldiers. They apparently are not able to strike on the mainland with telling force without sea transport and air cover from us as well as munitions and supplies. Neither can General Chiang sit as he now is — in comparative idleness — forever. He must strike soon aggressively in one form or another or fade out as a great force in the Far East. I formed the impression that Madame Chiang is still her husband's greatest helper when it comes to working with the United States but that her influence with him is not too great otherwise. General Chiang's son, General

Chiang Ching-kuo, whom I met, is being talked about more and more. Neither the Generalissimo nor his son speaks English. The son speaks Russian and received educational training in Russia where he was first a cadet in the military academy and then was sentenced to forced-labor camp for seven years for anti-Stalinist activities. It is possible that the son might come into power in his father's footsteps and then, in Oriental fashion, and being married to a Russian woman, might not hold fast to the views of the present Nationalist leaders about the West and Russia. There are some within the ranks of the Nationalist Party who have fears or doubts about this. Some of these people would be prepared to take over power if necessary to perpetuate present policies. And so there are possibilities ahead that could generate not a civil war within China — which has been going on for a long time — but a civil war within the ranks of the Nationalists. In the meantime, seventy per cent of all the expenditures on the island of Formosa are supported by American dollars. If some one does not get busy every bullet fired by the Nationalists on the mainland to repatriate the Chinese will have cost its weight in pure gold many times over.

I returned also to Japan and what I saw there by way of food, freedom, and prosperity led me to the thought that the way for a nation to go forward fast is to get into a war with the United States and lose it by unconditional surrender.

Two dinners in the Palais Elysée in France certainly merit some detailed reporting but I can only say that other than its charming hosts what stands out in my memory connected with this palace is an enormous bathtub in an enormous bathroom. It is reserved for royal visitors. It looks like the kind of bathtub that should have been in the Palace of the Kings at Versailles but wasn't.

I have told about going behind the Atlas Mountains to see the Sahara Desert. But I also went to Lapland to see the reindeer, to Australia to see kangaroos in their natural haunts, and to Iceland to see the midnight sun and to play golf at two o'clock in the morning. These strange places and scenes have an uncontrollable attraction for me. As a result of seeing the Broadway show titled *The King and I*, I decided to go to Thailand and to Thailand I went. It was worthwhile both from the standpoint of the people and the beautiful temples. I was there when Vice-President Nixon and his wife arrived on their round-the-world good-will trip and attended the state dinner in their honor as well as the dinner given by our Ambassador William Donovan. At these functions the princes of the royal family wore those long baggy fold-over-and-under trousers seen on the male members of the cast in the show that had intrigued me into making the trip. And then there was the other Broadway production, *South Pacific*, which caused me to go to the island of Bali and watch the native dances. The Balinese were not quite up to their billings so far as I was concerned but I will never regret the four days I gave to this side trip while on my way from Thailand to Australia.

Adventure is always just around the corner, and I can turn that corner mighty fast.

I went to Argentina by airline with Floyd just before this book went to press. He went there on business. I went along for company, and partly to go over the galley proofs with him en route. But the portions that remained unchecked on arrival at Buenos Aires remained that way until the publishers started breathing down my neck on my return to New York four weeks later. The four weeks were packed full.

President Perón sent me in his executive plane to see the aircraft factory at Córdoba. In that plant they were building a medium-sized transport and a jet fighter. Also they were building an automobile with a plastic body — which, because of the economics involved, makes sense to me for automobiles as well as for certain types of planes. When President Perón received me on my return from Córdoba, I told him how intrigued I was by the plastic automobile and he promptly presented me with a beautifully done scale model of it which was on his desk at the time. President Perón has a great warmth of personality and he is the acme of courtesy. The Sunday we were in Argentina, he had us out to his country place (called La Quinta) for a walk around the grounds and for lunch. La Quinta is an estate of about two hundred acres on the outskirts of Buenos Aires and on the bank of the Plata River. It was given to the nation about fifty years ago by a wealthy landowner on condition that it be lived in by the President not less than five days a year. President Perón has turned the grounds over to a girls' organization similar to our Camp Fire Girls, and the youngsters were out in force that particular sunny Sunday. President Perón rides a motorcycle as a hobby. On one, and dressed with open-neck shirt, sweater and skull cap, he came to the gate to meet us, and at the time of our arrival was refereeing a basketball game. Those girls wandered around with the President as they would with a much-liked older brother, while he showed us their boathouse, gymnasium, restaurant and playgrounds. Two of the hundreds joined us for lunch in the President's house and later a whole group of them on motorcycles acted as our escort to the main gate. President Perón was most informal. He keeps no regular staff of help in this week-end hideaway. The man who cuts the lawn during the week served us at the table.

I headed north to Rio de Janeiro, where I had some official business to attend to for our Civil Air Patrol. But I saw little of that beautiful city because our Ambassador, James S. Kemper, and General Leigh Wade, head of our Air Force Mission in Brazil, had arranged other wonderful plans. With one of our Air Force officers who was stationed there and an officer of the Brazilian Air Force, I flew to a landing strip that had been cut a short time before in the dense jungle in the center of Brazil, about nine hundred miles north and west of Rio de Janeiro. At our landing spot on the shore of a river a tribe of aborigines had their fishing outpost. About sixty men, women, and children were there. I experienced another "first" on stepping out of the plane. I was the first white woman they had ever seen. What's more, they wore no clothes. Our own faces stand the violent changes of climate because they have been kept bare. Well! These Indians — with much darker skin than the copper hue of our North American Indian — were *all* face.

They were most friendly — like curious, playful children — and crowded about us wherever we went. They were mostly intrigued by my blond hair and constantly stroked and gently pulled it until I finally covered it up with a scarf. They also pulled up my skirt to look at my silk stockings and to flip with delight my elastic girdle. The Brazilian official had told me they would be curious, friendly, and, if not insulted, harmless, and I did my best to be nice to them. Finally, however, I went into the plane and changed into slacks and gave one of the women my silk stockings. I slept that night in the plane, without fear, although the tribal people, out of pure curiosity, seemed to be wandering about all night in the moonlight.

In the morning, these naked men, women, and children crowded about in a circle while I cooked eggs on a small gasoline stove we had brought along. Then we watched them cook their meal. It was done by putting a monkey and a parrot — fur, feathers, entrails and all — on a fire. They also had fish and a sort of bread made by grinding the root of a certain kind of tree. They used bamboo spears for hunting and fishing. They always crowded about but looked clean and smelled clean. Each time I handed a bit of sausage or a tangerine to a grown-up, he would first smell it and then give it to a child. One of the men went through my handbag the way a child would, and while showing him the contents I found two or three mints which, after the testing sniff, were relished by the children.

A woman made motions that she wanted my shirt so I went back to the plane and brought her my extra one. (We had also brought along some beads and hard candy for barter.) Each man wore loosely around his waist, as sole adornment, a string of small, homemade stone beads of about the diameter of a pencil. One of the tribesmen took his off and gave it to me in exchange for a handful of blue beads. The women wore around their waists similar loose strings, which looked like strands of thread made by rolling fiber of some kind against their bodies. The strings looked like three or four fish lines twisted together. I have two of these strings, one of which came to me from the body of a virgin and one from the body of a married woman. The two strings are slightly different but are not intended for the purpose of covering or concealing anything. When the girls of the tribe reach puberty they are tied in a hut for six months, during which they are taught to roll the fiber into strings and are given other training. Then they are turned loose to get husbands. If a girl is rejected by the man she chooses, she is destined, I am told, to become an old maid. Death by being tied to a tree in the jungle is the sentence for molesting a virgin. Dr. Kinsey should revise his ideas of morality by going to the heart of Brazil and studying these aborigines. I intend to go back some day in an amphibian and learn a lot more about them.

Peru and Bolivia were next on my homeward trip but I will leave their stories, like those of India and Egypt, for the travelogues. One incident, however, I must tell. My flair for picking up hitchhikers paid off in a big way. I had gone from the ancient city of the Inca Empire called Cuzco to the remains of that enormous ancient stone structure (as large as a couple of city blocks) called Machu Picchu. I had a private train consisting of a hybrid between a wooden, boxlike automobile and a very small gasoline-driven coach. It was fiesta day in that area and all the men were gaily drinking *chicha*. I quickly recognized it to be what I knew as "knockum" during my childhood. When sugar cane is crushed and the juice boiled in a kettle, a skim comes to the top. If that skim is put into a barrel and fermented, it becomes "knockum" and "knockum" when distilled becomes moonshine. While I was examining the ruins, my driver imbibed a little too much *chicha*, and as a result we eventually went off the track through a half-open switch.

Prior to that time, when passing a small way station, a non-English-speaking Peruvian (who turned out to be an engineer) thumbed for a ride and I took him into the car. When we went off the tracks, he left his bag behind and disappeared. He actually scaled a cliff and walked five miles to the next station for help. Along about dark, back he came on a handcar with eight *chicha*-happy Indians. After much trial and error combined with loud jabbering, they got the car back on the tracks. Its doors were sprung and its wheel flanges badly nicked, but slowly we made it down to where an automobile could be obtained.

How could I write a book about myself and not say something about the cosmetics business with which I have been continuously identified since I was about ten years of age?

In Sherlock Holmes fashion, I deduce either that the Garden of Eden had a moist climate, making for a soft velvety skin and peachbloom complexion, or that Eve, concurrently with her creation, was provided with cosmetics and the skill to use them properly. This deduction is based on the statement in the Good Book that God, after creating Eve, looked upon her and it was good.

Unless make-up is properly applied, it had better be left off entirely. Face rouge that looks like consumptive fever spots and overly red lips with smear lines pointing to those fever spots do no credit to the person concealed behind such a bad camouflage. I personally do not use fingernail polish because it does not seem to harmonize with my personality or my work and only calls attention to my large hands. Cosmetics are to help nature, not to offset nature's basic correctness. Coloring should be a delicate additive to make one look like a portrait by Howard Chandler Christy, rather than one by Picasso.

It is woman's right, indeed her duty, to be as presentable as circumstances of time and purse will permit. Fifteen minutes a day, if properly allocated, is all that is needed for this, but that fifteen minutes gives an end result that is emotionally satisfying.

I have known many women who were spending more on cosmetics and beauty treatments than on food. And they looked better for it in two ways. Most people eat too much anyway. During the depression of the "thirties" I was partner in a small chain of small, cheap, mass-production beauty shops in New York City. After working hours at Antoine's (where a charge of forty dollars was made for a hair dye), I would go to one of these shops and supervise the work of the operators, most of whom were just out of a beauty school. There we gave three services for a dollar. An operator was permitted to do only shampoos for her first week on the job, preparations for hair wave during her second week, only hair waving during the third week and so on. The customers were mostly working girls or those hoping to get work, and we kept open until eleven o'clock evenings. I have seen plenty of these people cash dole or relief checks to get a beauty treatment. And well they might because to get a job they had to be presentable.

When I returned from my air training stint in California with a pilot's commercial license under my belt, I was ready to step back into the business I had actively engaged in most of my life. I had started at the bottom and wanted to end at the top. No longer did I want to go on the road — the air road — selling for some other concern. I wanted to sell my own products. I certainly had learned the hard, laborious way how to perfect such products. With a cosmetic chemist, whom I took from a toilet goods subsidiary of one of the major oil companies, and the help on a consulting basis of an expert in perfumes, I opened a laboratory in Roselle, New Jersey, and I also opened a luxurious beauty salon in Chicago. In that salon with my products in plain bottles with typed labels, I obtained customer reaction and developed sureness.

Pogue's in Cincinnati and Halle Bros. in Cleveland were my first two accounts for Jacqueline Cochran Cosmetics, and they became customers both because of my aviation activities and the desire of some aviation enthusiasts in the stores to help me to a start. That was nearly twenty years ago and it has not been easy going during the intervening years. Only recently have I developed sufficient volume to operate at a profit, which means that people now buy millions of dollars' worth of my products a year through thousands of outlets. I have a payroll of several thousand dollars a day to meet. It's a narrow-profit-margin business I am in. I would be very happy with a margin of five per cent on sales.

Some years ago, I was asked to make a speech about the cosmetic industry before the Harvard School of Business. I researched and discovered that men buy an enormous quantity of cosmetics. Men buy about forty per cent of all the deodorants and many tens of millions of dollars a year of hope — by which I mean hair tonic. And men buy an astronomical quantity of mustache wax. That and snuff seem to be two staple products in this country, although one seldom sees a waxed mustache or a snuff sniffer. Two things happened as a result of that Harvard speech. Almost immediately several of the young men in the graduating class applied to me for jobs. Also as a result of my research, I went into the business of selling men's cosmetics. I did this by buying

Parfums Charbert, which had, besides its women's line, a well-established men's line. Later I also took on, for better rounding of my business, the American distribution of the Nina Ricci French perfumes. So now "Jacqueline Cochran" has two cosmetics children. With all these perfumes and scents, my business at least will always "smell good" even when through depression or otherwise business in general "stinks."

I'm not always in the front office on Fifth Avenue or on the road. Often I am puttering in the laboratory. To develop a really new and extra fine item gives me a great thrill. This I succeeded in doing with my "Flowing Velvet." Women in moist climates, like England and Ireland for example, usually have good complexions. Women in dry climates usually don't. I went about it to find an oily base that would emulsify, maintain its integrity at widely different temperatures, absorb quickly through the skin and leave a moist and almost imperceptible dewy residue. To try to imitate is to compliment and in this way I have had plenty of compliments from competitors with respect to my Flowing Velvet. But I am positive, for basic reasons, that they can't make the grade.

Sometimes a situation is presented that results in a new product. Floyd was troubled with cracked lips in the dry hot air of the desert. The usual aids seemed to give only temporary relief and indeed to make matters worse in the long run. I had some of my lipsticks made up for him without any color pigment. They worked perfectly not only for him but for his numerous friends for whom he kept depleting his supply. Then some test pilots started using them for high-altitude work and also some golfers and surf bathers, all with enthusiastic approval. So I changed the ingredients slightly and added a bit of sun-repellent and put the item into my Charbert men's line as "Lipsaver."

This cosmetics business is a full-time job for me as top boss. I should not be twins, as the saying goes, but should be quintuplets.

If I were quintuplets, one of me would spend her time entirely on the domestic side, another would fly, another would be a full-time cosmetiste, another a rancher and another would certainly by constant play get her golf score down below the middle eighties where it now stands. But there are so many things to do beyond what these five could thus do that I believe, on second thought, I can't settle for anything less than octuplets.

That arrangement of being many people would also spread the surgical operations around on a more equitable basis. When I was fourteen or fifteen, I had acute appendicitis. A young doctor took the appendix out at a very little cost. I mean immediate cash cost, because that operation cost me plenty in every way over the years. I was, I guess, the first warm body he had ever operated on. Adhesions formed which required more operations which seemed to cause more adhesions. Other surgeons in later years started mining me for talcum. It seems that the first young doctor knew about putting talcum powder on his rubber gloves. But he put on too much and a large part of it stayed inside me and formed what I refer to as little barnacles. Finally, Dr. "Randy" Lovelace, following my experience while flying a jet plane without a "G" suit, did an operation to end all further operations. It is called a Noble Plication. One of the seven major operations I have had through the years on my "tummy" (which in consequence rates a zipper) occurred while I was working for Antoine at Saks-Fifth Avenue. During my recuperation period, I could not take the long hours of work on my feet. But neither could I stand inactivity. So I satisfied a long-standing secret ambition to dance professionally. I obtained a job as a dancer in the show that was being put on in the Roxy Picture Theater in New York City, which was then new and taking second place to none. The Music Hall had not yet been built. Imagine dancing this way to take things easy while recuperating from an operation. I did this for about a month.

Also in addition to these abdominal operations and a radical sinus operation, I have had three eye operations which were nearly tragic. So far as I knew, my eyes were perfect but about a year after I obtained my pilot's license I was turned down on my physical examination because of a muscular eye imbalance which it was said approximated twenty per cent. I was about to lose my license and through friends went to the chief doctor of the Aviation Department in Washington, D.C., who recommended an eye operation and, at my request, suggested a certain surgeon in Philadelphia. To Philadelphia I went and had a "tuck" put in the muscle of one eye and a "buttonhole" in the muscle of the other, in order to tighten and to weaken them respectively. When the bandages were taken off several days later, I was cross-eyed. In what approached a panic on my part, I started consultations with the field of specialists and finally had corrective surgical measures. This operation left me cockeyed. As soon as the wounds had healed, Dr. John H. Dunnington did a third operation, after which my eyes appeared normal but in fact had about the same imbalance that I had at the start. While my one eye was still bandaged from the last of the three operations, I went out in my plane to see if I could do take-offs and landings. I had a friendly pilot sit beside me at the dual controls for safety. Wiley Post flew with only one eye, which meant without the benefit of depth perception, and I felt that I could do the same. I succeeded in obtaining a waiver from the official doctor in Washington which stated that it was for a five per cent eye imbalance. Thereafter throughout the years I flashed that waiver when appearing for a physical. Recently — through the aging process, I guess — my eye muscles have come into balance. But during the intervening years I never had depth perception, never used more than one eye on take-offs and landings and, what's more, never made a bad landing. Depth perception for a pilot — who in fact does not look down at the ground just below him while landing — is overemphasized in my opinion and I am the *living* example of what I mean.

These operations not only interfered with my flying and my life generally, but were very trying on Floyd. When I could, I tried to get through surgery before he could find out about it. In the summer of 1953, when "Randy" did that Noble operation, I flew myself into Albuquerque, reached the hospital at two o'clock in the afternoon and was in surgery an hour later. On arrival in Albuquerque, I called Floyd's secretary in Los Angeles, where Floyd was at the time, told her I was going up in the mountains that afternoon with "Randy" to see an Indian and could not be reached until the next day. It was technically true. "Randy" took me into the "heights" with anesthesia and the scrub nurse was a Navajo Indian girl — and an exceedingly competent scrubber-upper she was.

This is enough about the cosmetics business and operations. I have other things I want to say before the gong is sounded on this Chapter "Thirteen."

Now I am going to express some personal views even though in abbreviated headline form.

I have been exposed through the years to a lot of good intellects at work audibly. Few people get such a kaleidoscopic panorama of life and views as I do. I see Mrs. Richwich by evening and the girl behind the counter by day. On occasions I have had tea with a king or queen and dinner with a mechanic. From Sawdust Road to the Diamond Horseshoe at the Metropolitan Opera House takes in a lot of territory and a lot of diverse viewpoints. There is a constant flow through our ranch house of scientists, industrialists, professors, judges, artists, pilots, and military leaders, as well as a sprinkling of crackpots. The whole makes the pattern of the kind of democracy we enjoy in America today.

These people pour out great knowledge in diverse ways. And such knowledge properly correlated and harnessed is potent.

Most of our knowledge is born with us as instinct. That's why newborn babies get along with their breathing and eating and exercising. Our subconscious mind does most of the work of thinking for us. The conscious thinking bears about the same relationship to the subconscious as the little piece of ice sticking up above the water bears to the enormous iceberg below surface. The French scientist and author, du Noüy, in his book *Human Destiny*, sets out to prove that the mind of man is the only thing that is developing through the ages. He satisfied me on the point. There must be a pool of intellect that draws on the experience of all the little segregated portions farmed out to the millions of brains at work around the world at any given time. Into and out of that pool feed streams of intellect and experience. Some of the sludge is cleared away in the process. One trifling increment to the whole over an entire generation and the forward stride is fast, considering the age of the universe or even the much lesser age of Man. Whenever I want to get a proper perspective of the place of Man on earth, I go out onto our ranch lawn and look at the moon, planets and stars through our rather large-sized telescope. The moon is so near that light reaches us in less than two seconds, and I look at it closely with landing fields in mind. Then I take a look at one of the distant stars and realize that it may have been extinct before Man came first into being, as it takes the light from some of these stars millions of light years to reach us as against the two seconds from the moon. When one considers that the billions upon billions of balls of fire called stars keep going on and on in accordance with a pattern, that by studying the corona of the sun (which is the earth's most important star only because it is comparatively close by) we can now forecast to a degree what our weather will be or when we can get good radar reception or have a radar blackout in case of a necessary long-distance air offensive; and that the mind of Man is gradually taking the ascendancy over everything else — one must believe in an ordered whole and divine planning and a continuation of life after bodily earthly death. Religion can be that simple. It does not have to be complicated. I'm satisfied if my body goes back to nourish and create flowers. It is only human to think of afterlife in terms of one's own personality and the things that we do and like here and now. But to live on, as part of the never-ending stream of intellect, as a part of an infinite and divine planning, should be sufficient.

In America, we have the so-called freedoms; the run-of-mine man on the streets gets opportunity to form an opinion about public matters and has both a choice and a voice. But he shouldn't be making the choice or shouting too loud on matters of national or international importance unless he knows what he is talking about, and oftentimes he is confused by the babble of crackpots, partisans or the out-of-balance urgings of minority groups.

What we have today in America is wonderful measured by anything we know in history. But we are not going to enjoy it long if we don't watch out. Point to all the democracies in history. Then try to figure out why they have all failed in time. They don't need to fail. Democracy properly defined is, in my opinion, the best form of political society of all. But it carries with it the seeds of its own destruction and those seeds must be searched out, isolated and sterilized.

We are spending many billions of dollars a year now on defense. Defense against what? Against Russia. What's more, almost everything we are doing with that money is being shouted about in the halls of Congress, in the press, and over the radio. We are giving the benefit of our technological progress to our potential enemies hot off the griddle and thereby saving our potential enemy time and money. Is it possible that freedom of speech and of the press will end up in the destruction of freedom? At least those with tongues and pens who reach great audiences should do a little self-monitoring.

Are we preparing to fight a war like the last one, or a new kind of war? It's going to be a new kind of war without the shadow of a doubt and it's going to break out suddenly on the home front. There are no front-line trenches for guided missiles with atomic or hydrogen bombs as war heads. I am sure too little of our funds are being spent on free-thinking schemes of research and development for the future and too much on trying to make a little better something we had and used in the last war.

We have the greatest industrial potential in the world. It licked Hindenburg and the Kaiser and it licked Hitler. But it took time to get into high gear. There may be no time again. Pearl Harbor was a minor example of what could happen on a nationwide scale. When I hear it said that five hours after the enemy strikes, we will return destruction to their own factories and lands, it makes me sick at the stomach. That five hours is at least four hours and fifty-nine minutes and fifty-nine seconds too late. And I have cut this timing short by at least a second.

But I do not believe armed warfare to be the present stategy of Russia. Her leaders must know where a present wide-scale war will end for them, whether it be at the end of five hours or five years. They want for the present to bore from within. They want our own people, as a whole, to surrender politically. That means that discontent and class hatred must be bred in our land. A depression would act as a trigger mechanism for such an internal upset. Russia, I believe, wants more than anything else a depression in America.

Depression can be brought about by many circumstances. It

is a complex life we are in with its myriad of impacts. Each one has his little bit to do and somehow out of what could be chaos comes a semblance of order and routine. We get our food not knowing how it is grown or distributed and we read our press and listen to our politicians.

Depressions are unnecessary evils. The answer is not entirely in work but work creates abundance, and where there is abundance there should not be want which nourishes political upheavals. During World War II a part of the people made enough goods to support themselves and the millions under arms, plus enough more to ship quantities of goods to be blown up at sea or in the air or on lands abroad. Close to fifty per cent of our national income was devoted to support of armed forces by way of goods for them to eat, wear or destroy in use, and yet we prospered. What an abundant life we could all have, therefore, now that there is no war, if we would each just choose to put in a good day's work. I am in favor of fewer hours of work if the end result is better for the people involved. But I see too many Huey Longs and their successors, whether in the guise of politicians, labor leaders or cranks who are whooping up the cry for fewer hours of work, for its own sake. We are in a machine age and I would like to see the machine do it all. But there must be a substitute outlet for the energies of the people.

A few days in the British Crown Colony of Hong Kong gave me a rather vivid and startling vision of what our American future may be. In an area about nine miles square, comprising the small island of Hong Kong and the tip of the neighboring Chinese mainland peninsula, there were crowded together more than two million people. They were nearly all Orientals and their living space was about twelve times more congested than New York City's Manhattan Island. This population was down to a half million at the end of the Japanese occupation, then it skyrocketed, then business fell off again when trade with Red China was practically eliminated. But the people of Hong Kong are getting along. True they carry on clandestine trade with the Chinese across the bamboo curtain. But Hong Kong is more and more turning into the markets of the world a great supply of low-priced goods, measured by American cost and price standards. Fine Japanese silk which I had purchased in Kyoto, Japan, was transformed overnight in Hong Kong into dressing gowns, evening coats and pajamas. Along the roadside in rows that extended for blocks sat cross-legged Chinese doing this needlework by night. A single electric wire extended overhead down this line of hand labor with one light bulb over each workman. Fine workmanship was shown and at a fraction of the cost of similar work at home. But it was not this hand labor in the raw that gave me the greatest pause. In large Hong Kong factories I saw American basic plastic material being turned by American machinery, guided by never-tiring Oriental hands, into all sorts of finished products that were being shipped out to undersell us in the markets of the world. A machine that works twenty-four hours a day will beat the product cost of one that works but half time and a machine needs very little rest. The human who tends these machines can multiply his industry many times over by more constant effort than we Americans are used to. When we give to the Hong Kongs of the world our raw materials and our tools and equipment and then our "know how," what have we left? Continued American leadership requires much more attention to be paid to the four-letter word *work* (particularly in *working* the machine), without the application of which we can become a prostrate, stagnant America.

Furthermore there is no good to be served by one third of a nation trying to take for itself what another third has in somewhat additional measure.

Have you ever figured out how much the rest of the people would be helped if every person in the United States with over

$100,000 in property had it taken away from him and spread about equally among the others? Well, it would hardly get the others a ham sandwich apiece. And they would be far worse off the next day because their sandwich would be gone and there would be no place to lift the next one. Furthermore, their future would be cut off because each American now has the prospect of moving upward into that lush bracket, which isn't so carefree or lush in any event when one gets there. But one likes the chance and gets it. Most American millionaires of today were poor boys forty years ago.

It's an interesting intellectual exercise to figure out what the millionaire does with his dollars. He eats three meals a day that probably are no better than the meals eaten all along Main Street; he wears one suit at a time and has a few extras in his closet. He rests in one bed, enjoys the same radio, newspaper and jokes that all the rest of us do. His money goes in one end of the slot and comes out the other in the form of purchasing power spread around as wages or in other distributions. He supports charities with his excess, if any, but more likely than not, he is actually cash-poor most of the time and worried with the same kind of worries that trouble all the rest of us.

When the leaders of a democracy devote their time to stirring up one group against another in order to lead a "cause" and thereby to justify themselves being elected, the seeds of destruction of democracy are being sown. When one group wants to live by taking things away from another, another form of government will ensue unless the movement is stopped.

It is not necessary to be a millionaire if you can live like one, and we all can if we let up on the jangling of discordant notes and work together as a national team.

These are some of the thoughts of a person who came from nowhere, but neither at the start nor on the way ever got irked by the thought that someone else had something that she didn't have. She wanted the nice things, it is true, but had no idea of getting them except through the expenditure of initiative and honest energy. This same girl thinks now as she always has, that opportunity and incentive are the true heartbeats of happiness. They are kept by letting the other man hold on to the benefits of his enterprise and not by taking it away from him through a false will of the so-called people spoken on the political platforms, echoed in Congress by a man who usually knows better, and then plugged into a law. The people in leadership should lead as statesmen. Americans are honest and really don't want hokum.

Will Rogers used to say he only knew what he saw in the newspapers. That's pretty much true with respect to most of us if all means of communication are included. That's true in Russia also. It's necessary to get our facts straight, and they can't be received straight unless they are so given.

I have had a life of ups and downs and contrasts. There have been plenty of valleys. I like to think of the high points. In this connection my thoughts turn to an evening just before the presidential election in 1952. I was the special guest of His Eminence Francis Cardinal Spellman at the dinner he gave in the Grand Ballroom of New York's Waldorf-Astoria Hotel for the Alfred E. Smith Memorial Fund. The charge was $100 per plate, but I was "for free" sitting there on the dais. Candidate Dwight Eisenhower was seated about four feet away from me. Earlier in the year, as previously related, I had made it a particular objective of mine to get him to run for the Presidency and I was particularly pleased and proud that night because the race was about over and the running in the home stretch was good; and I had purchased an expensive and elegant gown for the occasion. Around my neck hung a very unusual diamond pendant that had come into my possession from an Indian maharajah through the mediation of Cartier's and by the financial grace of Floyd. On my wrist was a miniature diamond airplane set in a bracelet with back-ground of sun, moon and stars, designed by Floyd, and presented as his trophy for one of my flights; and on my ring finger was a square-cut sparkler of proportions.

The occasion was soul-stirring. As I looked down and over the sea of twenty-five hundred human faces, made only partly dis-tinguishable during convocation by the glow of tallow candles which cast their shimmer against the rose and gold-leaf-covered walls of the enormous room, I had come over me that same strong sense of infinity and divinity which I have often experienced fly-ing alone, high above the earth, among the stars.

As I settled down into my bed that night, I began reminiscing and thinking of the contrasts that life had held for me. I thought of the sawmills and hunger and work, of the earthquakes and hurricanes I had gone through, of my many sicknesses. And I thought of my private audiences with His Holiness and of my visits with royalties and of my war service and decorations. And also I thought of Floyd and how privileged I had been to spend nearly twenty years with such a rare and unique person. Most people think of him in terms of big finance. He is to them a "tycoon" who makes decisions involving millions and they are interested in whether or not they are going to have a profit or loss as a result of his decisions. But I always think of him as be-ing one of the gentlest, kindest, and most generous human beings I have ever known. There are literally scores of people he has looked after and taken care of. He now has some twenty women (I always refer to them as "his women") whose husbands have passed on or are sick or no longer able to provide adequately for their families, whom he guides in their investments and advises as to what they can or cannot spend — in other words, for whom he makes life better. This takes a great deal of effort and time out of his life, already overburdened with work and responsi-bility. I feel that Floyd has lived and is living a completely selfless and saintly life. He is never too tired or sick to do something for the other fellow. (I have had to "sneak" this comment about him into the book after he read the last proof copy.)

As I fell asleep that night, happy and contented, Sawdust Road and the cotton mill served as a background for my dreams. I was not less happy on that first mill job. Happiness is a relative thing. Even a mangy cur with fleas is happy and contented when the fleas are removed, but Fido the Great will sulk when he doesn't get his homogenized milk or ground porterhouse. Today I possess one feeling that is very satisfying and sustaining, and which I wish I could give to all my friends: I can never have so little that I haven't had less.

Man has seemed dedicated through the ages to the creation of a new environment for himself followed by an adjustment or attempted adjustment to that environment. Gunpowder, printing and the wheel have all been highspots in this march of man. But it seems to me that at no time has there been such a sudden rush forward, such an environmental change for man as during this last quarter of a century brought about by a web of radio and television networks and airlines — and I am fearful that I have used the word "web" correctly. The faraway peoples of the earth have become our neighbors. We see each other's table fare and clothes and habits with much consequent highlighting of the haves and have nots. Russia and China are not countries we hear about from a returned traveler with a lag of a year or more in time. These lands are closer, measured by knowledge of what is going on or in transportation back and forth, than were Richmond and Washington, D.C., in the days of our grandparents.

I have helped bring about this crisscrossing of the world by airlines, this speed, this force known as aviation, and sometimes I wonder if it has been for the good. As I took that moonlight walk about Rome I was struck by the fact that Christianity, which is the simplest of spiritual products, had gathered force while the

ornate marble and granite of paganism had crumbled. But sim-
plicity can be overdone too. Mahatma Gandhi went to that extreme and I saw little in India to justify that swing of the pendu-
lum.

It's clear that we are in a world of flux today. Aviation to date
has been something always close to power and force and strife.
It could bring so much. But it has not brought peace. Rather it
has caused us to consider dispersing our industries and our population — to run from each other. Our leaders float in a new
atmosphere where diplomatic landmarks have disappeared. In
this period of world turmoil and doubt and competitive drive
we are trying to reorient ourselves, to find a new framework to
cling to. Perhaps all of this is putting temper into the quality of
man. Perhaps a human being of greater force and character and
spiritual vigor and strength will emerge to take dominion over
what appears to be at least the rumblings of an approaching
violent chaos.

I hope we shall see this progress, and not chaos. I hope to live
to see the day when man has justified himself by taking control
for constructive ends over the recent space- and time-consuming
and energy-producing products of his scientific advancements.
They are worthless unless they contribute or will contribute to
the happiness of human beings. When that time arrives we can
be confident of the poetic prophecy that with respect to the air
age every new phase "is but a camp for the night in man's eternal
flight."

I will then have the extreme of satisfaction that I flew — not
only the early planes but their aerodynamic children and grand-
children. And I will be there on the aerial sidelines cheering
with my last breath those who are carrying on.

EPILOGUE

THIS book has been written primarily for the millions of our youth of today who have the frustrating feeling that yesterday's generation had more opportunity, tomorrow's generation may have things better, but today is tough.

Every generation has its rough roads and its barriers to surmount.

My story went from sawdust to stardust. Only because of this was it written. While I hope it brought reminiscences to some oldsters, it was chiefly designed to motivate those who are behind me in years and are looking wonderingly and perhaps with fear toward the new horizon.

What I have done without special advantages, others can also do.

I hear far too much about the desire for security. I do not believe there is such a thing as financial security — at least with satisfaction. Certainly it does not come from a private pension fund or a government's promise of poor bed and board after most of life has been spent idling around waiting for such a payoff.

My message to America's youth is to flex your mental muscles and get cracking under your own power. Derive emotional satisfaction from a good try and then another and another and still another if the first ones fail. In the case of an airplane, speed is determined by the outcome of the conflict between thrust of the power and drag of the plane. So it also is with humans. If you will open up your power plants of vitality and energy, clean up your spark plugs of ambition and desires, and pour in the fuel of work and still more work, you will be likely to go places and do things.

The formula for success has many components. There is never precisely the same mixture. A drop of luck can substitute for a dash of opportunity. But in every well-blended recipe for success will be found, in addition to honesty and as main ingredients, determination and tenacity and a substantial portion of skill and experience which come with the trying. There will also be found imagination and faith which bring the other elements together as a potent whole.

This land of ours still has its Sawdust Roads and Tobacco Roads that I knew in my childhood. And it will always have these places because some people prefer to live that way rather than to work. But I have seen most of the rest of the world, and the poorest one third of our people live in abundance compared to the top one third of most of the other peoples of the world.

What we have here in the United States, good, bad and mediocre taken into account, is the best the world has ever known.

Let's not let it be pulled down — either by carelessness, indifference or idleness.

JACQUELINE COCHRAN